CREATING SCHOOLS

WHERE STUDENTS AND TEACHERS WANT TO BE

Published by Melbourne Books
Level 9, 100 Collins Street,
Melbourne, VIC 3000
Australia
www.melbournebooks.com.au
info@melbournebooks.com.au

Title: Creating Schools: Where Students and Teachers Want To Be
Author: Michael Lawrence and Dr Fabio D'Agostin
ISBN: 9781922779366
Publisher: David Tenenbaum
Cover Design: Holly Lambert

A catalogue record for this book is available from the National Library of Australia

CREATING SCHOOLS

WHERE STUDENTS AND TEACHERS WANT TO BE

MICHAEL LAWRENCE AND DR FABIO D'AGOSTIN

M
Melbourne Books

Praise for Testing 3,2,1 ...

Lawrence's book is a lot more than just an indictment of Australia's current education system (including issues relating to standardisation, teacher status, funding – which is given due prominence – and student wellbeing). It is a well-researched "call to arms" for the current system to change and a brief history of how Finland's education system produced "the world's most literate citizens". Lawrence then describes how several trips to Finland prompted a complete re-evaluation of an education system he had been part of for 30 years; there was a definite disconnect between the routines, habits and activities he had practised in his career in Australia and those of the Finnish teachers he observed and worked with during his time in Finland.

For all of our belief in grades, testing and competition, Lawrence points out an embarrassing fact: these things aren't working. In fact, they are probably making Australia's education system worse, as evidenced by steady declines in international tests such as the Programme for International Student Assessment (PISA) over the years.

— *Wade Zaglas, The Education Review*

NAPLAN has failed miserably and our curriculums are now tied to endless testing that is comparative rather than focusing on improving an individual student-based system that better meets the unique needs of students.

— *Maggie Dent, Author, Parenting & Resilience Educator*

Part memoir, part investigative journalism, part call-to-action, this easy-to-read and highly compelling plea for an improved education system can't be ignored... Lawrence reminds us that we can (and must) do better.

— *Jared Cooney Horvath PhD, Educational Neuroscientist, Melbourne Graduate School of Education, University of Melbourne and author.*

"This is a must read for all teachers who find themselves blindly having to follow compliance regulations and for those seeking clarity on what is going wrong in our classrooms."

— *Robin Nagy, Educational Consultant at Effort Tracking.*

Lawrence outlines the differences in the Finnish and Australian education experiences and the reader not only sees the chasm between them, but also understands that like the proverbial domino effect, everything has to change if anything is to change. Because although Testing 3, 2, 1 focuses on the impact of NAPLAN and other testing regimes in Australia as a tipping point for the woes that beset education here, even a move away from this algorithm driven, outcomes, or standards-based educational approach will not alleviate the inherent issues faced by educators and students on a daily basis. By looking at all the issues the author explores, it's easy to understand why.

One teacher, with thirty years' teaching experience under her belt, but completely burnt out, has joined those leaving the profession. She says:

"Teachers are no longer seen as a valuable resource in this quest for bettering our world through nurturing responsible, intelligent, creative young people. They are now simply seen as employees who just need to do what they are being told to do, by the educational academics, administrators and the parents. And the list of what they have to do to keep their job is increasingly being filled with administrative tasks to justify either their existence or that of the academics who keep coming up with them, leaving less and less scope for teachers to actually be the professional educators they were called and trained to be."

The book is a salutary reminder of the cost of an education system, such as we have in Australia, which is based on standardised testing – that one size fits all approach which, as he points out, makes testers a fortune, produces pretty flowcharts, and provides parents with 'data' to assist in their school choice for offspring, but ultimately has very little to do with student learning.

There is much, much more in this book which one would hope might be a wakeup call to every parent, every student, every prospective teacher.... it will take an entire societal, economic, cultural shift to move the goal posts as he is the first to point out. Lawrence does a great service in this book in exposing that need.

— Loudmouth Magazine by Mandy Stefanakis, Ph.d

I can safely say that Michael Lawrence has captured the essence of the Finnish education philosophy in Testing 3,2,1. His thoroughly researched insights on relevant issues in comparing the Finnish educational system with the Australian make this book an essential read for our Education students and staff alike at Tampere University.

— Mikko Turunen, lecturer in Education Pedagogy, Tampere University of Applied Sciences and Professional Teacher Education, Tampere, Finland

Thanks to Kerri and Helen, Peter, Ryan, Brodie, Luisa, Theo the many friends and colleagues who have endured our discussions on education (sometimes whether they liked it or not!). This could not have happened without your support.

CONTENTS

INTRODUCTION

At the time of writing – 2024 – Australia's education system finds itself at a serious juncture. Thousands of teaching positions remain unfilled across the country. Actual numbers are very hard to obtain, and educators have told us that they are not allowed to talk about the staffing issues they face. We have been shocked at the number of teachers who have communicated to us, or publicly expressed via social media, a desire to leave the profession in the near future. An education union survey put the figure at around 40%!

This fits with predictions that the 'teacher shortage' (we always use this term with reluctance, as there is no teacher shortage – just a shortage of teachers who are prepared to teach in the current system and its conditions) will be at its worst in 2025. There are thousands – possibly tens of thousands – of excellent ex-teachers out there who are no longer teaching.

The damaging impacts of too few teachers in schools are being felt now. Students, whom the education system is supposed to be all about, are bearing the brunt of the crisis.[1] If we grow the Australian population aged under eighteen by only 6%, we must increase the school teacher cohort by 6% just to maintain current

---

1 Simon Kuestenmacher, "A growing problem looms for Australian schools as teachers flee," *InDaily News* April 15, 2024.

teacher to student ratios. This means we must add 23,000 teachers to reach a workforce of 414,000 by 2034.

A nationwide survey of independent, Catholic and government schools found that Australia's school system continues to experience widespread staff shortages, with 92% of respondents saying they had significant difficulties in attracting and retaining staff, and 97% reported being severely impacted by workload concerns.[2]

We see the damage everywhere in schools. Some are resigned to the fact that they won't be fully staffed for the year and there are reports of some schools with up to fifteen ongoing vacancies. Many of these schools cope by combining classes, resulting in increased class sizes. Echoing COVID lockdown practices, some schools organise online classes. Or – in surrender – they just send students home early. The words 'crisis', 'desperation' and 'alarm' are all applicable.

We need to shift our focus beyond simply addressing the shortage of teachers. Instead, we must strive to elevate teaching to one of the most sought-after professions in the nation, drawing in our brightest young minds. If you want to learn something, you want to be taught by someone who is excellent at that skill. You certainly do not want to be taught by someone who was not particularly good at it, but is working as a teacher because the criteria to get into that profession were easily met and they had few other options.

We are amazed that, despite such an enormous crisis in teacher numbers – not to mention record numbers of students who have either left school prematurely, or have 'quiet-quit' school and are just doing the bare minimum to stay out of trouble until they are able to join those who have left – the media still devotes considerable time to criticism of the teaching profession.

---

2 Robert Henebery, "Global study highlights critical importance of teacher wellbeing," *The Educator Australia*, April 11, 2024.

We need to return to valuing teacher professional judgement, not hiding behind mountains of collected, but never used, data; and once more place attention on the intellectual work of teachers to ensure our classrooms are dynamic, engaging environments, and not one-size-fits-all buzzword-ridden templates.[3]

This book tackles the big issues of Australia's 'teaching crisis'; from a loss of teacher autonomy and respect, to increased pressure from lobbyists on policymakers, to the real and tangible impacts on students today – who are dropping out in record numbers.

How we treat and support our teachers in the education system becomes the lens through which our students receive and view education, and then the lens through which they view the world outside of education.

Our education system can be characterised by trust, innovation, creativity, autonomy, critical thinking, collaboration and inspiration ... or blighted by excessive compliance, control, dependency, micromanaging, standardisation, meaningless competition, arbitrary ranking and superficial judgement.

We are all a part of that choice. *We* are creating society.

---

3 Jane Hunter & Don Carter, "Disquiet in the playground: Explicit teaching and other buzzwords," *The Education Review*, July 16, 2024.

TEACHERS

'The reasonable man adapts himself to the world; the unreasonable man persists in trying to adapt the world to himself. Therefore, all progress depends on the unreasonable man.'

— *George Bernard Shaw*

'... the term evidence-based is used not to invite questions but to discourage them, much as a religious person might seek to end all discussion by declaring that something is "God's will." Too often, the invocation of "science" to defend traditionalist education reflects an agenda based more on faith than on evidence.'

— *Alfie Kohn*

Australian schooling is beset by a set of serious challenges, and governments have decided to disregard the failure of their own policy logics and instead blame teachers, school leaders and students. A key tactic has been to claim that teachers are not implementing 'science': Australian schooling policy is now being framed inside of a so-called Science of Teaching (SoT) paradigm (otherwise termed 'what works', 'school effectiveness' or 'learning science'). Those governing – and their knowledge brokers – attempt to close down debate by claiming that any critique is ignoring the (their) 'science'. But no policy should be above reproach – and certainly not this one. Against the so-called SoT, a good social science, by definition, is sceptical, transparent, humble in its truth claims, explanatory, non-coercive, works off critique of its own truth claims, sensitive to how power works on and through knowing, context dependent, and theory-practice challenged.[4]

A push towards direct instruction, resourced with generic scripted lessons which can be (supposedly) 'taught' by teachers either unqualified in that subject area, or with less than a university qualification, is an alarming development, particularly at a time when teachers are facing criticism over pedagogical choices such as the teaching of reading. Ultimately, the victims are the children.

In a disturbing development in New South Wales, teachers and administrators who have publicly questioned the move to direct instruction have found themselves stood down and silenced. Such intimidation will see our brightest, most creative minds steering clear of teaching for some time.

It was education neuroscientist Dr Jared Cooney Horvath[5] who pointed out that at medical conferences, there are many presenters who are doctors and nurses, and similar for most professions, but at education conferences and on government panels almost all presenters are academics or bureaucrats, with hardly any teachers. The same is obvious when reading the aforementioned criticisms of teaching and the education system in Australia: the noticeably absent voice is that of teachers.

---

4 Robert Hattam, 1st Emeritus Professor Education Futures at University of South Australia, LinkedIn July 22, 2024.

5 Jared Cooney Horvath, *Stop Talking, Start Influencing – 12 Insights from brain science to make your message stick* (Dunedin: Exisle Publishing, 2019).

Cooney Horvath tells a story about being invited to join a state government curriculum-setting body to deliberate on changes. After several hours of consultation related to content that teachers would be mandated to teach he asked the group, numbering dozens, 'who here is a teacher?'. There were none. Upon his observation that the absence of teachers presented an issue for the body, they conferred over his concern and soon satisfied themselves that it was indeed fine for the curriculum decisions to be free of teacher input.

It is difficult to count the number of 'think tanks', advisory panels, academics, religious groups, testing organisations, and others who feel it is their role to publicly comment on all areas of the education system. As mentioned previously, there is currently a huge push towards 'direct instruction', (we look at this in some detail later) which seems to follow on the back of the previous week's criticism of how reading has been taught. The connection between the two is unclear, and both claim to have 'evidence' to support them.

> ***'... at a time when Australia needs to be advancing as a highly developed knowledge economy. And a "what works" learning science purports to be the truth but then its evidence is shaky. Instead of reflecting on their own policy failure, governments push the blame onto schools' leaders, teachers and students. All we hear ad nauseam is that teachers aren't implementing the science!'***[6]

Decades after the restrictions and limitations of direct instructional pedagogies were recognised, they have seemingly been rebirthed and promoted as a salvation for education. In truth, direct instruction never went away, it is the most obvious way that anyone might think to teach. But we are aware of little evidence (claimed

6 Hattam, LinkedIn.

or actual) in the latest incarnation that addresses the flaws that originally led many educators to consider alternative classroom practices. Why now the orchestrated push? What do we know now about direct instruction that eluded us for so long? Who benefits?

As for the timing, why are these things being thrust into the public eye right now? Is there something 'they' don't want us to look at (the 'teacher shortage', school funding, growing inequality in the school system, record student absenteeism, student mental health issues)?

Is there a plan to ease the teacher shortage by rolling out video versions of direct instruction lessons to those schools that cannot find the required teachers? If they have done the groundwork to convince us that direct instruction is best practice, then they could announce that these video lessons are a wonderful opportunity for the more disadvantaged schools (for these are the schools most likely to have a shortage of teachers) to now have access to the best teachers. This would not be possible if we had not first been convinced that direct instruction (little else is possible on a video) is best practice.

DISCOVERIES FROM UNESCO

An April 2024 United Nations High-Level Panel on the Teaching Profession recommended (these recommendations were supported by the United Nations Educational Scientific and Cultural Organisation – UNESCO) among dozens of things:

- **Teachers are the central element in the transformation of education systems**
- Education goals should aim to promote varied and well-supported learning pathways for success in life. **Learning should be based on principles of cooperation and solidarity, not exclusion and individualistic competition,** and should foster relationships, empathy, compassion, ethics and environmental and social consciousness

- Governments should fully implement enabling rights for education and decent work for teachers, in line with international standards, including freedom of association and collective bargaining, **freedom of expression, freedom of thought and academic freedom**
- **Funding for public education should be guaranteed at a level of at least 6% of gross domestic product and 20% of total government expenditure**, as set out in the Education 2030 Framework for Action, and should allow for increasing investment per capita in education
- Long-term funding for well-qualified and well-supported teachers is an investment in the quality and sustainability of education systems and is more efficient than short-term measures to fill teacher gaps, which result in high turnover and attrition. Governments should invest in teachers through competitive salaries and incentives; high-quality, accessible and affordable teacher training; and continuing professional development (CPD) and quality teaching and learning materials; as well as through the provision of qualified education support personnel
- **The status and dignity of the teaching profession need to be protected and elevated**
- **Teacher status and dignity are also directly related to teachers' ability to influence policies regarding their work, including curricula and pedagogical practices. Policies should ensure teacher agency and autonomy based on knowledge, competence and responsibility within education goals, and should foster a climate of trust and respect between school authorities, communities, learners and teachers.** Governments should also ensure that teachers and their organisations can engage in social dialogue, including collective bargaining, and policy dialogue on all matters affecting the profession
- **To inspire and attract young people into the profession,**

countries should promote public recognition of the teaching profession through advocacy and coherent policies, messaging that acknowledges teachers' social importance and professional expertise, and recognition of outstanding teachers

- **High-quality initial teacher education and training should be publicly funded for all prospective teachers**, including through stipends and other monetary and non-monetary incentives
- Teachers at all levels should at minimum have a first-level higher-education degree, and ideally a master's degree or equivalent
- Initial teacher training and CPD need to be transformed to prepare teachers to be leaders in a new learning environment and in new roles. **Teachers should be prepared to be not only providers of information but also active and innovative guides and leaders of their students' learning and social development process, in order to support the development of higher-order thinking skills, problem solving and the ability to learn independently and cooperatively**
- Teacher training should prepare teachers to provide learner-centred quality education that is holistic, transformative, inclusive, effective and relevant, including through mother-language based education, where appropriate
- **To strengthen collaboration further, governments should foster local, regional and international teacher collaboration through partnerships between educators and schools to share best practices and resources**; develop repositories of open digital educational resources; **create exchange programs for teachers and foster research collaboration;** and develop and maintain digital platforms that connect teachers, researchers, policymakers and organisations
- Governments should develop policies that set out clear career pathways and include resources and staff dedicated to teacher professional development and lifelong learning within defined vertical and horizontal career paths.

- The digital revolution and artificial intelligence must be pedagogically harnessed by teachers and integrated through active and human-centred teaching and learning methods and practices. **Such tools should not become a substitute for teachers, but rather should empower teachers to guide their learners' quest for inquisitive, critical, creative and lifelong learning**
- **Teachers need autonomy and pedagogical choice in how they use technology to ensure that a given technology improves learning**
- Teachers and their organisations should engage in research and dialogue with education systems and teacher training institutions in order to **ensure that teachers can play a leadership and innovation role in relation to new subject matters, pedagogies and technologies within a learner-centred approach.** Part of this work should be the creation of strong partnerships between innovative schools and teacher preparation programs that enable prospective teachers to learn in practice as well as in theory
- **Student engagement and the meaningful participation of students in the co-creation and evaluation of teaching and learning should be regarded as a fundamental value and integral building block of educational quality**[7]

These are just a few excerpts from the more than fifty-nine recommendations of the panel. Unfortunately, for a wealthy country such as Australia we are failing to achieve many of these goals. We have highlighted in bold text a few of the areas we are clearly not meeting.

The alarming advent of scripted direct instruction lessons which can supposedly be 'taught' by almost anyone, opens the door to a teacher qualification which is not university or degree-based, but the result of 'on-the-job' training much like an apprenticeship. We

7 UNESCO, *Recommendations and summary of deliberations of the United Nations Secretary-General's High-Level Panel on the Teaching Profession*, (Geneva: International Labour office, 2024).

have seen schools already using 'scripted' lessons, often taken by teachers teaching out of field. A script has no regard for student interest, independence or autonomy. An assembly line model of instruction where any employee in the factory can read the script for any lesson cannot be what we want for the future of education.

And as the world's leading education systems move towards flipped learning and continue to create intrinsic motivation and love of learning while developing student independence, creativity and mental health – in a system where teaching is a respected and highly sought profession – we in Australia do the opposite.

A similar move toward scripted lessons has been suggested in New Zealand. Dr Sarah Aiono recently commented on this:

> *'I find the recent comments from the Ministerial Advisory Group, suggesting that "teachers can't be curriculum designers as well as teachers," deeply troubling. Good teaching goes beyond merely delivering a curriculum. It involves making informed adaptations to ensure that the material is relevant, engaging, and accessible for all students.'*

Dr Aiono continues:

> *'Unfortunately, many of my colleagues are being sold a story about the "help" the curriculum designers are providing teachers – who are already overworked and juggling many challenges within their classrooms – by designing a curriculum in a way that teachers can confidently pick up and "deliver" without too much thought (and thus save time). However, this is not "help"; it is more a handicapping of the very creativity that underpins the professionalism of teaching that ensures a*

> *rich, responsive level of practice that differentiates poor teaching from excellence. A teacher who has the autonomy to truly respond to their learners, from a place of deep understanding of their children and their needs, is a highly skilled practitioner, operating at an exceptional level within the profession."*[8]

Every day, teachers make countless informed adaptations to meet the individual learning needs of their students. Our classrooms are not 'one-size-fits-all'. Children arrive with a vast array of learning needs, backgrounds, and ways to connect and engage. Some students thrive on visual learning, while others need hands-on activities to grasp new concepts. Some require additional support in literacy and numeracy, while others excel and need to be challenged further.

In dismissing the role of teachers as curriculum designers, we risk turning our classrooms into sterile environments where learning is a checklist rather than a journey.[9]

Positioning explicit teaching (ie. direct instruction in this case) in opposition and superiority over inquiry-based teaching creates a false binary. This is constructed through misunderstanding and misrepresentation of inquiry-based teaching. It neglects the essential inclusion of explicit teaching within inquiry-based teaching along with a range of approaches necessary to build relationships between teaching and learning with the diversity of students.[10]

But direct instruction has existed – and been in practice in

---

8 Dr Sarah Aiono, "Being Sold a Story: Teachers as Curriculum Designers – Teachers Are More Than Just Curriculum Deliverers," *Curiosity Creator* (Substack), June 27, 2024.

9 Aiono, "Being Sold a Story".

10 Nicole Brunker, "Escape Oppression Now: Disrupt the Dominance of Evidence-Based Practice," *EduResearch Matters*, June 13, 2024; John Sweller, "Why Inquiry Based Approaches Harm Students' Learning," *The Centre for Independent Studies*, August 11, 2021; C. E. Hmelo-Silver, R.G Duncan, & C. A. Chinn, "Scaffolding and Achievement in Problem-Based and Inquiry Learning: A Response to Kirschner, Sweller, and Clark (2006)" *Educational Psychologist* vol. 4, no.2 (2007), pp. 99–107.

many places – for decades. Does the 'evidence' for it really stand up? We have been to dozens of schools in the last few years, and we hardly see anything but direct instruction. Why is this being done in such a public manner when surely some upskilling of teachers could take place without turning it into an open forum on criticising the profession?

If we are to really understand anything, we are best served by first experiencing it first-hand in a relaxed, exploratory, holistic way, not as a series of discrete parts like the way we tend, for instance, to teach mathematics (first comes counting, then adding, then subtracting, then multiplying, etc.). When we break things apart like this, we remove the complex connectivity that stands at the centre of life itself. We would never think to teach children about soccer by first showing them a photograph of a ball. We all know, intuitively, that this removes the ball from the world of physics, sport, teamwork, and play, rendering it meaningless.[11]

TEACHERS IN PUBLIC DISCOURSE

With direct instruction, the teachers' work is simplified, supporting arguments that anyone can teach. Initial teacher education is denigrated for developing pre-service teacher ability to engage with the complexity of teaching. It also supports a return to the reproductive model of teacher training which is absent of critical thinking, reflection, and engagement with theory and research. Ultimately, the status quo is maintained.[12]

Bill Jacob, a math professor at the University of California, Santa Barbara, reported, 'the use of problem solving as a means of developing conceptual understanding [in math] was abandoned and replaced by direct instruction of skills' in California ... even

---

11 Teacher Tom, "Why Schools are so Threatened by Children at Play," *Teacher Tom* (blog), August 16, 2024.

12 Brunker, "Escape Oppression Now".

though the available research actually tended to point in the opposite direction (and still does). Indeed, Jacob added, the phrase research-based was just 'a way of promoting instruction aligned with ideology.'

There never seems to be any consideration for what students and teachers think about this criticism. What are the implications of being part of a 'profession' where everyone seems to feel entitled to criticise your practices?

Teachers, teacher unionists and a majority of educational administrators are well down the list of people whose opinions matter. The voices of politicians, wealthy industrialists, sandstone university academics, members of partisan think tanks, journalists, social media commentators and even celebrities are all more powerful than the thoughts of most Australian educators. What is the impact on recruitment of future teachers when being told how to practice your profession is so public and prevalent?

In the subordination of teachers, research is pre-digested into easy-to-read summaries for teachers to know the practices being prescribed are 'evidence-based'. Such pre-digestion of research is selective presentation of evidence to promote desired practices. It further removes teachers from engagement with research evidence.

Australian Education Research Organisation (AERO) latest guide, 'Assessing whether evidence is relevant to your context – For educators, teachers and leaders' directs teachers to AERO's own materials.

It neglects key aspects and oversimplifies, leading to errors.[13]

Is there a fear that we could see change which involves allowing teachers and students to think for themselves?

One only has to witness the noise that comes from political circles when there is a change to the history curriculum regarding Indigenous relations to the early settlers to see that many

---

13 Nicole Brunker, Escape Oppression Now: Disrupt the Dominance of Evidence-Based Practice, from EduResearch Matters, June 13 2024

politicians clearly believe that teachers teach *what* to think rather than *how* to think.

Emeritus Professor of Education Futures at University of South Australia, Robert Hattam noted: 'Australian educators are now being forced to adopt so-called evidence-based practices. Those who are harassing teachers often claim privileged access to scientific truths. But then so-called evidence-based practice has been framed up by claims about meta-analyses of randomised controlled trials (RCT). There is no scientific rationale for such a claim which I read as a tactic in a paradigm war that distorts educational policymaking. Those making policy too often fail to read the archive of educational research and followed this with a list of examples of research to support this.'[14]

Are we following the US trend of rewriting history and banning books?

Surely, we are not letting a desire to control the narrative get in the way of ensuring our country's children get the best education possible?

As the Australian crisis unfolds, many publicly debated measures such as those relating to money and curriculum appear tired before they are even tried. Should there be a point of debate

---

14 Examples include: Adrienne Alton-Lee, "Meta-analysis in education: How has it been used?" *The Australian Educational Researcher*, 2003; Daniel T. Willingham, "On the dangers of meta-analyses in education," *Education Next*, 2015; John W. Creswell, "Challenges of meta-analysis in educational research," *Review of Educational Research*, 2017; L. Greer et.al, "Publication bias in education research: A meta-analysis of meta-analyses," *Educational Research Review*, 2020; Jeffrey S. Bowers, "The limits of meta-analysis in educational research," *Educational Researcher*, 2021; Stephen J. Valentine and Patricia J. Cooper, "The Dangers of Meta-Analysis in Educational Research: A Critique," *Educational Research Quarterly*, 2016; G Biesta, "Why "what works" won't work: Evidence-based practice and the democratic deficit in educational research," *Educational Theory* vol. 57, no.1 (2007), pp. 1-22; A Keddie, "Disrupting the pathways of disadvantage: The problematic promise of John Hattie's Visible Learning" in T. Barkatsas & N. Binns (Eds.) *Teacher preparation and professional learning in Australia* (Singapore: Springer, 2016); B Lingard, "Policy borrowing, policy learning: Testing times in Australian schooling," *Critical Studies in Education* vol. 51, no.2 (2010), pp. 129-147. W Sawyer, "Critiquing the evidence-based education movement: The dangers of "what works" approaches," presented at the American Educational Research Association Annual Meeting, Washington DC, 2016.

in our discourse, it revolves around the understanding that the resolution to Australia's current education crisis won't emerge from incremental changes to teaching programs, educator salaries, student loan burdens, or the provision of prepackaged lesson materials (which are also an excellent way to control the narrative!)

Rather, the solution lies in elevating teaching to a position of the utmost esteem and desirability. It must become a profession that captivates the most accomplished, determined and dedicated young individuals as they conclude their secondary education and contemplate their future paths. Anything less than this undermines our nation's most valuable asset: its children.

> ***'It's disheartening when a teacher's spark for creativity is extinguished by the pressures of standardization and bureaucracy because it is their spark that often ignites the excitement of learning within their students.'***
>
> *— Dr Brad Johnson*

We are often asked if Australian teachers are at a world class standard. A CEO from an international education organisation looking to set up schools in Australia asked me if I (Michael) thought he would be able to find excellent teachers in Australia, and suggested that he thought he might have to source them from overseas. In the last few years, we have visited dozens of Australian schools and have always been impressed with the dedicated and hard-working teachers we have encountered. To function effectively in an Australian school in the current environment is an achievement in itself.

But many of our best teachers have left the profession. Those who care most about the students are often the ones who find it most difficult to apply standardised practices, and be judged by standardised tests. We have also removed our teachers' autonomy:

their ability to use their professional judgement, knowledge and experience to make decisions about their practice.

> ***'We can't expect teachers to work 60–70 hours per week or more, but then tell them to self-care. Maybe leaving is their self-care?'***
>
> *— Dr Brad Johnson*

When I (Michael) visited China, I often asked guides about political issues within the country and it quickly became obvious that as they had never had the opportunity to vote for their political leaders, they saw little point in debating or even discussing their actions. This is what we have done to Australian teachers: having lost their professional autonomy to micromanaging policymakers, many have stopped looking into alternative practices within their profession. Effectively we have transitioned the teaching profession to a clerical delivery position (see 'The GERM' later in this chapter for more details).

Australian teachers and school administrations are generally gagged. There are few, if any, forums for constructive input, observation and commentary. Educational authorities determine course structures and content, policies and direction, frequently in the absence of input from actual educators. They are regularly influenced by powerful lobbyists, including religious organisations, industrial groups, think tanks and some tertiary institutions. These entities tend to be completely shielded from accountability in relation to the dire state of many aspects of Australian school education.

Further examples of 'evidence' disseminated to teachers in pre-digested formats include CESE's (NSW's Centre for Education Statistics and Evaluation) Cognitive Load Theory: research that teachers really need to understand which is based on a paper widely critiqued as a strawman fallacy. CESE's paper is then relied upon by AERO (Australian Education Research Organisation) in their presentation of evidence for cognitive load theory to teachers.[15] Pasi Sahlberg believes that, 'The successful transformation in education systems requires that teachers and principals are really involved as partners in co-creating new education systems and that schools provide students with real opportunities to use their voices and engage in incorporating and guiding their own learning inside and outside the school.' [16]

SCHOOLS WHERE TEACHERS WANT TO BE

In this text, frequent references are made to Finland and Estonia, primarily because they are nations where teaching stands out as a prestigious career option, and students consistently express high levels of satisfaction with their educational experiences. Both from the perspective of students and educators, the deliberate avoidance of standardisation in any guise acknowledges the uniqueness of individuals involved. A plethora of neuroscience and relevant research underscores the connection between this autonomy and satisfaction, reduced anxiety, and increased motivation.

In 2017, 67% of UK schoolteachers were reporting feelings of stress – by 2023, that figure had risen starkly to 78%.[17]

In a report published in 2020 by the Finland Ministry of Education and Culture on the attraction factors of teacher education, more than 6,300 upper secondary school students (Finland's population is less than a fifth of Australia's) reported what would make them interested in the teaching profession. A common theme was that, 'as a teacher, you can make the work your own'.

---

15 Brunker, "Escape Oppression Now".

16 Pasi Sahlberg, "Sata 24", presentation, Croatia 2024.

17 "Teacher Wellbeing Index," *Education Support* (UK), accessed August 2024.

A recent study conducted by Oxford University's William Fleming delved into the impact of various workplace wellbeing interventions, including stress management, yoga, mindfulness classes, and wellbeing apps. Surprisingly, the findings revealed that almost none of these interventions had any statistically significant impact on worker wellbeing or job satisfaction. In other words, despite the time and money invested in workplace wellness programs, they often fall short of their intended goals.

Here are some key takeaways from the study:

- Costly Interventions: Companies worldwide spent a staggering $61.2 billion on wellness interventions in 2021, and this figure is projected to grow to $94.6 billion by 2026. Many of these interventions come with a hefty price tag and consume valuable employee time.
- Stress Reduction Matters: Rather than adding new coping mechanisms, the most effective way to improve employee mental health is by reducing workplace stress. Unfortunately, most wellness programs fail to address this critical aspect.
- Underwhelming Impact: Workplace wellbeing initiatives, including stress management courses, mindfulness training, and wellbeing apps, rarely lead to significant improvements. They don't enhance employees' sense of belonging, reduce perceived time pressures, or strengthen workplace relationships.
- Mixed Results: Some interventions even had negative effects. For instance, resilience and mindfulness training slightly worsened employees' self-rated mental health.
- Real-World Evidence: A US study involving nearly 33,000 employees found similarly lacklustre results. Despite wellness interventions, there was no significant difference in physical health markers, healthy behaviours, healthcare spending, absenteeism, job tenure, or job performance.

So, while companies continue to invest in wellness programs, it's essential to focus on meaningful stress reduction strategies rather than merely adding more tools to employees' coping toolbox. After all, a healthier workforce benefits everyone in the long run.[18]

PRIORITISING TEACHER AUTONOMY: CREATING SCHOOLS WHERE TEACHERS WANT TO BE

What do the countries where teaching is a top career choice do differently?

Autonomy consistently arises in global research across many employment sectors as a key condition for satisfaction, challenge, positive self-efficacy beliefs and ultimately professional longevity. The education systems in countries where no issues with teacher recruitment and retention exist are characterised by respect for teachers as key decision makers and independent agents of learning within their own classrooms.

Teaching is often cited as the most popular career choice for young people in Finland. This popularity has waned somewhat, with one in six applicants now gaining entry compared with just one in ten a decade ago. The Finnish teacher is a highly respected professional with great autonomy. A 2012 survey asking what it would take for them to consider leaving the profession saw the loss of this autonomy as a top response, above money.[19]

This high demand to enter the profession ensures that only the brightest, most appropriate applicants gain entry. At least one teaching university holds what amounts to an audition as part of the selection process, ensuring that not only are the successful applicants academically suitable, but that they are also predisposed

---

18 Andre Spicer, "Work 'wellness' programmes don't make employees happier – but I know what does," *The Guardian*, January 18, 2024; William J. Fleming, "Employee well-being outcomes from individual-level mental health interventions: Cross-sectional evidence from the United Kingdom," *Industrial Relations Journal* no. 55, no. 2 (2024), pp. 162-182.

19 Pasi Sahlberg, *Finnish Lessons 2.0* (New York, Teacher's College Press, 2015).

in other ways to the requirements of the teaching profession.

It is rare for a teacher to leave the profession in Finland. While teacher pay there is similar to that of Australian teachers, the conditions under which Finnish teachers operate are very different and comprise the main reason for the popularity (and success) of the profession there. Perhaps the best illustration of this is Pasi Sahlberg's response to the question about how to best evaluate teachers.

'In Finland, we don't ask "How can we evaluate teachers?" we ask, "How can we best support teachers?"'

The Finnish teacher is a trusted professional, and to be conducting frequent performance evaluations would be undermining this trust. They are given great autonomy to interpret and construct curriculum and assessment as they see fit for their students. Interference in this area would be seen as a breach of this professional autonomy and unacceptable. This is one of the reasons why the teaching profession is able to attract excellent candidates. The Finnish teacher's assessments are trusted. As one Finnish educator said to me during a discussion about Australia's standardised testing regime, NAPLAN, 'Why don't they just ask the teachers?'

> ***'Most of what teachers do in the classroom is an interpretation of the science. The teacher's job is to learn the science and make the best possible teaching decisions in the light of it.'***
>
> *— Anna Geiger*

There is considerable truth to this. When I (Michael) had my own Grade 3/4 class, I had notes and data on when each student had mastered the six times tables - and all the others - and exactly where they were at with spelling, sentence structures, reading etc. The data from the NAPLAN tests, which arrived the year after they had done the test, contained nothing I did not already know, and I knew it in far greater detail. And my notes and data were changing at least every week, whereas the NAPLAN results were already six months old when I got them.

Our insistence on micromanaging our teachers and students with things like NAPLAN, standardised curriculum and ongoing evaluations and assessments (see 'The GERM' in the next few pages) has seen both teachers and the students lose the motivation and enthusiasm that autonomy and trust brings. And this is at the heart of the success of the Finnish system.

A Finnish teacher completes a master's thesis involving research into practice. It is designed to create a 'highly developed problem-solving capacity that derives from the teacher's deep understanding of the principles of learning and allows them to create "powerful learning environments" that continually improve as they learn to engage in a cycle of self-responsible planning, action and reflection/evaluation.'

This is 'intelligent accountability' in a context where external student testing is rare, but analysis of practice and student learning is all pervasive.[20]

When I asked a Finnish colleague how their students had managed through the period of remote learning, the response was, 'They have tried to not let it impact their studies'. Here in Australia, many students saw remote learning as an opportunity to disengage. Such is the difference between having ownership over something and having it thrust upon you.

Most Finnish teachers are quite happy to teach in a way that they know will have better outcomes in the long term rather than teach to a test.

---

20 Linda Darling-Hammond, *The Flat World and Education* (New York: Teachers College Press, 2010).

A recent research paper set out to determine whether a state's big standardised test measures student learning, teacher effectiveness, or something else. The answer, it turns out, is something else.

'The tests are not measuring how much students learned or can learn,' says Tienken (one of the researchers). 'They are predominately measuring the family and community capital of the student.'[21]

In Australia, it has been observed that final year exam performances are also often a measure of something other than learning – a student's postcode.

THE GERM

When Professor Pasi Sahlberg coined the term Global Education Reform Movement (GERM) he was talking about the countries that have employed a number of education policies and reform principles to try to improve the quality of education and fix the apparent problems in public education systems. This is the direction Australia has taken and adherence to it has curtailed any genuine innovation for decades.

Standardisation

Outcomes-based education reform became popular in the 1980s, followed by standards-based education policies in the 1990s, initially within Anglo-Saxon countries. A widely accepted – and generally unquestioned – belief among policymakers and education reformers is that setting clear and sufficiently high-performance standards for schools, teachers, and students will necessarily improve the quality of expected outcomes. Centrally prescribed curricula – with detailed performance targets, frequent testing of students and teachers, and test-based accountability – have characterised a homogenisation of education policies worldwide,

---

21 Jamil Maroun and Christopher Tienken, "Research Shows What Standardized Tests Actually Measure," quoted in *Forbes Magazine*, Feb 10, 2024

promising standardised solutions at increasingly lower cost for those desiring to improve school quality and effectiveness.

Focus on core subjects

Basic student knowledge and skills in reading, writing and mathematics are elevated as prime targets and indicators of education reforms. As a consequence of accepting international student assessment surveys, such as PISA, TIMSS and PIRLS, as criteria of good educational performance, reading, mathematical and scientific literacy have now become the main determinants of perceived success or failure of pupils, teachers, schools, and entire education systems - all at the expense of social studies, arts, music and physical education.

Low-risk ways to reach learning goals

This minimises all innovative approaches, and limits risk-taking in schools and classrooms. Research on education systems that have adopted policies emphasising achievement of predetermined standards and prioritised core subjects, suggests that teaching and learning are narrower and teachers focus on 'guaranteed content' to best prepare their students for tests. The higher the test-result stakes, the lower the chances of any innovation in classroom learning.

Use of corporate management models

This label includes educational policies and ideas that are lent and borrowed from the business world, and which are often motivated by political goals and economic profit, rather than by moral goals of human development. Such initiatives limit the role of national policy development and enhancement of an education system's own capabilities to maintain renewal, and perhaps more importantly, it paralyses teachers' and schools' attempts to learn from the past and also to learn from each other.

We have asked education leaders about their professional reading, and it is amazing how many of them are reading business instead of education texts. We are aware of a popular online educational leadership course, Leading People, run jointly by the Harvard Graduate School of Education and the Harvard Business School. Although the program is well-intentioned, it promotes several hard-nosed business practices, such as the use of simplistic evaluative metrics and processes for naming and shaming allegedly unproductive employees, as effective measures for teacher management.

We believe that typical company workforce approaches are often jarring within school contexts. Our students are not business clients, they are our partners, and they should reap the highest profits. Our most valuable products can never be quantified or itemised on a balance sheet. Teachers should be primarily accountable to their students, not to their line manager. We do not work on production lines, we deal with young humans and the wonderful, imponderable, immeasurable and inspiring worlds in which they live. Schooling is a unique enterprise that is not well emulated by standard business models.

Test-based accountability policies

Raising student achievement is closely tied to processes of accrediting, promoting, inspecting, and, ultimately, rewarding or punishing schools and teachers. Success or failure of schools and teachers is often determined by standardised tests and external teacher evaluations that devote attention to limited aspects of schooling, such as student achievement in numeracy and reading literacy and exit examination results.

This does not imply that education standards, focus on basic knowledge and skills, or accountability should be avoided in seeking better educational performance. Nor are we suggesting that these ideas were completely absent in education development in Finland. But, perhaps, the implication is that a good education system can be created using alternative approaches.[22]

THE CURRENT SYSTEM AND ITS FAILINGS

As one Finnish teacher asked me (Michael) in reference to our current 'education crisis': 'So they would rather go without teachers than look at changing the practices driving teachers away?'

I was speechless. The willingness of the Finns to openly discuss issues within their system and schools is the polar opposite to our 'method' of ignoring the issue, never speaking of it, and dismissing any suggestion to improve it, unless it comes from the government. Of course, governments do not have the specialised knowledge or experience to make these calls, and when they do they are often reverting to the practice of micromanaging teachers and further eroding their last shreds of professional autonomy.

The removal of the competitive framework within which Australia's schools operate will immediately encourage collaboration and cooperation.

> ***'… evidence and science were employed to justify all sorts of educational approaches, as seems to be the case with a label like "best practice." But these words are almost always used to defend traditionalist practices such as direct instruction and control-based interventions derived from Skinnerian behaviorism such as Applied Behavior Analysis (ABA) and Positive Behavioral Interventions and Supports (PBIS).'***
>
> *— Alfie Kohn*

'Many people,' Sahlberg writes, 'think that in today's highly competitive and fast changing era, children need to learn how to

---

22 Salberg *Finnish, Lessons.*

compete and become winners. However, my point is the opposite. The best way for students to adapt to competition and change is to teach them to cooperate, because in such a complex and ever-changing environment, creativity and adventurousness are more necessary, and these qualities can be nurtured and born only in an environment that encourages cooperation. So as an educator, I would not encourage students to study for the sake of competition and to win. On the contrary, I want to give them a relaxed and cooperative environment so that they will have those precious qualities of creativity and adventurousness – and be given opportunities to make mistakes – that they need to face challenges in the future.'[23]

We are aware of many Australian schools where staff have been instructed to not comment on issues regarding staffing and other policies. There are also many stories of schools which have used alternative methods (to the GERM) with great success and been virtually ignored by the media (government bureaucracies are usually behind the decisions on which schools get media attention).

Boosters of the Science of Teaching (SoT) are attempting to narrow and strangle the definition of what constitutes good science and then shouting down anyone who contests their truths. It's now a key tactic that anyone who contests policy is told they are ignoring the science. I'm saying, 'yes, we are ignoring your science actually!' The SoT also pushes highly scripted teaching approaches, and whenever possible, proposes the further erosion of the professional autonomy of teachers.[24]

We spoke with school leaders who understood that what they were doing was not working – and had a wealth of data to prove it – and they could see how the practices we talk about in these pages would change things, but there were still only a few leaders prepared

23 See Zoey Zheng, "Pasi Sahlberg : Teachers need a sense of mission, empathy and leadership," LinkedIn, Febrary 3, 2018.

24 Hattam, LinkedIn.

to put the needs of the students above anything else. We spoke with principals who told us that they have had no improvement from practices such as the department's High Impact Teaching Strategies - and they then admitted that they were not aware of any schools which had seen improvements from them - yet they were mandating them to the entire school!

Teaching must be valued for the complex, 'problematic' practice that it is. Wider understanding is needed on how teachers have and do use evidence to build a relationship between teaching and learning to support other teachers and school leaders, along with teacher educators and PSTs. Teachers have been making evidence informed decisions for action long before the emergence of evidence-based practice ... evidence is not proof, and that evidence cannot speak for itself, rather evidence must be interpreted.[25]

We are aware of teachers and even department heads who have been performance-managed out of their positions for questioning the standardised curriculum they have been mandated to use. Ironically, we know that the teacher is the most important component in the educational chain, 'accounting for about 30% of the variance in student achievement'.[26] Yet we continue to marginalise those teachers who so much as question the standardised methods and teaching to the test.

Australia's adherence to its outdated, ineffective system is akin to the United States' reluctance to move away from its gun culture. The evidence is clear and the number of lives (and careers) destroyed are incalculable, but there's a stubborn resistance to change that is hard to explain to someone with any perspective on the situation. Indeed, there have been professional consequences and gag orders for some who have been seen to not toe the line.

The Finnish teacher is well aware that standardisation is poor

---

25 Brunker, "Escape Oppression Now".

26 J Hattie, *Hattie Ranking: 252 Influences and Effect Sizes Related to Student Achievement*, 2017.

practice which ignores the differences between students, putting the desire to collect data ahead of the students' best interests (ahead of all interests of the student).

The Finnish National Curriculum includes the statement: 'Every student is unique and worthy just as they are. Everyone has the right to grow up into a fully rounded person and member of society. For this to happen students need encouragement and individual support. They need to feel they are being listened to and respected within the school community, and that the community cares about their learning and wellbeing.'

> *'... the term evidence-based sometimes functions not as a meaningful modifier but just as a slogan, an all-purpose honorific like "all-natural" on a food label. Rather than denoting the existence of actual evidence, its purpose may be to brand those who disagree with one's priorities as "unscientific" and pressure them to fall in line.'*
>
> — *Alfie Kohn*

Retired Queensland principal Chris Gold described the reasons why Australian education leaders are reluctant to change:

> *'I see good leaders kowtow to authorities to get ahead. It's cringeworthy ... to recently hear of the increased oversight and direction to dumbing down and further crowding of curriculum ... It's fear of the system, the system fears reduced funding, and the government looking for scapegoats ... Until we get back to what you talk about – trust and perfecting the craft of teaching and love of learning – we will continue on the slippery slide.'*

Finnish teachers looked at me (Michael) as if I were nuts when I described the NAPLAN tests given to children as young as eight. With shocked expressions, they asked why Australian teachers allowed this to be done to such young children. They then suggested that (of course) the results of these tests should lead to increased funding and assistance for those students and schools that did not do well.

> ***'In reality, no controlled study then or since has, to the best of my knowledge, ever demonstrated any benefit to high-stakes testing - other than the tautological claim that it raises scores on those same tests. The damage done to the quality of teaching and learning by NCLB has been incalculable.'***[27]

I didn't immediately understand the concerns of my Finnish colleagues, as – like most Australian teachers – I had come to accept NAPLAN as a normal practice. I was mistaken, and later in this text we discuss students whose self-belief in a subject was destroyed by NAPLAN, and some who attempted to take their own lives during the test.

> ***'We do not work for administrators, central office personnel, superintendents, heads of school, boards of education or parents. We work for kids.'***[28]

The Education Trade Union (OAJ) in Finland has been a strong advocate for the high professional autonomy of teachers. The

---

27 A Kohn. See also Deborah Meier et al., *Many Children Left Behind* (Beacon Press, 2004); and Gerald W. Bracey, "The Condition of Public Education," *Phi Delta Kappan*, October 2006, pp. 151-53.

28 Eric Sheninger, *Disruptive Thinking in Our Classrooms*, (Chicago: ConnectEDD Publishing LLC, 2021).

organisation includes practically all Finnish educators, ranging from early childhood to university and polytechnics. School principals are also members. OAJ is a substantial stakeholder in education and has a strong influence in maintaining a priority on the professional autonomy and voice of teachers in terms of curriculum, pedagogy and policymaking.[29]

This is one of the reasons why teaching is such a highly respected and popular vocation among young people, often ranking above law and medicine as a career choice. On graduating, the teacher swears an oath known as The Comenius Oath (much like medicine or engineering), which assures the children's best interests are always first and ethics are the teacher's priority. It is this oath which ensures that the best interests of the students always come first. The teacher is responsible for the wellbeing of the student.

There is no singluar 'Finnish method', except to say that the teacher is continually reviewing their own practice, and anything less than that which is proving successful, backed by neuroscience and research, is discarded.

The system is constantly evolving. The trainee teacher is encouraged to study best practice and try to improve it; innovation is always encouraged in the belief that without it there can be no improvement.

It is not that Finland has dashed ahead of other countries, rather that others (Australia, the United States, the United Kingdom) got caught up in the standardisation of curriculum, in the pursuit of grades on standardised tests (the GERM), and evidence-based practice which means that we effectively stopped all innovation and progress.

---

29 L. Hannu et al., "Three Orientations for Understanding Educational Autonomy: School Principals' Voices from Australia, Finland, and Jamaica," *Journal of Educational Administration and History*, vol. 53, 2021.

> ***'We want our teachers to focus on learning, not testing. We do not, at all, believe in ranking students and ranking schools ... In Finland, having happy children is the most important thing, we want to bring back the joy of learning. When you go to schools here, you see happy, active and engaged pupils.'***
>
> *— Kristiina Volmari from the Finnish National Agency for Education*

Once we standardise, the message is, 'Stop! Don't change a thing, just learn what is on the test and let's get these grades.'

If we view education as a business then we may feel justified in treating students as products, parents as customers and teachers as employees. Using this business model, we are in competition with ourselves. ATAR and NAPLAN results compare one school to another. If one compares favourably, then the job is considered done.

If Australian education were a genuine business, it would not be allowed to continue using outdated practices that were not successful. It would have a research and development arm.

But what of the students who were not part of the successful business?

What of the teachers who walked away from the system because they love learning and working with young people and don't like being just 'employees' delivering test content?

How do we compare with the rest of the world? Particularly those countries that are open to educational change, building a love for learning (as opposed to a love for winning the grades contest), and preparing for the unknown future rather than the known past?

Are we happy to centre our entire system around those students who do well in a test/grade-centred environment, and dismiss those who don't do well as collateral damage, or even victims of friendly fire, 'who should have worked harder and deserve to fall behind'?

A Finnish teacher Arto Kaukko, who worked in a Victorian (the State, not the era!) school lasted six weeks and told his story in a recent edition of *Opettaja*, the magazine of the professional body in Finland under the headline:

> ***'While working in Australia, Arto Kaukko realized what it would be like to be a slavish implementer of the curriculum. In Finland, the goal of teachers' pedagogical autonomy is for everyone to learn to think about things independently and critically.'***

He estimated that we were thirty to forty years behind and described Australia's education system:

'They believe that education develops best when schools are made to compete with each other. Trying to hold on to the reputation of the school may lead to the teacher not being allowed to upset the parents,' he told the magazine. 'I didn't treat students like a flock of sheep that should be herded and humiliated. I didn't agree to that.' [30]

A recent study at Curtin University found: 'The vast majority of teachers are considering leaving the profession because they have very poor work-life balance. Our teachers are telling us that their workloads are unmanageable and unrealistic.'[31]

'It is paramount that state governments initiate immediate and tangible reforms when it comes to workload. We simply cannot continue to expect our teachers to carry all the requirements being

---

30 A Kaukko, "Finland relies on teachers' pedagogical solutions – in Australia, class teacher Arto Kaukko had to print lesson plans on the classroom wall," *Opettaja Magazine*, 2021.

31 Brett Henebery, "'Cruel' wellbeing approach adding to teachers' stress – study," *The Educator*, 27 February 2024.

put upon them and not burn out or become seriously demoralised about a job they undoubtedly love, especially when it comes to making a difference in the lives of the young people they work with.'[32]

A large part of the problem is that the majority of this work is compliance work involved with curriculum and assessment which has been imposed upon the teacher with little or no consultation.

VIOLENCE AGAINST TEACHERS

48% of the 2300 principals who took part in the Australian Catholic University's (ACU) annual principal safety survey reported experiencing or witnessing physical violence, and about 54% were threatened with violence.[33] There is a likely association between these figures and our standardised system treating the students as pawns in the collection of data and grades, keeping interactions impersonal and mechanical. Student behaviours can only be worsened by a lack of autonomy and recognition of personal needs.

> ***'... It was the searing mental and emotional load that came with supporting young people from psychologically complex and often heartbreaking circumstances. It was buckling under the expectations of systemic pressure to score higher in standardised testing despite vastly different cohorts. It was the dance between instilling high expectations with students while parents entitled their children to denigrate the importance of education and disrespect staff.***
>
> ***What would it have taken for me not to leave? Ultimately? Trust. We need to start trusting our teachers, because***

32 S Karnovsky and Brad Gobby, "How teacher wellbeing can be cruel: refusing discourses of wellbeing in an online Reddit forum," *British Journal of Sociology of Education*, 2024

33 Australian Catholic University, "The Australian Principal Occupational Health, Safety and Wellbeing Survey 2023," (Melbourne: Australian Catholic University, March 2024).

when you remove bureaucracy from wonderful and compassionate people, it's amazing what you can achieve.'

— Peita Mages, Winner of the Minister's Award for Excellence in Teaching.

'... Paperwork now consists of documenting every conversation with a parent, every behavioural incident, collating results and recording them to get 'the data', not to mention completing all the risk assessments and all of the other paperwork to keep admin ticking boxes for their bosses.

The expectation is that you will attend camps and functions outside of school hours with no recognition or reimbursement of any sort...

In the end I had to get out, away from the system that was destroying my mental health and my joy of teaching.

How do you fix this broken system? By providing admin time or assistants to help teachers do the admin... And by allowing them to have time to do their job, which is teaching.'

— Fiona Reed, 35 years of experience

Newspapers reported that WorkSafe found 'teachers (who were) facing up to twenty violent and sexist attacks every day from students at their Victorian school need psychiatric support'. WorkSafe also found, 'the level of assaults, threats, harassment and gendered and racial abuse directed by students at their teachers throughout 2022 and 2023 left most of the staff at Warrnambool

College ... in an unacceptable risk of psychological injury.' Teachers spoke of 'being forced to flee and lock themselves in offices after being pushed, shoved and threatened, with disturbing accounts emerging of groups of students targeting staff with antisemitic and other forms of racial abuse.'

The (education) department rejected the WorkSafe direction to provide an on-site mental health worker, saying, 'Warrnambool is far from the only school in the state dealing with workplace violence' and the provision of a mental health worker at one school would 'have implications for every government school where incidents of workplace violence occur.'[34]

There is no precedent for workplace conditions such as this outside of war zones. Police officers would not expect to face violence on a daily basis. The fact that this is occurring in many other schools should certainly not be grounds to reject recommendations designed to resolve the issue.

The expected response to this would be to clamp down or even implement a zero-tolerance approach to discipline (the report suggested that this had taken place: the department cited extensive efforts by the school to manage student behaviour and protect staff), but does this get to the heart of the problem?

Such student misbehaviour is almost always pushback against what students see as attempts to coerce them into participating in something they don't want to. It's likely that many of these students regularly attend football or netball training and have little difficulty with the compliance rules in place at these.

We can be sure that the teachers are not the only ones traumatised by the violence and abuse going on at this school.

Whenever we see situations such as this in schools, it is rare for anyone to ask why the students are behaving in such a way. In any

34 "Legal Fight Over Help for Teacher," *The Age*, July 6, 2024.

other industry, a change in customer behaviour will be followed by research attempting to find if the customer perception has changed, or the business' product is no longer what it once was.

How can we be claiming to be 'child centred' when we will not compromise in any way on our requirements from the students: if our only solution to the above issue is to clamp down on student discipline and recommend a mental health worker for the traumatised teachers? How can we claim to be respecting the teachers involved when we challenge the recommendations that help teachers deal with a problem, especially when we have not even been able to reduce the problem in any way?

A search for policy response to 'student violence' from the Victorian Department of Education online resources[35] unhelpfully led to a discussion on adult-on-adult misbehaviours. This is in line with workplaces in general but totally misses the most critical contemporary issue – student violence in schools. Further searching found details of end-game procedures, including how to implement suspensions and expulsions. But the Department line is thin on how the need for such admittance-of-failure measures can be avoided.

The closest Department advice on student violence is given in relation to managing behaviours. It states, 'Schools are expected to consider, explore and implement positive and non-punitive interventions to support student behaviour...'. Great in principle, but lacking in impact unless everything that leads a student to extreme acts, like all forms of violence, is considered.

We need to look deeply at school organisational structures, our teaching approaches, our curricula, our responses to student concerns, our own respect for teachers (let alone from the wider community) and our respect for students as the valuable,

---

35 See "Information for Schools," Schools Victoria, September 9, 2024.

precious individuals they are before we will get anywhere. One of the simplest and possibly most productive starting points for addressing the crisis of student violence is to ask, are our students happy, and the related question, are our teachers happy?

TEACHING IS CONTEXTUAL

The most effective teachers in our schools exhibit a variety of different qualities, often associated with the subject context. What works for one may not be appropriate or useful for another. Perhaps the best guide to describing how teachers can do great things is by starting with a set of successful student outcomes and working backwards. The following sketches may all be considered representations of student success. We have seen them all throughout our time in schools.

Mimmy

She was a high academic achiever. Mimmy worked hard and understood the association between her efforts and outstanding outcomes. She had a series of great STEM teachers, expert people, passionate about their subjects, communicators of fantastic ideas and exemplary role models for Mimmy. She knew what sort of adult she was going to be.

Christos

He came a long way in six months. Christos now comes to school more often than he stays away. Christos found a teacher who 'got' him, maybe even thought he was ok as he was. Christos was never the best behaved or smartest student in class, and he hated always being compared to the good ones. This teacher didn't do that; she tried to understand what made Christos do the things he did and never gave up with him. He felt alright when she was teaching him.

Jasmine
She drifted through primary into secondary without making any waves. Jasmine was quiet but never appreciated being told that. She got pass marks in most academic subjects without really standing out. But Jasmine realised one day that she had a talent for working with textiles. Her textiles teacher was like her: low profile, unassuming, but highly interested in textiles and appreciative of Jasmine's beautiful work. Jasmine found what she really wanted to do at school and beyond.

Jose
He always tried hard but too often this was not enough. Jose didn't consider himself very bright, so many of his tests ended up in failure. One year, he found a teacher who told him he didn't get too hung up about Jose's results, it was his effort that mattered most. He taught Jose not to worry or fret over his marks. It was what he did before and after that mattered just as much. Once Jose understood that his tests were also part of his learning, he became more relaxed and could start to work out what he was doing wrong himself. Jose thought his teacher's advice helped him a lot.

These four student cases are a small sample of the many ways in which a teacher can be great. A teacher's impact will depend on the context and circumstances of the learning situation as much as on the complexities of a student's character, self-perception, current strengths and challenges, hopes and ambitions and much more. The great teacher needs to deal with many affective and cognitive variables if any student is to succeed. There is no formula for this, only general principles that emerge from a consideration of what success looks like. Researcher Philip Jackson found that elementary teachers have 200–300 exchanges with students every hour (1200–1500 a day), most of which are unplanned and unpredictable and call for teacher decisions, if not judgments.[36]

We believe all students need to experience genuine care.[37] Care is not completely addressed by running a wellbeing program, teaching religion or providing courses in values, ethics and morals. These activities can help but care that is personalised and meaningful to a student, from a teacher's perspective, is much more effortful and integral to their practice. It is evident in their manner, approachability, the way they interact, talk, instruct, observe and notice, understand, encourage, wait, respond, respect and smile.

Relationship-building is another key attribute of a successful teacher. Relating to children differs greatly from relating to adults. The partnership is between unequal parties. The teacher often needs to draw from deep reserves of empathy, patience, humour, faith, humility and acceptance to establish a productive rapport. The building of positive relationships is usually a critical step in any process of teaching students. Teachers don't get far without it. The mutual respect and understanding that characterises strong positive relationships plays a significant part in a teacher's ability to manage students, another hallmark attribute in a successful teacher's professional skill set.[38]

Passion and expertise commonly surface as attributes of a great teacher: passion for a subject, expertise within it and passion for teaching it. The success of those who view school education as a long game, not something that is quickly ticked off on the way to another goal, is sustained by their passion. The business is necessarily lumbered with challenges – failure is only ever one bungled preparation or unforeseen circumstance away. It is the

36 Tristha Ramamurthy, "Teachers are the surgeons of the education," *The Times of India* 17 March, 2023.

37 See "The Importance of Supporting Students with an Abundance of Care," Catapult Learning, February 8, 2021.

38 See, J. Yassine et al., "Building Student-Teacher Relationships and Improving Behaviour-Management for Classroom Teachers," *Support for Learning*, vol. 35, no. 3 (2020), pp. 389-407.

teacher's passion that allows them to continually step through setbacks, learn from the experience and be better next time.

Students usually can't help but appreciate a teacher who loves and knows their topic, even if they don't get swept away by it themselves. They will always forgive a teacher whose lesson doesn't work but they know she is trying hard and won't give up on them. When the teacher's knowledge, ability and passion can be expressed and communicated through an accessible and engaging teaching practice, the appeal is complete. Anyone blessed with such qualities is well equipped to become a great teacher for many of their students.

A school that is replete with passionate, expert and caring staff is likely going to be a very good school. The capacity of teachers to work their own magic should not be constricted by their schools, it should be enhanced and celebrated. Teachers who are allowed to develop their personal teaching practices, play to their strengths, be informed by their professional experience and keep fresh through ongoing training, are an invaluable asset for any school.[39]

Teachers should be encouraged to put all new pedagogical initiatives through the 'pub test'. Will this work for my students in my classroom? They should be able to trial, adapt or discard and make their own professional judgements about the value added to their local practice. As the educational neuroscientist Jared Cooney Horvath advocates, teachers (informed by their own students' responses) need to be the ultimate arbiters of the success or failure of their methods, not putting blind faith in generic labels such as 'evidence-based'. Cooney Horvath states:

---

39 See Zayd Waghid, "Teachers Change Lives – But What Makes a Great Teacher?," *The Conversation*, 7 March, 2023; "The Most Important Qualities That Make a Good Teacher," *Teachers of Tomorrow*, 30 July, 2023; "What Makes a Good Teacher?," Open Universities Australia, 3 June, 2022.

'Accordingly, although drawing on educational research is worthwhile and can help align thinking, pedagogical decisions must always be ceded to the experts in pedagogy: namely, teachers.'[40]

The last thing any school should want is for their teachers to be distracted by endless data-gathering demands; compliant with rules and procedures that do not strongly contribute to teaching and learning in their classroom; straitjacketed by mandated pedagogies and ideologies; and implementing policies that nobody really understands. Great teachers do not need herding. Education systems and administrators need to back their teachers and respect, trust and put faith in them to create optimal levels of student nurturing and academic development. Australia appears to be failing in this regard.

A 2022 research survey report[41] showed seven out of ten Australian teachers do not feel respected, the same proportion admitting to contemplating leaving the profession. Nine in ten felt politicians don't respect teachers. Externally imposed data-gathering and processing directives – such as the requirements associated with NAPLAN testing – were cited as a factor in the issue for many teachers. The researchers wrote:

'Teachers are experts. They care about children and their learning. They're professionals with deep knowledge and experience, but too often this isn't reflected in policies, nor the associated political and media commentaries ... We need to trust them, and value their training and expertise.

---

40 Jared Cooney Horvath, "Why You're Probably Wrong About the Science of Learning," *Tes Magazine*, 1 May, 2024.

41 "When it Comes to Teachers, Respect Takes Many Forms – And All Matter," *Monash University*, 16 December, 2022.

> ***We need to believe they're teachers because they care about our students and our communities.'***

A teaching workforce that is backed by administrators, media and political leaders should be the natural drivers of great education in Australia.

We glimpsed what this could look like at the Tampere Classical School in Finland. The Finnish senior school years structure is not all about university entrance. There is room for localised courses that contribute to a valued final school certificate and are free from state controls. Teachers are encouraged to be creative with courses and meet their students' interests. We saw a class full of enthralled students like Mimmy and they thought their freewheeling teacher was great. They were being dared to comprehend as he presented, Eddie Woo style, a model of consciousness based on advanced mathematical and metaphysical ideas. It was Year 12 education, but not as we know it here in Australia.

TEACHER TRAINING

We are concerned that preparing great teachers is not necessarily on the agenda of Australian education authorities. A frightening report of a planned future for Australian initial teacher training (ITE) was prepared by Skourdoumbis and Rowe (2024)[42]. We believe the plan is not to effectively address the assortment of crises in Australian education, a few that we have discussed, but to extend the plight in which many schools find themselves.

A 2023 Australian government report, 'New Beginnings', initiated the reform response to pressing issues in education such as the acute teacher shortage. The government authors identify several organisations – including the Australian Institute for Teaching and

42 A Skourdoumbis & E Rowe, "A critique of 'Strong Beginnings' initial teacher education reforms: mandating neuroscience as core curriculum within the 'what works' movement," *Australian Education Research* (2024).

School Leadership (AITSL), the Centre for Independent Studies (CIS), and the Australian Education Research Organisation (AERO) – as key drivers of an ideologically based conservative reform agenda. The proposed policies represent a major shift towards a 'what works' approach and is based on a heavily scripted and frequently contentious set of principles and practices.

A major concern is the promotion of 'brain-based' learning principles, chiefly in the form of neuroscientific findings. Skourdoumbis and Rowe express a high degree of alarm related to the nature of the utilised neuroscientific evidence. They warn:

> *'... we question neuroscience in education as a "value-free" approach, drawing on critiques and limitations of brain-based education; we put forward the risks of a brain-based approach as potentially dehumanising for students, establishing oppressive technologies as located within eugenics ...'*

Skourdoumbis and Rowe are further concerned that the reform approach is based on a deficit model of teachers, requiring high levels of micromanagement, compliance and mandating. This perspective is the polar opposite of the approach we believe is needed for the development of great teachers.

The authors of the study report that a standing assumption of the reforms is that teacher quality is in decline and that teacher-sourced concerns such as excessive bureaucratic workloads are ignored in the reasoning. Perhaps the most concerning aspect of the policies is the misuse of neuroscience to construct a narrow and simplistic concept of learning. Neuroscience generally precludes the investigation of social processes and interactions.

Thus, any claim for learning to be solely a province of neuroscience dismisses a large body of long-established educational understanding. For example, Vygotsky's theory of sociocultural learning and constructivist principles related to the formation of knowledge, is ignored. What is left is a skeletal, vastly over-simplified cognitive model of how learning occurs, to be inculcated into trainee teachers. Does anyone really think this will improve teaching?

The study authors point out that the rendition of learning as a totally explicated biological and cognitive function of the human brain opens the way to potentially authoritarian leveraging. If everything to know about learning is known and controllable, why should any other views be tolerated? Fukuyama's *End of History* may have its counterpart in the 'End of Educational Research'.

Skourdoumbis and Rowe suggest that back in the classrooms, absolute notions of mental states like the 'novice' and the 'expert' brain, promoted by 'brain-based' advocates, can be damaging ideas if teachers (and students) use the labels to inform student self-images. The authors conclude that Australian teacher training is being moved away from viewing education as a 'human event of communication, meaning making and interpretation' and towards 'cause-effect relationships'.

We do not understand how such a mechanistic concept of learning can bolster the teaching profession, let alone serve the students in our schools. We believe neuroscientific findings add valuable elements to our understanding of learning, but they cannot serve as the all-encompassing foundational principle. To believe that selected cognitive transactions within the brain form the total of an individual's learning is a flawed conceptualisation of academic ability.

A disturbing corollary of such a narrow idea emerges from the question, what do we conclude when a student fails in their learning? And there will always be academically failing students, for reasons other than limitations of memory. Under the memory process-only definition, heavily promoted by AERO and other organisations, the issue will ultimately reside with the student. Failing will solely be an indication of a mental deficit, inadequacy or lack of natural ability and capacity. If such conclusions are reached with a number of students of similar demographic – neurodiverse, ethnic backgrounds or gender – then we stand atop the eugenicist's slipway.

A compounding issue stemming from exclusively 'brain-based' views of learning is the invitation to honour direct-instructional pedagogies as the prime, if not only, optimal teaching approaches. The empty vessel to be filled is back in town. The AERO[43] online resource site presents an exhaustive collection of reports and advocacy promoting the merits of explicit instruction. No alternative pedagogies are mentioned: it's as if nothing else exists.

So, the coming generation of teachers is to be fitted with knowledge of a single, fully determined path to all learning and a one-size-fits-all pedagogical shop. If only education were that simple. We are alarmed to think that this may be the future for ITE. The art and sophistication of effective teaching practices are threatened by the bludgeoning mandate of a privileged pedagogy – direct instruction. Coupled with the contentious 'what works' agenda, which amounts to an extremist position on learning, the quality of Australian school education can only be driven backwards.

THERE IS ANOTHER WAY...

Experienced teacher professional development is the important extension of ITE. No teacher can ever reach a stage where nothing more can be learnt or improved. Both pedagogical and content knowledge are always works in progress, and how teachers engage with the upkeep can add both to their job satisfaction and their value. Effectively managed, professional development can be a key ingredient of a satisfying and rewarding teaching career.

---

43 See, "Welcome to AERO," *Australian Education Research Organisation.*

Research by Canadian academic Professor Shelley Peterson[44] into how teachers may be retained in education suggests that much more can be done in the ongoing training space than is currently promoted by Australian governments. Peterson emphasises the value of 'generating teachers' excitement about teaching' through empowerment and positive collaborative relationships. We rarely encounter such worthy phrases – 'teacher morale' is another – within the millions of words published in the name of improving Australian education.

Peterson's idea is to place teachers as the drivers of their own classroom research. They are often better situated to identify the learning needs of students within their own classroom contexts than the credentialed bureaucrats, knowledge brokers, assorted academics and other remote promoters from whom teaching advice and mandates are typically sourced. In her method, teachers are given licence to identify the issues that they face, create relevant questions for research and generate the local data that they need to inform themselves of solutions.

Peterson's initiative comes under the umbrella of 'action research', where a teacher embeds an investigation within their professional practice. I (Fabio) conducted my own action research as the core activity in my PhD program. Along with touring the Finnish education system, it was the most valuable professional development I have ever undertaken. I selected a theme that had eluded all of my decades of formal training and in-servicing – the nature of student emotions in relation to academic work. My study allowed me to explore a frontier of learning that is still, unfortunately, a largely unknown wilderness.

The knowledge I gained and the reflection on my own teaching that this opportunity allowed are unsurpassed in the advancements

---

44 Shelley Stagg Peterson, "Letting Teachers Choose What They Want to Learn Supports Teacher Morale – And Yields Better Teaching," *The Conversation*, 23 August, 2024.

that I made as a teacher. It generated evidence for my previously held intuitions, personal self-image and experiential beliefs, some of which were affirmed, others unsupported. The project was mine, conceived out of my own observations, wonderings and preoccupations. One intriguing facet of my exploration, the emotional response differences between direct instructional and student-centred forms of teaching, tapped into an issue which has raged for decades.

Peterson's findings resonated with me. She found that teachers responded with ownership, enthusiasm and affirmation of themselves as professional educators when entrusted with the power to guide their own development. They saw immediate relevance and benefits for their own practices, outcomes that are often elusive when teachers are directed to do things on the assurance that evidence exists, somewhere. Perhaps above all, Peterson reported that teachers found new reasons to believe in their profession and enjoy their work. The importance of Peterson's results is obvious in an era when demoralised teachers are abandoning schools in devastating numbers.

Peterson's advocacy points in the opposite direction to what is going on in many parts of Australia. A policy recently advertised on the NSW Education Standards Authority website (August 2024) includes 'compliance training' for all teachers.[45] Compliance with what? 'Deliverers' of professional development by 'providers' for a start. The EduResearch Matters blog noted that, 'This suggests that teachers may continue to have little say in the kind of PD that matters to them ... The use of the term "providers" again suggests a view of PD as something "delivered" to teachers rather than something they actively engage with and have ownership over.'

---

45 See Nicole Mockler, Meghan Stacey, Claire Colledge & Helen Watt, "Professional Development: The Minister Claims She Trusts Teachers. But Does She Really?," *EduResearch Matters*, 23 August, 2024.

STUDENTS

'What society does to its children, so will its children do to society.'

— Marcus Tullius Cicero

'... many young people avoid school due to anxiety, like canaries in coalmines they warn that many schools damage mental health – by punishing failure to learn, and enforcing petty rules and detentions, isolation rooms and exclusions. Ofsted bullies teachers, who frequently feel forced to bully students, who, unsurprisingly, often bully peers, in a pyramid of fear and coercive control.'

— Prof Priscilla Alderson, Institute of Education, UCL

'... chronic absenteeism is a canary in a coal mine. The implication is that schools as we have known and run them for generations need to change. I pray that's so because the other possibility is nearly overwhelming to consider: that the canary is a large and growing cadre of disengaged and disaffected young people, and the coal mine is much, much bigger than just school.'[46]

46 Robert Pondiscio "*A new lost generation: Disengaged, aimless, and adrift,*" from the Thomas B. Fordham Institute.

A 2024 report on government services told us that one in five Australian school students do not complete their thirteen years of primary and secondary education, and half of students are absent for 10% or more of the school year, qualifying them for the 'chronically absent' label. Victorian Education Department data shows that the number of students being homeschooled jumped 112%, from 5333 in 2018 to more than 11,332 in 2022.

In Tasmania, only 53.1% of students get to Year 12.[47] While this figure is 82.6% for Victoria, it is 41.6% for the Northern Territory and 70.5 % for New South Wales. University of Tasmania vice-chancellor Rufus Black said the figures showed why fixing the education system needed to be made a top priority.

'By the time we get to 2050, 80% of all jobs are going to require tertiary education – uni or TAFE. That means 90% of kids need to be finishing school, ready to go to uni or TAFE,' he said.

'We're so far short of that at the moment, we're barely above 50% of kids completing school with the qualifications we need. So we've got to care about education.'[48]

In 2023 the attendance rates for students in Years 1 to 10 was 88% – down from 92% almost a decade earlier – and 38% were absent for more than twenty days a year, which is considered to be 'chronically absent'.[49] The average Victorian secondary school student in 2024 was in the process of accumulating almost an entire year of absence from school.[50]

The nationwide survey of independent, Catholic and government schools, found a staggering 98% of educators reported an increase in student mental health issues, with school refusal rates more

---

47 The Australian Government, *The Productivity Commission*, 2024 (Canberra: The Australian Government, 2024)

48 Adam Langenbern, "University of Tasmania vice-chancellor Rufus Black sounds alarm over state's public education system," *ABC News* Thu 6 Jun 2024 at 7:10pm

49 Mridula Amin & Sascha Ettinger-Epstein, "The Kids Who Fear School," *ABC News*, 29 April, 2024.

50 See "Alarming reasons why more kids are skipping school", *The Herald Sun* 6 April, 2024.

than tripling over the past year from 6% in 2023 to 21% in 2024.[51]

Dr Pamela Patrick from Monash University's School of Psychology said she believes students might not see the relevance of school.

'Emerging data from a parent-teen dyad study of teens with school non-attendance concerns has revealed that bullying and a disconnect between reality and curriculum taught in classrooms are two major reasons for the rise in school non-attendance rates,' she said.

'Add to this, the fact that many found a new way of schooling that suited them fine during the pandemic, bringing into question: "Why the need to change?"'

The data also found 200,000 students, 5% of the school-age cohort, are 'severely absent', and a further 50,000 are 'detached students' (not enrolled in a formal education program of any type).[52]

Recent reports from the UK, where parents are fined (the fine was recently increased from a base of £60 to a maximum of £160) suggest that, 'Most recent figures show that in the last academic year (2022/23), one in five pupils were persistently absent from state-run primary and secondary schools'. Many UK parents are taking their children out of school for holidays, which can be up £1600 cheaper during the school term than during the holidays.[53]

A BBC investigation has found the number of children moving to home education in the UK is at its highest level since the pandemic, and has risen by 22% in the past year. Councils received almost 50,000 notifications in the last academic year from families wanting to take their children out of school. This does not include children already being home educated.[54]

---

51 Ideagen, "Education Crossroads: Navigating Teacher Shortages, Safety Concerns and School Refusal Trends" (Australia: School Governance, 2024).

52 The Productivity Commission, 2024

53 "Some parents think their kids don't really need school anymore," *Manchester Evening News*, 17 March 2024.

54 Alix Hattenstone, "Move to home schooling biggest since pandemic," *BBC UK* 3 June 2024.

Where did we ever get the crazy idea that in order to make children do better, first we have to make them feel worse? Think of the last time you were humiliated or treated unfairly. Did you feel like cooperating or doing better? And you are not a child!

Student non-attendance rates can be driven by many factors, including health issues, parent attitudes towards scheduling holidays and homeschooling, or online learning trends. Of all reasons for absenteeism, school-refusal is of major concern. A 2024 Productivity Commission report stated that 45% of Australian students over the preceding two years had missed 10% of school days. This figure had doubled compared to long-term rates.

STUDENT MENTAL HEALTH

A staggering 98% of Australian teenagers report feeling anxiety or pessimism, and one in five rated their mental health as poor, a new nationwide research shows. According to the Monash University survey, which involved more than 600 young Australians aged between eighteen and twenty-four, just 46% rated their mental health as good or excellent, and around 20% received mental health support. Importantly, 10% of young people sought it but did not receive it.[55]

Dr Lucas Walsh, director of the Monash Centre for Youth Policy & Education Practice (CYPEP) and lead author of the Australian Youth Barometer, said this finding is particularly troubling. 'To paraphrase my friend and co-author Blake Cutler, "young people are not thriving, just surviving".'

'Schools that have a whole of school focus on wellbeing, but tailor for the needs of individual students, are more effective at creating an environment for all students to thrive and build individual as well as collective wellbeing,' Raise's Data and Youth

55 The Australian Youth Barometer, developed by the Monash Centre for Youth Policy and Education Practice (CYPEP) in the Faculty of Education at Monash University, Aug 2024.

Insights Director, Lucy Snowball added. 'Growing research, including research from the Life Course Centre at the University of Sydney, is showing that teacher wellbeing is heavily linked to student outcomes and performance.' Snowball said schools that focus on teacher wellbeing alongside student wellbeing will see benefits not only for student wellbeing but also student academic confidence and performance.

'One strategy that schools can use is to have a diverse range of programs available that are targeted and appropriate for the group of students that are aimed at collaborating with students and actively seeking their input into the design of strategies and to assess how they're working,' she said.[56]

Given the reasonable assumption of associations between student happiness at school and school attendance, Australian absentee rates are alarming. The most recent figures equate to a full year of schooling lost through Foundation to Year 10. This duration coincides with our own professional estimates that students today are often a year behind in their academic development compared to their counterparts twenty years ago. Shouldn't we do something about this? Can we at least try to make schools happier and more satisfying places for students to attend?

We recently witnessed a principal request that all Grade 3 boys meet in the assembly area at lunch time. Recent school satisfaction survey data said that nearly 80% of them were not enjoying their time at school. Following the usual greetings, the principal explained that she had looked very closely at the survey results, and she was very disappointed that such a small percentage of third-grade boys said they did enjoy school. She then proceeded to warn them that they would need to improve their attitude in future or there could be a lot more lunch time meetings like this.

---

56 The Australian Youth Barometer.

We are reminded of the comedic line, 'The beatings will continue until morale improves.'

It seems that we are inclined to speak about a desire for student wellbeing, and prepared to introduce programs to encourage wellbeing (mindfulness, yoga, exercise, sleep, 'improving your attitude'), but somehow unwilling to look at what it would take to make school a place where wellbeing programs are not required.

Imagine that your boss at work controlled you the way a teacher controls children at school. You are reprimanded even if you are a minute late. You are not allowed to leave your seat while at work except at specified breaks. You are not allowed to compare notes with, or even talk with, your co-workers except at specified times when you are given permission. To go to the bathroom, you must ask permission. You are told minute by minute what you must do and how, and everything you do is judged and ranked in comparison to the work of your co-workers. You are told exactly what to wear and how to style your hair, and other aspects of grooming and you could be sent home for not complying with any of these.

And suppose your employer also required you to do more work at home, every day, and encouraged your loving spouse (or friend) to be sure you do that work.

How would you feel? Imprisoned? Enslaved? Choked? Untrustworthy? Anxious about how you will be evaluated? Helpless? Depressed about having so little control over your life? Maybe you would even feel that life is not worth living. The fact that all this is being done 'for your own good' by people who love and care for you – people who claim that they are also teaching you about critical thinking – would likely make you feel even worse. You must be truly incompetent if all this must be done for your own good. If all this were done by people who hated you or were exploiting you, at least you would have the satisfaction of anger about the injustice. Your unhappiness would turn outward (as anger) rather than inward (as depression and anxiety).[57]

STUDENT WELLNESS IN FINLAND

In valuing holistic growth, the Finnish system not only focuses on academic excellence but also places a strong emphasis on character development, social skills, and emotional intelligence. In this nurturing environment, students are encouraged to explore their passions, experiment with various subjects, and develop a lifelong love for learning. Ultimately, the Finnish education system's student-centric philosophy equips students not only for academic success but also for leading fulfilling lives as well-rounded individuals.

This student-centred approach also promotes a healthy teacher-student relationship, enabling educators to provide personalised guidance and support to individual learning journeys. Consequently, students feel empowered to take ownership of their education, leading to higher intrinsic motivation and a lifelong love for learning. By valuing comprehensive education over rote memorisation, Finland's education system continues to cultivate well-rounded individuals equipped for the challenges of the modern world while nurturing their mental and emotional wellbeing.

By prioritising not only academic success but also the emotional and social development of students, Finland demonstrates how an education system can play a pivotal role in promoting mental health and preparing students for a balanced and fulfilling life[58].

While the Finns are currently questioning the impact of digitalisation and AI in their system (and asking how much of the shift is driven by budget cuts) and the extent to which 'the education system allows for social mobility and helps to overcome existing

---

57 Peter Gray, "Letter #41. How the Leash Chokes the Spirit," Substack, 22 May, 2024.

58 Finland Education Hub, Aug 23, 2023.

inequalities based on socio-economic status, language, place of birth or residence, religion and disability,'[59] the Australian system seems to be shamelessly attempting to widen these inequalities.

The Finnish local schools principle means that almost all children and young adults attend the school closest to their homes, pre-empting divisions according to family social status. Since schools maintain a reliably high standard, parents are generally satisfied with their local schools, and elite private schools have not emerged alongside local comprehensive schools. Subject to licensing, private schools exist to some extent, but they also receive state funding and follow the national curriculum, and are obliged to include pupils from the local district.[60]

Australians have always considered their country to be a place where everyone gets a 'fair go' and we have no doubt that our national founders had no intention of recreating the social class divides they had left behind in the mother country. We do not believe that the private/public school divide is desired by the majority of Australians, rather that it is a response to the gradual downgrading of funding for government schools by governments that were implementing policies far more extreme than they would publicly admit.

Within a period of fifty years, Finland has progressed from austere conditions to the global cutting edge, proving that education can transform a society. An equal education system and high-quality teaching in schools have played a significant role in this process. For example, recent studies have shown that Finland is the happiest country in the world, with the least corruption.[61]

Students in Finland work with teachers to create their own

---

59 "*Finland: UN expert says education system must address new challenges to continue to deliver on its promises*", 29 November 2023, United Nations Office of the Human Rights Commissioner.

60 Tim Walker, "The Simple Strength of Finnish Education", This is Finland, 2016.

61 K Lonka, "Education lifted Finland out of poverty, but we need to keep developing to remain at the cutting edge," *University of Helsinki*, December 2019

education; meaning they have ownership and responsibility for it. In Australia, we impose an education on students. I (Michael) recall a conversation with a Finnish colleague where I asked how their students had coped with remote learning. Her response was that students had been determined to not let it affect their learning and were really missing their time at school.

The Finnish education system creates independent, passionate learners who are not there because they want grades. They are autonomous learners who become lifelong learners and successful, responsible citizens.

Education writer Amanda Ripley queried Kim, an American exchange student in Finland (who had obviously seen both sides of the equation) about this phenomenon. Kim told her: '... there just seemed to be something in the air here. Whatever it was, it made everyone more serious about learning, even the kids who had not bought into other adult dictates.' Kim's mention of 'other adult dictates' referred to the fact that these students were still rebelling against the adult society around them, but neglecting their education did not appear to be among their choices for this rebellion.[62]

We witnessed this in several Finnish schools. By making education a partnership between the teacher and the student, many of the things students see as needless constraints and compliance are removed and students and teachers are working together.

LEARNING VS CONFORMITY

We were always impressed with the Finnish educators we saw who could tell a student that everything they are doing at school is about the student and developing a love for learning. If we were to say that to our students in Australia (or the United Kingdom or United States) the student could respond by asking, 'Why are you

62 A Ripley, *The Smartest Kids in the World* (New York: Simon & Schuster, 2013).

so concerned about the socks I am wearing that you are prepared to remove me from my learning environment if I don't conform to what everyone else is wearing?'

The Finnish educator would suggest: 'If you have the neuroscience to show that students learn better when wearing a particular colour of socks, then we will look into it. Otherwise why would we waste time on such trivial things?'

Indeed, the message these policies send to students is that we are more concerned with conformity than with learning or wellbeing, and that it is okay to dig in and be stubborn about a trivial point. To the students who are from a strong family background, these things are not an issue, but for the student who has a troubled background, the controlling nature of many of our compliance rules can be triggering if not very difficult for their family to arrange. A recent letter to a newspaper highlighted the case of a Year 7 student who was given a warning about the colour of the stitching on her shoes, which was followed up within days by a detention for the same offence as the parent had been unable to replace the shoes immediately due to the costs involved. The school no doubt invoked claims about being a child-centred, critical-thinking teaching, evidence-based practice following, educational institution!

The Finnish educator is ensuring that students enjoy the school environment by starting the year with games and activities focused on fun. The Australian educator is starting the year by ensuring that students are compliant. There is a wealth of neuroscience explaining how the stressed brain is very inefficient at learning, yet it is one of the pieces of evidence conveniently ignored by the educators who throw around the term 'evidence-based' when it suits them.

As educators we find it concerning that we are obliged to say to a student that their education at this institution will not commence until they conform with these rules.

We are not suggesting that schools remove all uniform regulations, but try writing a list of the school's priorities, and if uniform is not above learning, then treat it as such. If uniform is one of your top priorities, we would question your desire to create a school where students want to be.

> ***'Strict enforcement of uniform, punishments for infringements of draconian rules and the liberal use of isolation and exclusion have created a harsh culture in many schools. If the rigid and narrow curriculum – with reduced opportunities for creativity – plus endless testing is added to students' experiences, it is hardly surprising that they are anxious. Such a culture is anti-educational and anti-learning.'***
>
> *— Dr Lorna Chessum, Former principal lecturer in education, Brighton.*

WHAT IS STUDENT WELLBEING?

If parents were asked what they want for their children, some might mention 'achievement' or 'success', but most would reply 'happiness', 'confidence', 'kindness', 'health' and 'satisfaction' and the like.[63] It should therefore be somewhat surprising that the data by which we measure schools is all about academic success.

What happens in school is key to understanding whether students enjoy good physical and mental health, how happy and satisfied they are with certain aspects of their life, how connected to others they feel, and the aspirations they have for their future.

Wellbeing is a dynamic state: without sufficient investments to

---

63 E. P. Martin et al., "Positive Education: Positive Psychology and Classroom Interventions," *Oxford Review of Education* vol. 35, no. 3 (2009): pp. 293-311.

develop capabilities in the present, students are unlikely to enjoy wellbeing as adults. The psychological dimension of students' wellbeing includes a sense of purpose in life, self-awareness, affective states, and emotional strength. It is supported by self-esteem, resilience, motivation, self-efficacy, hope and optimism. It is hindered by anxiety, stress, depression, and distorted views of the self and others.

There is also a social dimension – wellbeing can be influenced by relationships with family, peers and teachers, and social ties within and outside of school. The cognitive dimension refers to the student's ability to function fully in society, use high-order reasoning skills and solve problems alone and in collaboration. The physical dimension refers to health and adopting a healthy lifestyle and dietary habits.[64]

South Korea has experienced academic success in a system similar to Australia's. There, school starts at 8 am and continues until early evening before students head off to *hagwons* – private tutoring colleges. The government has introduced laws to prevent *hagwons* from operating after 11 pm and a branch of the police force conducts raids to enforce this. Parents take out mortgages to pay the fees and many tutors have become wealthy. The most well-known of these, Andrew Kim (said to be the world's highest paid teacher!) is not a fan of the system: 'I don't think this is the ideal way' he told writer Amanda Ripley, 'This leads to a vicious cycle of poor families passing poverty to their children', adding that in his opinion Finland had a much better system.[65] A cumulation of academic stress from long hours of studying in *hagwons* combined with the competitive environment triggered by the ranking system in schools tends to lead to poor mental health for students, an

64 OECD, "Students Well-Being: What it is and How it can be Measured," *PISA 2015 Results Volume III* (2017), pp. 59-66.

65 Ripley, *The Smartest Kids.*

unfortunate reality for many Korean teens. According to data from statista.com, South Korea's high school student suicide rate was four in every 1000 students in 2021, an alarmingly high statistic.[66]

A further consideration into student wellbeing in Australia is neurodivergence and disability: about four students in every classroom will have a language or attention disorder. While schools are legally required to remove learning barriers for students with disability, students first need to be identified as needing this support. A recent study by the Centre for Inclusive Education at the Queensland University of Technology found that more than two thirds of participants (69%) said some of their teachers talk too much.[67] Importantly, students also described the effect of too much teacher talk – including when teachers 'go off topic' – on their ability to sustain focus, attention and engagement. If this is the case, how can schools claim to be observing their legal obligation when they are implementing the direct instruction programs being mandated by government departments?

THE IMPORTANCE OF BREAKS

American teacher Timothy Walker taught in his homeland before moving to Finland (he married a Finn) and found it a culture shock to transition from a system that prioritised maximum hours and grades – a system he said nearly destroyed him – to one where in the first few days of the school year teachers played games with students and strove to ensure they were as happy as possible at school before commencing any formal lessons.

At first, Walker saw the Finnish idea of taking a fifteen-minute break for every forty-five minutes of instruction as an unproductive

---

66 Alexis N, "South Korea and Finland – role models for the ideal education system?" *The International School of the Sacred Hearts Student Publication*, January 11 2023.

67 Haley Tancredi, Callula Killingly & Linda J. Graham, "'My Brain Leaves the Room': What Happens When Teachers Talk Too Much?," *The Conversation*, 17 July, 2024.

use of classroom time. His Finnish students told him exactly how they felt when he pushed them past the usual break time. 'I think I'm going to explode! I'm not used to this schedule!' a fifth-grader told him on his third day of classes.

To test this idea, researchers took two groups and taught them a specific skill. After the first group mastered the skill, they took a half-hour break and learnt something new. Next day, the group was tested. They 'tanked' the test but tested well on the task they'd learnt last. The second group learnt the same skill as the first group and took the same half-hour break, but instead of moving on to the next task they went back and relearnt the first skill for the same amount of time. When that was done, they moved onto the new task. They went home, came back, and aced the first and second tasks. Brains are flexible – they are adept at learning new tasks. What this research suggests is that if you stop training a skill right after you've acquired it, the brain stays in its ready-to-learn state. If you then train on a second similar task while your brain is still in this plastic state, it overwrites the first skill. It's as if you hadn't studied the first skill at all.

'In the usual situation in which you stop training on a new skill immediately after you've mastered it, the area of the brain related to the skill is still plastic,' said Takeo Watanabe, a professor of Cognitive, Linguistic and Psychological Sciences at Brown University and an author on the study.

Before long, Walker changed his methods to those of his peers and incorporated the breaks. 'I no longer saw feet-dragging, zombie-like kids in my classroom,' he wrote. 'Throughout the school year, my Finnish students would, without fail, enter the classroom with a bounce in their steps after a fifteen-minute break. And most of all, they were more focused during lessons.'[68]

68 T. D Walker, *Teach Like Finland* (New York & London: W.W.Norton & Company, 2017).

NAPLAN

> *'I think in Finland teachers and principals would find it pretty insulting that someone would come and tell them what they need to do differently to fix a problem that's shown by data collected during one day a year.'*
>
> *— Finnish academic Dr Mervi Kaukko, now working at Monash University*

Pasi Sahlberg: 'Another reason why we are seeing more and more students around the world say that they are not engaged in learning in schools – and that therefore their sense of belonging to what is happening in their schools is declining – is that many schools continue to try to convince young people that if they want to acquire the necessary and useful knowledge and skills, they must do it in school and that they have learned to demonstrate it in standardised exams. Most young people today know that this is no longer the case. As schools continue to insist that students must come to school to gain knowledge from yesterday and memorise facts that have very little value in their lives, students will continue to lose confidence in schools. The solution is simple: to involve teachers and young people as key partners in reshaping schools so that teaching and learning are better balanced between understanding the past and actively co-creating the future.[69]'

We were horrified when Finnish educators asked how we could condone forcing children as young as eight to sit hours-long examinations. 'You are responsible for their wellbeing, so why would you allow this to happen,' we were asked accusingly.

We were at a loss to answer this question. Australian teachers

---

69 Pasi Sahlberg, 2024, from '24 Sata', Croatia.

must complete mandatory reporting online training each year to ensure that they understand their obligations regarding the reporting of any type of type of abuse or harm to children, but we are then expected to participate in high stakes mandatory (we have not seen children asked if they want to do it) standardised testing which does have serious (as the stories below confirm) consequences but we spend zero time looking into the suitability of this for our students.

In a recent discussion with one of my (Michael's) Year 8 classes about growth mindset thinking – the belief that basic abilities can be developed through dedication and hard work – a third of students admitted that the experience of taking the Grade 3 NAPLAN test (as eight- or nine-year-olds) had made them decide that they were 'no good' at mathematics. Some said they could actually remember making that decision. I couldn't help but wonder, 'How many of you have experienced similar moments with Reading, Writing, Spelling and Grammar (the other subject tested in NAPLAN)?' The nature of the NAPLAN test is that it presents progressively more difficult problems for the child to solve, until they eventually can go no further with that particular activity.

Children of this age naturally assume that if the problem is on the test, then there is an expectation that they will be able to do it. This has been their experience of testing thus far. And they certainly want to please the adults, don't they? Those who raised their hands were not the rebellious students – they were good students who are (and certainly were at the time of sitting the test) very keen to please their parents and teachers. They trust, or at least trusted, adults and teachers unconditionally.

In September 2018, news surfaced at a government inquiry of a Canberra fifth-grade student attempting to take his own life during a NAPLAN test. Reports detailed how Shane Gorman, the principal of Wanniassa High School in the capital's south, said a teacher had found the student attempting suicide in the schoolground after walking out of class during a NAPLAN test.

'People don't realise the stress it puts on kids,' Mr Gorman told the ACT inquiry into standardised testing.

'Indeed, principals across the country are reporting a rise in incidents of mental illness, particularly anxiety in students which the schools are not resourced to deal with.'

In a move that hopefully signals the start of a shift in attitude to the GERM in Australia, the ACT Government established the inquiry into standardised testing to 'examine its effectiveness and how it affects the mental health of students as well as the morale of teachers, as part of a push to change how data from those tests is reported.'

Mr Gorman said the student walked out halfway through the text – leaving a note – and then went to take his own life.

'He was going to end it,' Mr Gorman said.

Mr Gorman appeared alongside the ACT's education union secretary Glenn Fowler, who told the inquiry that the public reporting of NAPLAN data caused stress for students.

'If doctors said, in near unanimity, that a practice did more harm than good for their patients, would they be ignored for nine years?' Mr Fowler said.

Without being overly dramatic here, it is worth remembering that the Australian Capital Territory is the smallest (in size and second-smallest in population) state or territory in Australia and the only reason this case was brought to public attention is that the ACT held a (public) inquiry into standardised testing. This is an excellent example of failing to observe Dr Brad Johnson's mantra: 'data informs; but relationships transform. In education it is connection that matters most.' South Korea also experiences high incidences of teenage suicide, as does Japan, India, and many others due to the pressures of the education system. This is also an issue in Australia; however, strict media rules around the reporting of suicide, incidents involving children and school protocols mean that these are rarely heard of in the public arena. An attempted suicide from a fifth-grader in Canberra during a NAPLAN test was only reported on when it came out in a recent enquiry into NAPLAN in the ACT.

WHY ARE WE WHERE WE ARE?

> ***'What are our educational objectives? Students who learn a curriculum and regurgitate information become compliant adults and are great for making armies.'***
>
> *— Sanna Lukander, Finnish education writer and creator of the game 'Angry Birds'*

How do we explain why so much autonomy has been taken away from teachers and also from administrators?

Thinking about the obvious damage done to many young children forced to sit NAPLAN examinations, it is clear that if teachers do not speak up for the children, no one else will. The companies that prepare the tests make many millions of dollars from them; we won't be hearing much criticism from that corner. The states themselves and school principals are reluctant to be seen as unsupportive, hence they are called out as trying to hide 'poor performance' and end up losing students and funding.

So who is looking at the tests and asking if they are in the best interests of the students?

According to a study published in the Australian Journal of Language and Literacy reporting a survey of more than 200 Year 7 and 9 teachers across NSW in 2017, 'nearly 60% disagreed with the statement that NAPLAN provides important information on the literacy skills of students.'

Students attempting to take their own lives, and the majority of teachers believe it has little value ... Exactly what has to happen before we abandon this industrial-age practice?

If our goal is to create schools where students want to be, questioning every aspect of school and asking ourselves, 'Is this good for students and teachers?' is essential.

The answer regarding NAPLAN is clearly a 'no'. Ignoring this is as good as stating that teachers and students are not as important as the gathering of data.

As to the move to online testing and correction, the shift is subtle but important as Les Perelman, a former Massachusetts Institute of Technology associate dean and longtime critic of automated essay-scoring notes: 'The software can't tell you if the written answer is good, but it can tell you if it closely resembles the examples that the software has been told are good ones.'

Which hints at the philosophical issue here. Using computer scoring fundamentally changes the task. Instead of making a good-faith effort to communicate information to another human being, the student is now tasked with trying to meet the requirements of the software.

Perelman also notes that machine scoring 'teaches students to be bad writers,' with teachers incentivised to instruct children on how to write to a computer rather than to a human. The problem, he said, is machines are 'really stupid' when it comes to ideas.[70]

Teaching students to prepare for a standardised test goes against everything that we should be doing if we are to follow the motto experts agree will be necessary for the future: 'Don't prepare our learners for something. Prepare them for anything.'

Cognitive flexibility might just be the most important competency we can bestow on learners. 'Developing means to

---

70 Talia Richman, "Computers to Score Written Answers to Texas' STAAR Test," *The Dallas Morning News*, February 14 2024.

spontaneously restructure one's knowledge, in many ways, in adaptive response to radically changing situational demands.'[71] But how can we do this – is it even possible – in an inflexible, standardised environment?

Recently released research from Australian Catholic University suggested NAPLAN had 'strayed from its original purpose' of identifying struggling students by 'insidiously infiltrating everyday teaching and learning.'

At what point did NAPLAN go from a tool to identify issues with student learning to a scoreboard for the comparison and ranking of schools and students?

The study's lead researcher, Dr Rafaan Daliri-Ngametua, said the test had become so embedded in school-level decision making that it was undermining student learning.

Teachers interviewed for the research said their programs were now aligned with NAPLAN testing topics, while staffing decisions were also determined by who was best suited to NAPLAN's testing years.

'Greater accountability and data visibility of NAPLAN results has led to it covertly shaping everything from staff and resource allocation to curriculum decisions and teaching priorities,' Dr Daliri-Ngametua said. 'When performance and policy decisions are dictated by a narrow measure such as NAPLAN scores, it severely inhibits the capacity for educators to do things differently.'

'NAPLAN,' they continued, 'has become a dictating force in curriculum development, teaching priorities and resource allocation, making it a troublesome and influential policy driver.'[72]

---

71 R. J. Spiro & J. C. Jehng, "Cognitive flexibility and hypertext: Theory and technology for the nonlinear and multidimensional traversal of complex subject matter," in D. Nix & R. J. Spiro (Eds.), *Cognition, education, and multimedia: Exploring ideas in high technology* (pp. 163–205). (Lawrence Erlbaum Associates, Inc, 1990).

72 Dr Rafaan Daliri-Ngametua, "NAPLAN's covert influence on teaching and learning," *Australian Catholic University*, November 2023

Why is the same standardised test used to gain information from schools working with the same curriculum when there is no effort to ensure any equality in the facilities of the schools themselves? When the test highlights this gap, how are we bridging this gap and bringing the conditions of the worse-off school closer to the better?

Almost in parallel with NAPLAN, High Impact Teaching Strategies (HITS – a series of teaching strategies promoted by many Australian educational authorities) have also had a dominant presence in Australian education over the last two decades. And like NAPLAN, the advent of HITS has also had minimal positive impact on levels of student academic performance, composed behaviour, satisfaction and happiness within our schools. Both initiatives suffer from related brands of limitation. One only values learning that is easily measurable, and the other assumes all learning is directly teachable. These premises do not well serve Australian students and teachers.

The modelling of teaching and learning as purely cognitive transactions does not address many critical factors that sit outside the intellectual field but are deeply influential within it. For example, NAPLAN would be made substantially more useful and relevant if students were asked questions such as, 'What helps you to enjoy your learning at school?'. Responses to such questions could then be used to inform a richer, more powerful HITS regime. The acknowledgement that valuable learning lies beyond a NAPLAN score, and that there is much more to teaching than HITS suggests, is needed for Australian schools to achieve greater success in delivering quality education.

Standardised curriculum is not educational rigour – standardised curriculum is educational rigor-mortis.

THE 'WHY' OF LEARNING

Simon Sinek reminds us that the most important questions we should be asking begin with a focus on why.[73] If a student does not understand why they are learning something, the chances of them becoming engaged or inspired decreases dramatically. If you use learning outcomes or objectives (and there is little evidence to support them), they should include the 'why'.

Young children who are regularly faced with parental disapproval when they try to dress themselves and even anger when they get things the wrong way round, may eventually become passive recipients of adult direction rather than strive for independence and self-efficacy. This also happens when caring parents do everything for their child rather than give them opportunities to try, fail, try again and succeed.

Similarly, if students are faced with a rigid curriculum with no room for creativity, innovation or the potential to influence change, they may not see themselves as having any ownership of their learning, and perhaps not even try to become active, creative learners.[74]

For example, risky play and unsupervised outdoor activities, which might 'protect against the development of phobias' and reduce 'future anxiety by increasing the person's confidence that they can deal effectively with emergencies,' are often frowned upon. That last point is crucial, because dozens of studies suggest that happiness in childhood, and then later in adolescence, is driven by internal feelings of 'autonomy, competence, and relatedness' – and independent play, purposeful work, and important roles in classrooms and families are vital, early forms of practice.[75]

---

73 Simon Senek, "How great teachers inspire action," TED Talks, September 2009, video, 17:47.

74 Sue Roffey, *ASPIRE to Wellbeing and Learning for All in Early Years and Primary: The Principles Underpinning Positive Education* (Melbourne: Routledge, 2024)

75 Peter Gray, PhD, David F. Lancy, PhD, David F. Bjorklund, PhD, "Decline in Independent Activity as a Cause of Decline in Children's Mental Well-being," *Journal of Paediatrics* vol 260, February 23, 2023.

Many schools now include SEL (Social Emotional Learning) programs that teach tolerance and kindness, but thirty minutes a week cannot hope to make the slightest dent in a school where adults emphasise meanness-enforced compliance all day, every day.

If your administrators and teachers spend every day grinding down students to get them to fall in line and do as they're told, that is your SEL program.[76]

BUILDING INTRINSIC MOTIVATION

Agency is the practice of giving children choices where possible, encouraging them to have a voice in what concerns them, and guiding them to think through the consequences of different actions – not just for themselves, but for others. This enables them to develop self-efficacy, a belief that they can act – and that what they do has impact and matters.

A typical school day asks students to sit still for long periods, listen in large groups and follow a strict schedule that dictates when and how long they need to learn certain subjects. There are many reasons that this doesn't work for many students, yet our system demands that we choose efficiency and convenience over what works for cognitively diverse student learners.[77]

Students will develop a negative attitude towards school if the learning targets and topics set by the teacher feel meaningless, overwhelmingly difficult or tediously simple. A significant number of students learn to hate school, and as a result, hate learning during the course of their school years. These students may decide that learning, or indeed any academic related activities, are not for them and the course of their lives is permanently changed.

---

76 Peter Green, "ICYMI: Memorial Day Washout Edition (5/26)" *Curmudgucation* (blog), May 26, 2024.

77 Sachin Pandya, "My Students Can't Meet Academic Standards Because the School Model No Longer Fits Them," *EdSurge*, Jan 24, 2024.

> *'Kids walk into schools full of wonder and questions, yet we often ask them to hold their question until later, so we can get through the curriculum. We forget that our responsibility isn't solely to teach memorization or the mechanics of a task but to spark a curiosity that empowers the students to learn on their own. To wonder. To explore. To become leaders. We forget that if students leave school less curious than when they started, we have failed them.'*
>
> — *George Couros, The Innovator's Mindset*

American education writer Peter Green sums up the frustration with continual testing: 'Raising test scores is a lousy educational goal. There is no research to suggest that raising a student's score will improve their life outcomes. Nor is there any research to suggest that the tests are actual measures of educational quality or actual student achievement.'

'... from the classroom teacher standpoint, the tests are a black box. Teachers are forbidden to see the questions or the answers, and so the data is just a score. In my own classroom, with my own tests, I would give the test, then break down the wrong answers to see exactly what kinds of mistakes students are making. None of that is possible with the Big Standardised Test.'

'... one of the assumptions of this whole approach, which is that teachers either can't or won't do their jobs, and so some system of carrots and sticks must be devised to get them to do the work that they signed up for. Hill suggests a picture of teachers who just keep doing the same thing over and over, as if teachers are not motivated or capable of searching out other techniques and approaches.'[78]

---

78 Peter Greene, *Curmudgecation.*

'I undertake to act with justice and fairness in all that I do and to promote the development of my pupils and students, so that each individual may grow up as a complete human being in accordance with his or her aptitudes and talents.'

— *From The Comenius Oath*

CURRICULUM CONTROL

In the 1970s, both Finland and the United States were in the doldrums with their education systems. Within the next thirty years, Finland went from placing 25th in international rankings to first. By the time Finland was first (around the end of the millennium) the USA was 29th.

When a global recession occurred in the 1990s, Finnish government cuts in the education budget were applied at the top, rather than in schools and curriculum design, and development was handed to teachers. The national school inspectorate was abolished, and all assessment of students was left to teachers.

As a result of finding themselves even further behind in the rankings, the USA introduced standardised national testing (No Child Left Behind, followed by Race to the Top). Australia, which was not doing much better, introduced the NAPLAN (National Assessment Program, Literacy and Numeracy) tests soon after.

Decades later, Australia and the United States are still struggling to gain any traction with their education systems, while Finland has been, and expects to continue to be, around the top of the rankings for most subject areas. The former countries are also experiencing teacher shortages. Finland has also had to find extra teachers, but it is much easier to do so when teaching is often the most desired career for teenagers to the extent that less than 20% of applicants gain admission to study education. In comparison, a

2019 study found that teaching was the first-choice career for only 58% of Australian teachers. [79]

How did Finland manage to scale the heights of education rankings – whilst maintaining the interest and enjoyment of both teachers and students – at the same time that Australia and the USA were doing almost the opposite?

In a nutshell, Australia and the United States tried to narrow the focus of study to only the material on the test or assessments by controlling curriculum, and teachers. Finnish educator Pasi Sahlberg called this approach the Global Education Reform Movement (GERM), which used standardised tests to rank and compare schools, students (and even teachers), following the conservative political ideology that market forces and competition can create success and maintain competitive standards.

Students are acclimatised to a world of testing and numerical assessment, which dispels the appeal and meaningfulness of genuine learning. Instead of developing their own strengths and self-knowledge, children are now systematically compared to each other. Natural human differences – a lack of ability in one area and exceptional aptitude in another – are no longer seen as desirable. Instead, standardised learning targets require children to achieve an unnatural conformity. The result is that a significant proportion of students do not enjoy school and are not inclined to put any effort into their own learning.

> ***'Organisational or institutional abuse is the mistreatment of people brought about by poor or inadequate care or support, or systematic poor practice that affects the whole care setting. It occurs when the individual's wishes and***

---

79 Information Management and Management Science, *2nd International Conference on Information Management and Management Science 2019*, (New York: Association for Computing Machinery, 2019).

> ***needs are sacrificed for the smooth running of a group, service or organisation.'***[80]

The information to be learnt is considered more important than learning how to learn, and the amount that must be learnt is continually tested in a way that does not encourage children to creatively develop their strengths.

In Finland, students work to create their own education, and are given both responsibility for and ownership of their own learning. This system creates independent and autonomous learners who are at school because they want to learn, not because they want particular grades. These children go on to become lifelong learners and responsible citizens with confidence in their own abilities.

We are reminded of Education writer Amanda Ripley's observations of Kim, an American exchange student in Finland, who saw the way that student cease to rebel again their learning when it becomes something children have control over. Even students who didn't adhere to 'other adult dictates' felt no need to rebel against school because it didn't belong to adults: it belonged to them.[81]

We witnessed this in several Finnish schools. By making education a partnership between the teacher and the student, many of the things students see as needless constraints and compliance are removed and students and teachers are working together.

HOW CAN STUDENTS ENJOY SCHOOL?

I: There were smiles

As a student in the 1970s I (Fabio) got it. Traditional, conventional,

---

80 Organisation or Institutional Abuse," Buckingham-shire Safeguarding Adults Board, updated 2024.

81 Ripley, *The Smartest Kids.*

mainstream education worked for me. I lapped up the lectures, the monologues, the explaining, the direct instruction. It all made sense, and I thrived. My teachers talked as much as walked me a fair way down the road in every subject and I happily travelled the rest of the way to formidable final grades, enough to qualify for scholarships and any tertiary course in the country. However, I realised that for many of my peers, their journey was not so easy: it was hard, verging on impossible. At the time, I naively wondered what was so hard about the stuff we were being shown and told. I didn't know then, but such an awareness would occupy my thinking for the next fifty years.

In a grotesque incarnation of direct instruction, a history teacher I once endured dictated from a book all lesson, every lesson for twelve weeks straight. I remember, despite my hand cramping during each transcriptive frogmarch, finding interest and fascination in the early days of Australian colonial life. God knows what the rest of the class made of the lessons. I think the teacher hated us, but it was ok – we all hated him back. Although my history teacher was an extreme example of 'chalk and talk' without the chalk, the episode was a caricature for the limitations of direct instruction in reaching many students.

I was a newly minted teacher in 1983 and was teaching mathematics to a class of thirty-nine junior high school students. Not unusually for teachers of my background, I began teaching in the manner that had served me so well. In my best blackboard diction and my clearest instructional voice – I had already spent many years tutoring my struggling friends so was well-versed in the art of explanation – I taught algebra basics. The outcome was underwhelming. At least half of my students didn't understand most of what I was doing and several more had no idea at all. I had created the same situation that I had witnessed happening around me years before. My first big lesson in teaching.

So, what could possibly have gone wrong? Heaps of things.

My beginning assumptions of existing conceptual knowledge, terminology and operational skill levels varied tremendously in their validity across the class (even though the text from which I worked was nominally aimed at their year level). Many were not where I'd thought, and my lectures were largely lost on them. Others reached the limits of their attention spans, commonly around twenty minutes at the time, while I tried to hold the stage for half an hour or more. And then there were my problem solution steps, my reduction of processes into digestible chunks. I had always thought it was a fail-proof approach but again I was mistaken. Like in the metaphor of the chain's weakest link, students not understanding one line of working also failed the rest.

Maybe the most significant of my problems was the sheer boredom of my monotone voice on a topic that held little meaning, less context and no intrigue for students. There was also frustration, disappointment, hopelessness and feeling anxious about work that was impossible to do. My next big lesson: there is more to teaching and learning than delivering the purely academic or cognitive matter that fills our curricula. A *lot* more. I quickly realised that I needed to curb the negative emotions arising in association with my teaching if I was to get anywhere with my academic agenda.

I wanted to alter the confusion, boredom, anxiety, disengagement, despair and anger that arose in my classes. The anger was an emotional response of particular interest to me. My well-behaved class was characterised by a core motivation to learn. The frustration some were feeling boiled over into anger because they were not learning. As for despair, it was generated in students facing situations that were beyond their ability to control but mattered a lot. The tears were one manifestation of bewilderment, but the loss of confidence, self-belief, composure and determination was a dead end for learning. Despair is one of the most academically debilitating emotions of all.

I asked myself, 'What emotions linked to learning do I want

instead?'. Interest certainly, hope, curiosity, pride and satisfaction – a list any teacher would desire. But I went further: how could my students be *happy*? When I looked within my own student experience, I realised that the pursuit of happiness lay at the heart of my motivation, drive and success. I applied myself to my learning primarily because it made me happy. The happiness itself was tied to academic achievement, progress, growing self-belief and the experience of enjoyment. I have since come to know the latter source, enjoyment, in the context of learning activities, as possibly the most powerful classroom influence I have ever encountered. My response was to step into unfamiliar territory.

I needed to move beyond the main planks of my teaching, including repetitive instructional teaching practices such as lecturing and notes transcription, that I found were linked to negative affective responses. How could my students feel happy about their work and happy about themselves as capable mathematics students? What activities could I set up for students that presented valuable learning opportunities and were inherently interesting, motivating and enjoyable? This aim pointed me towards the unconventional.

I latched onto the *Reality in Mathematics Education* lesson series.[82] This was a resource designed to serve as an alternative or perhaps complementary approach to lessons based solely on textbook use. The lessons featured tasks which encouraged students to investigate and explore open-ended problems, contextual applications of mathematical skills and mathematical modelling. As the title implies, contextual relevance was a priority, already a departure from my initial teaching. Importantly, the material allowed me to exit centre stage and made the students themselves the drivers of what may be learnt.

The lessons directed students to explore, investigate, measure

---

82 See Charles Lovitt & Ian Lowe, *RIME*

and analyse. There were group tasks, outdoor challenges, invitations to discuss, debate and share. Students had to move and do rather than sit and listen. Often enough there was not just one right answer, just good and better answers – a giant step away from the conventional work I had been presenting. The acceptable responses to some tasks also challenged me, sometimes making me a student in my own class. In such situations I unexpectedly found myself experiencing heightened levels of enjoyment and interest as well.

The approach allowed me a comparison of student responses to contrasting styles of teaching. Changes in elicited emotions were evident: I saw fewer indications of boredom, such as daydreaming, procrastination and off-task behaviours. Student interactions, both among peers and with me, reflected enhanced levels of interest. There were smiles. I was encouraged when voices carrying tones of excitement and enjoyment sometimes replaced the student quiet that often accompanied my instructional lessons. It seemed that the previously commonplace anxieties were less evident, making for more relaxed classroom environments. My formal monologues reduced in frequency and length and were often replaced by conversations with students.

The unconventional tasks I tried did not always work. There were occasions when, usually for reasons I had not anticipated, students did not find activities interesting or engaging. Sometimes the issues involved insufficient existing skills, unclear demands or contexts that were simply not appealing. Nevertheless, feedback from students and my own observations led me to believe that deliberate lesson design for positive affect was often a key factor when welcome feelings such as interest, enjoyment and enthusiasm were experienced.

I noted several circumstances that could be influential in determining whether a lesson would succeed. These included the mood in which students began lessons, the amount of classroom space, available time, levels of harmony within peer groups, student beliefs, attitudes and habitual behaviours. Many other factors were probably also operative. Any or all of these circumstances could compete with my activities in any lesson to shape the emotional responses of students.

It was actually a much more challenging way for me to teach than my instruction-based lessons. There were fewer certainties about the way lessons might unfold and more messiness, although mathematicians will point out this is truer to the real uses, purposes and applications of mathematics in our lives. Regardless, the outcome of students being happy about the mathematics they were doing was a priceless reward for me, uplifting, energising, motivating. I spent the next forty years of my career seeking the same result and was thrilled every time it occurred. If possible, I would spend another forty years looking for the same treasure.

II: The Lip-Sticked Pig

My early forays into the reinvention of mathematics as an enjoyable pursuit were of course performed in the context of a beginning teacher finding his feet in the classroom. Perhaps my perceptions were not so much about pedagogy or students as about me stumbling towards a base level of professional teaching that is top-heavy with explicit instruction. For various reasons, I have been part of the problem often enough. Many students trained to 'shut up and listen' develop the idea that passivity – cognitive and physical – is a key behavioural theme in their education. They adopt views of themselves that match their treatment: their heads will have knowledge poured into them through their eyes and ears. If only it were so. Over the years I became better at what I did, including delivering direct instruction in more sophisticated ways, such as embracing the *I do, we do, you do* principle. I became more aware of student body language and facial expressions: visual cues linked to levels of engagement and focus.

By reading the classroom more effectively I could sense the real-time impressions that my talk and directions were making. I could make decisions about the lengths of my lectures, the difficulty of my examples, the understanding of my terminology and the following of my solution steps. By adding variation to my delivery style, posing easily answerable questions and interspersing sessions with student action, my instruction became more textured and less likely to induce the deep student torpors that I had seen all too commonly. But my improvements were a little like lipstick on a pig: the inherent failings of relentless direct instruction were never far away.

There are at least two major problems with direct instruction. One of the big issues presented by pedagogies based on direct instruction is the educational vision they promote. If students are treated as empty vessels to be filled by the teacher with knowledge and skills, and the subject content is explicitly described, worked and demonstrated with the expectation that students will copy and reproduce, what are they encouraged to think learning is? What do many students make of mathematics when it is presented in the style of mimicry? The answers are not what mathematics should be.

In a usually forlorn attempt to counter such thinking, I have long prefaced my explicit instruction to students with the message, 'You're not learning while I'm showing you what has to be learnt – that comes later'. Even that's not completely correct. It is impossible to show a student how their own conceptual knowledge will evolve. They can witness someone who has developed a concept demonstrating what they can do, but that is a long way short of coming to know it themselves. The influential Russian psychologist, Lev Vygotsky, investigated how children develop conceptual understanding. In his findings, the teacher practice of trying to teach concepts is 'educationally fruitless' resulting in a 'meaningless acquisition of words'.[83]

A simple exercise I have played with dozens of times over the years is to perform a quick mental calculation out loud with a spontaneous sum that appears difficult, such as seven times fifty-seven. I will answer three hundred and ninety-nine within a couple of seconds, using a break-up, distribution and subtraction technique starting with turning fifty-seven into sixty take three. Students are usually astonished, often checking with a calculator in disbelief that the sum could be done so quickly. I always explain the process and assure students that there is no magic involved and they are as capable as me to do such calculations. But few take up the challenge to develop the same ability. My concept of mental number chunking and multiplicative distribution is not their concept.

Furthermore, when the teacher is perceived as the master and transmitter of all knowledge and skills, they are viewed less as a role model and more as a performer. A student's common classroom perception is that teachers are metaphorically there to dance and sing and if they do it well enough, learning will automatically occur. This, in my experience, is an unfortunate risk of routine direct or explicit instruction – responsibility for learning actions is outsourced to teachers.

In academic terms, constructivist principles of learning are relegated by direct instructional approaches to teaching. Constructivism maintains that learning occurs through students doing something themselves or within a group.[84] They do not rely on

---

83 M. E Gredler "Understanding Vygotsky for the classroom: Is it too late?" *Educational Psychology Review*, 24(1), (2012) 113–131.

84 See Saul McLeod, "Constructivism Learning Theory & Philosophy of Education," *Simply Psychology*, February 1, 2024.

supplied recipes, algorithms, solution steps or formulae. Students make their own way, building on what they already know and finding motivation in meaningfulness through context, challenge, curiosity or a number of other means. Constructivists maintain that learning will proceed differently for every individual, a belief that has little room within the herding of direct instruction. Direct instruction can guide the direction of learning, but the learning occurs beyond the telling. The theory remains one of the more compelling explanations for how students develop knowledge and abilities.

Deeply embedded student beliefs are hard to dislodge. It becomes even harder when they are affirmed by curriculum and assessment policies that promote reductionist subject visions. Such approaches present course content as shopping lists of sharply defined, mostly low-level cognitive skills. This is easily and commonly done in mathematics and accommodates direct instruction as an effective stock form of teaching. Subject content can be presented according to ordered teaching schedules along with the accompanying (wrong) assumption that learning follows in the same linear manner.

Assessment tasks can be designed to closely correspond with taught content and students trained to follow a tightly orchestrated cycle of instruction and familiar knowledge testing. In environments where Australian NAPLAN results and any number of other standardised evaluations create tremendous pressure to be seen to perform, it is understandable that many teachers feel the need to 'teach to the test'. I am aware of many schools where 70% or more of students routinely receive A or B grades in internal tests and exams, likely evidence that cycles of direct instruction and prepped assessment are heavily in play.

Despite my misgivings, every time I open my mouth in the classroom I am directly instructing. Some measure of teacher talk is unavoidable. Some things are most effectively relayed verbally to all students. My issue is with extent and purpose. My favourite form of talking is when I tell an anecdote, to stimulate student discussion, set contextual background or perhaps motivate a class. It's a great way to project your character and connect as well. I can be conversational, informal, and equal with my students. Their talk is worth just as much as mine. It is usually one of the most relaxing and enjoyable things I do in my classroom.

When the instructional purpose is formal telling and explicating, teacher talk loses its connective property and diminishes student autonomy. I become the authority, the expert and my words constitute the learning. The listening rules of teacher monologue descend like *Get Smart's* cone of silence. I tightly control verbal interactions and order the attention of students, who are no longer participants but become targets of my talk. When I detect distraction or loss of focus, I berate with lines like, 'You better hear me out now because this is as good as I will ever explain this stuff'. As for eyes glazing over, I don't really have any lines. I am not always proud of my teaching.

Anything that might minimise the use of direct instruction in the classroom is worth considering. Flipped lessons, which can take instruction outside of the classroom and gives students control through fast playing of videos or focusing only on highly relevant excerpts, is one promising idea. It could free class time for the types of rich activities and interactions that foster the development of high-order levels of thinking – although this idea comes with issues such as the immense amount of teacher resources (particularly time) needed to create quality viewing content and the student motivation needed to play instructional videos that give no opportunity for questioning.

A harder but ultimately more fruitful road would be to design a series of classroom activities and tasks that foster conceptual understanding and indirectly invite students to master the fundamental, routine skills that tend to be a catch cry of direct instruction advocates. In mathematics, times tables, basic operations, fractions and decimals can all be included in the set of foundational concepts. In each of these areas and others, it is possible to create problems embedded in contexts of relevance, curiosity or intrigue for students.

Within the solution process, the need for basic mathematical knowledge becomes apparent to students as 'just in time' skills. Students establishing for themselves a reason for learning particular skills can be a powerful way of fostering motivation. An added benefit of developing skills through problem solving compared to direct instruction of course is the demand for higher-level thinking. Rather than coming to view the acquisition of basic skills as the only goal of mathematics, students may rightfully realise that such development serves more powerful purposes. Pehkonen et. al. prioritises problem-solving ability on the same level as learning routine skills.[85] This view departs from the direct instructionalist principle of basic skills and knowledge always preceding higher-level thinking.

My second issue with explicit instruction lies in the affective domain. It has been common, for decades, to be part of conversations with adults where the discussion turns to school mathematics and the recalling of negative classroom experiences. Often enough they involve teachers doing a lot of talking but not making much sense. Undoubtedly, there would have been a lot of sense in the instruction, but this was not how it came across. If negative sentiments form the enduring classroom impression, this is a significant failure for us teachers and invites the question, how can mathematics be enjoyable? Others have arrived at the same question. Brown et. al. surveyed 1500 secondary students in

85 Erkki Pehkonen, Liisa Näveri & Anu Laine, "On teaching problem solving in school mathematics," *CEPS Journal* 3 (2013) 4, 9-23.

seventeen schools and found, 'An analysis of the effects of schools demonstrates that enjoyment is the main factor differentiating schools with high and low [mathematics] participation indices.'[86]

III: Where is the Fun?

I (Fabio) once had a senior high school mathematics class that I secretly dubbed 'Guantanamo Bay'. The title referenced an infamous quote from a former US Vice President, Dick Cheney, who described inmates of the prison there as 'the worst of the worst'. The phrase can also be seen as an unkind commentary on the harshest outcomes of ability-streaming. My class were together because they had long been failed by classroom mathematics: they hated mathematics, and they barely tolerated mathematics teachers. Even the students called themselves the 'spud' maths class, because potatoes are (as they explained to me) the 'dumbest' kind of vegetable.

Their course was taught from a standard textbook, the type that has examples of how to do the sums at the start of the topic and then rows and rows of practice questions. A great fit for a direct instructional approach to teaching the course but also a big reason why my class had arrived at Guantanamo Bay. I threw the book away. I replaced it with activities, challenges and problems drawn from several alternative texts like the *Mathematics at work: Modelling your world* series.[87] The material featured tasks which encouraged students to investigate open-ended problems, explore contextual applications of mathematical skills and construct mathematical models.

We spent the year making and playing, discussing and debating,

---

86 M Brown, P Brown & T Bibby, "'I would rather die': reasons given by 16-year-olds for not continuing their study of mathematics,' *Research in Mathematics Education*, vol. 10, no. 1 (2008) 3–18.

87 Ian Lowe, "Mathematics at work: Modelling your world," *Australian Academy of Science* vol. 1, no. 2, 1988.

designing and measuring, calculating and checking, creating and evaluating. It was energetic, indoors and out, problems were posed and solved: it was mathematics, but not mathematics as the class had previously known it. We enjoyed what we were doing. We had *fun*. The standing school rules for this class were that it was mercifully exempt from the final end-of-year exam that had to be sat for all other subjects. However, my students demanded that they sit an exam, such was their belief that they had learnt something to show. They were delighted when it was done.

Of course, I did some direct instruction: it's unavoidable, just undesirable as the only form of pedagogy. I would set the scene at the start of lessons, elaborating the challenge and describing what I expected students to do. At strategic intervals I would focus everyone together, to update work progress, summarise key findings, bridge a common impasse or provide a brief forum for the exchange of ideas and thinking. These forms of instruction were very different from standard lecturing. There was usually a self-evident need for me to talk and students generally welcomed my interventions. I became a useful resource, fostering the learning agenda rather than imposing it.

Perhaps my Guantanamo Bay story and other similar situations over the years were outliers, distorting my conclusions and beliefs about optimal pedagogies. After all, we tend to mainly notice only the views from the roads that we travel. Generalisations can only gain traction through deeper investigation. Do students learn more effectively when they enjoy what they are doing? Is direct instructional teaching really as limited as I imagined? I had the opportunity to explore these questions, and more, through my PhD study that was finalised in 2020.[88]

The seeds of my study could be traced all the way back to my

88 Fabio D'Agostin, "Task-Related Emotions in Mathematics Education," (Doctorate, Deakin University, 2020).

original observations around student enjoyment and different forms of teaching in mathematics. I wanted to trace the sources of enjoyment, happiness and other positive emotions in the context of teaching. As emotions go, negative feelings such as boredom, frustration and sadness were also of interest to me. The scope of my study encompassed quite different teaching approaches, the opposite ends of the pedagogical spectrum that had long intrigued me. It was conventional, instruction-based teaching versus student-centred activity or inquiry teaching.

I investigated a class that I taught at the time, which posed advantages and disadvantages for my study but proved to be a powerful way to gather authentic data. The Year 10 students were a middle ability stream, probably representative of most high school mathematics students. They were on a pathway towards studying the most common form of state senior mathematics in their final year. The investigation consisted of ten lessons: five taught through explicit instruction and five taught through progressive inquiry approaches. It aimed to identify associations between different forms of classroom activity and student emotional responses.

To begin, I searched for visions of ideal outcomes from prominent mathematics education advocates. It seemed logical to start with the desired endpoint before looking into the teaching processes that may take students there. This was a revealing exercise. Expectedly, their visions were filled with higher-order cognitive abilities, painting a portrait of a student that any mathematics teacher would be delighted to call their own. But there was more. The ideal student outcomes were also characterised by affective qualities including positive attitudes, beliefs and feelings. I was encouraged that my own convictions, developed through decades of experience, found some academic support.

Figure 1 was adapted from my PhD thesis. On either side it lists the cognitive and affective attributes generated through an ideal mathematics education, as advocated by academic experts in the field. The middle section presents the types of classroom activities and teaching approaches that are also advised for the ideal learning outcomes to be achieved. Although the academic sources have not been updated over the last ten years, the cited experts represent advocacy that has essentially remained intact for many decades.

It can be argued that qualities such as rote recall and ability to implement familiar procedures should appear in the outcomes list. Development of such skills are often the central or even only mission of many mathematics courses. Appropriately, experts do not recognise these abilities as endpoint outcomes. They are sometimes important stepping stones in achieving higher levels of thinking, but a valuable mathematics education should not stop there, perhaps not even start there. The development of a 'mathematical disposition' requires many more cognitive and affective layers beyond the acquisition of basic or procedural competence.

The most remarkable aspect of the tabled vision lies in the suggested classroom approaches and activities to drive success. Explicit instruction is conspicuously absent. But that makes sense. How can you foster 'independent decision making' through lecture? How can a student develop 'persistence' through having it explained? How can a talk on dealing with 'uncertainty, ambiguity and error' teach its practice? Perhaps these qualities can be role-modelled by a competent teacher in an instructional mode: it is something I have tried endlessly. However, it has always been a poor substitute for students getting their own hands dirty.

I once set a task that required students to elaborate and clarify

Cognitive Outcomes

Development of deep and interconnected concepts (Stein et al., 1996) TASK PROPERTIES 1, 7

Development of mathematical disposition (Henningsen & Stein, 1997) TASK PROPERTIES 4, 5

Development of ability to deal with uncertainty, ambiguity and error (Doyle, 1988) TASK PROPERTIES 1, 5, 7, 8, 10

Elaboration, clarification and reorganisation of thinking (Hiebert & Wearne, 1993) TASK PROPERTIES 5, 12, 13

Development of ability to comprehend, interpret, flexibly apply knowledge and assemble information (Doyle, 1988) TASK PROPERTIES 1, 2, 4, 5, 7, 8, 10, 13, 14

Development of ability to conjecture, abstract, explain, validate, challenge (Lampert, 1990) TASK PROPERTIES 2, 3, 4, 5, 13

Development of independent decision-making ability (Doyle, 1988) TASK PROPERTIES 3, 4, 10, 12, 14

Persistence through task accessibility (Stillman, 2004; Sullivan, Aulert & Lehmann, 2013) TASK PROPERTY 6

Associated teaching/ task properties

1. High level problem demands (Doyle, 1988; Sullivan, Clarke & Clarke, 2009)

2. Mathematics accessed through a model, opportunity for design (Sullivan et al., 2009; Clarke & Roche, 2009)

3. Imaginative content including practical investigation (Gorard & See, 2011; Grant & Searle, 1997)

4. Novel, unfamiliar problems (Doyle, 1988; Sullivan et al., 2009)

5. Provision for classroom discourse (Hiebert & Wearne, 1993)

6. Accessible content (Stillman, 2004; Sullivan, Aulert & Lehmann, 2013)

7. Truly challenging, not just a mask for algorithmic practice (Stein et al., 1996)

8. Contextualised and practical setting/authenticity (Sullivan et al., 2009)

9. Humour and play-like activities (Astleiner, 2000)

10. Open-ended solution space (Sullivan et al., 2009)

11. Scope for group collaboration (Sullivan et al., 2009; Gasser, 2011; Glaser-Zikuda et al., 2005)

12. Student-centered instruction (student agency) (Glaser-Zikuda et al., 2005)

13. Requirement for communication of reasoning, written or oral (Stein et al., 1996; Lampert, 1990)

14. Several possible solution strategies (Stein et al., 1996)

15. Clearly outlined, differentiated expectations and adequate time for learning (Glaser-Zikuda et al., 2005; Gorard & See, 2011)

Affective Outcomes

Development of courage and risk-taking demeanour (Doyle, 1988; Lampert, 1990; Stein et al., 1996) TASK PROPERTIES 4, 5

Interest and engagement (Sullivan et al., 2009; Gorard & See, 2011; Grant & Searle, 1997) TASK PROPERTIES 3, 6, 8, 9, 12, 15

Sense of ownership and personal meaningfulness (Sullivan et al., 2009) TASK PROPERTIES 6, 8, 11, 12, 15

Satisfaction, confidence and positive self-concepts through student agency (Glaser-Zikuda et al., 2005; Sullivan, Aulert & Lehmann, 2013) TASK PROPERTY 12

Experience of enjoyment or fun/pleasure (Sullivan et al., 2009; Glaser-Zikuda, et al., 2005; Astleiner, 2000; Gasser, 2011; Gorard & See, 2011; Grant & Searle, 1997) TASK PROPERTIES 3, 9, 11

Figure 1: Task properties and their associations with positive cognitive and affective outcomes

their thinking around a set of problems featuring applications of sequences and series. Students were required to explain the outcomes of their investigation to the rest of the class. One of my best students felt anxious about this aspect of the work, angrily telling me, 'You don't talk in maths!' He was right, in a direct instructional sort of way. Of course, you would object if you believe that is how mathematics is learnt. Everyone knows that it is only the teacher who does the talking.

Students exhibiting many of the tabled ideal cognitive and affective outcomes do exist. And explicit instruction does not appear to hurt them. For this small minority, it is possibly an efficient way to alert them to the direction their cognitive development needs to take before they go away and learn. As for the majority, probably around 70% or more of any unstreamed or unselected student group, there exists a huge distance between explicit instruction and the cognitive qualities that are the hallmarks of mathematical education success.

Considering the affective outcomes, perhaps a highly talented and entertaining lecturer might foster interest and engagement – the Australian educator Eddie Woo is an example – but positive student affect related to valuable learning generally eludes direct instruction. Positive affect, particularly enjoyment, is recognised beyond my table as a powerful influence in learning. For example, neuroscientific research has established that cognitive processes tend to occur concurrently with the activation of feelings, not necessarily in sequential order but possibly as mutually supporting events.[89] Task-related enjoyment and happiness are key beneficial feelings in this confluence.

The argument for pursuing positive emotional outcomes is also strengthened by the long-established awareness that negative

89 C Hinton, K Miyamoto & B Della-Chiesa, "Brain research, learning and emotions: Implications for education research, policy and practice," *European Journal of Education*, vol. 43, no.1, 2008.

feelings, such as boredom, anxiety and fear, act strongly against learning.[90] Even the most developed, most effectively implemented forms of direct instruction are highly vulnerable to driving such negative emotions. Perhaps unfairly, the immediate example within the direct instruction umbrella that comes to mind is the technique of 'choral response', where all students are asked to simultaneously respond out loud to a prompt.

I can imagine a group of earnest Year 2 students all confidently replying 'minus' to a question about the sum that needs to be done. All except one who unfortunately, discordantly, obviously, yells 'plus'. That would not be a pleasant experience for the child and an event that could initiate all sorts of lasting ill-effects. Even within the group of children all crying 'minus', there would probably be several who have mastered the art of slightly delaying so that the more confident and able students set the correct answer.

An appeal of direct instruction for some educators and administrators is the hard sell it offers. Content is pushed out at rates that too often have nothing to do with how students learn: a great way to squeeze a crowded curriculum into a tight teaching schedule but oblivious to the depth, quality or extent of learning. Learning is assumed to occur metronomically and be measurable in intervals of perhaps as little as twenty minutes. Quick evaluation systems such as 'traffic lights', thumbs up/down or mini whiteboards can be used. But to measure what? Rote recall, listening skills, mimicry?

Assumptions about pre-existing mathematics knowledge for an average class, where ability levels typically vary over at least a four-year span, can be wildly inaccurate for many students. Instruction supposedly consolidating and building on a notional starting foundation can generate bewilderment, boredom, confusion,

---

90 R Pekrun, *Emotions and Learning* (Geneva, Switzerland: International Academy of Education (IAE), 2014).

frustration, anxiety, anger, satisfaction, happiness, interest and sadness all within the same room at the same time. And that encapsulates a major concern with direct instruction – it is commonly a blunt instrument, tone deaf to the student emotions that may arise. And unfortunately for a sizable number of students, direct instruction is not much fun.

Regardless of my perceived limitations of direct instruction, it has long been a dominant teaching approach in a majority of schools. It was an established pedagogy at the school under research and formed five of the ten lessons in my PhD program. Apart from an initial teacher-led discussion to stimulate interest, these 'routine' lessons were conventionally structured. A set of notes were written on the whiteboard for transcription by students. An obvious issue with this activity is the channelling of cognitive thinking into one of its most menial forms.

Then followed verbal instruction or lecture, including walk throughs, shared practice and independent consolidation opportunities. Being clear is a clarion call principle from proponents of direct instruction and has always guided my delivery. An often unavoidable result of 'being clear' is the reduction of theoretical content and worked examples to easily digested components. This effectively presents mathematics as a body of steps, procedures, algorithms and single-sequence actions that can be neatly written in a summary book. Students develop the belief that their written notes contain the entire body of knowledge and abilities. Being neat and complete is hence the key to mastering mathematics – a highly limiting and ultimately dead-end way to appreciate the subject.

We mathematics teachers can get away with this if we don't move beyond basic knowledge and skills – and some of us never get much further. As for teaching conceptual understanding, direct instruction can only scratch the surface (see the chapter of this book titled '*Looking Under the Bonnet of Learning Science and Direct Instruction*'). No teacher can ever 'clearly' describe the depth, complexity, utility, strengths, applications and limitations of even something as fundamental as the decimal number system. To adequately grasp the concept requires a level of individual immersion that cannot be reached with direct instruction. Vigorous teacher guidance and orchestration, as helpful as it appears, inhibits the quality of student experiences needed to establish a deep individual understanding.

A typical measure of the extent to which conceptual understanding has been achieved is to gauge performance on 'unfamiliar' problems. If a student has not rehearsed their response to an encountered question, they need to draw on their own inner resources – particularly their conceptual understanding. Identification of appropriate skills, selection and adaptation of standard solution processes, modelling given situations using mathematical constructs, devising solution strategies, results evaluation – all these abilities can only develop from a strong inner conceptual foundation. Direct instruction is not great on the 'inner', it is very much teaching from the 'outer'.

After the lecture component of routine lessons came the familiar worksheet practice. A sheet was issued containing several questions that closely resembled the worked examples of the lecture session. Students spent the rest of the lesson time applying the solution processes that they had been shown. It was an adequate way of establishing basic ability, accessible to all students so long as there was nothing in the teacher's instructions that carried incorrect assumptions of existing knowledge. Students tended to become helpless when this happened.

It was generally a safe approach to teaching. Course content was systematically covered and the teaching-learning-assessment sequence was neatly finished by setting topic tests full of problems that were similar to those that had been rehearsed in the worksheets.

Students tended to be satisfied as they negotiated the symbiotic relationship between classroom and assessment content. It is a very common form of doing mathematics, an arrangement that is widespread throughout our schools. However, it also confines the subject to a small cage. And like any caged animal, vital qualities are lost.

The remaining five lessons of my research presented students with open-ended challenges, unfamiliar problems, modelling tasks and game analysis. Students entered into genuine collaborations that required discussion, elaboration and debate. They were required to create solution processes and evaluate their findings. I monitored, guided, hosted and answered questions with more questions, offering oblique support when students struggled. These 'rich' lessons were everything that 'routine' lessons were not.

Student emotional responses during all lessons were appraised through experience sampling (students selected suitable emojis while they were engaged in activities), observations, visual and audio recording and post-lesson interviews. The rich lessons were associated with significantly more positive emotions, mainly interest and enjoyment, than routine lessons. Many rich task properties were identified as key ingredients. The list included accessibility, meaningfulness, challenge, open-endedness, opportunity for design, novelty, modelling, whole class discourse and student agency.

The last item on the list, student agency, resonates with our argument that teacher autonomy adds to teacher satisfaction and enjoyment. The principle of derived happiness through responsibility for one's own decisions and actions is not limited by age. Apart from enhanced levels of interest and enjoyment, student agency also promotes a wealth of highly desirable academic qualities. Students gain confidence in acting independently, learn to identify the demands of given problems (or even formulate the problems themselves) and devise solution approaches and strategies. Having to construct your own communication of mathematical thinking is also an invaluable experience.[91]

The positive emotions that arose during routine lessons were associated with a much narrower band of task properties than were found in the rich counterparts. Accessibility, or the scope for making progress during an activity, was a factor in common with rich lessons. The characteristic emerged as a transcendent property, the takeaway being that whatever way a teacher wants to teach mathematics, their academic demands must be achievable at some level by all students. When students believe they have no pathway forward, no learning is possible.

Ironically, an argument used by proponents of explicit instruction is that 'clear' explanations and demonstrations optimise accessibility. This has never been my experience, in my work or in my PhD study. What can go wrong? Those invalid assumptions of pre-existing knowledge for a start. I have spent my professional life tripping over students who are left dumbstruck by my thinking that the incidental fractions that arise in some solution processes are no issue at all. An unexpected problem that arose during the PhD study came from my belief that everyone knew about supplementary angles adding to 180 degrees. That one threw up a roadblock for several students that voided the learning value of the lesson.

There are also considerations related to working memory and the high variation that exists in any average class in relation to the number of ideas that can be juggled at any given time.[92] It is often challenging to synchronise the delivery of explicit instruction

---

91 See Figure 1, Task properties and their associations with positive cognitive and affective outcomes.

92 See Conway, Andrew, and others (eds), *Variation in Working Memory* (New York, 2008; online edn, Oxford Academic, 22 Mar. 2012).

with the pace of student comprehension. Get that wrong and confusion is a typical outcome. Slow down the delivery to catch all students and you risk affective fallout including boredom and disengagement. It only takes one poorly or mistakenly comprehended term, a brief moment of distraction, the confusing influence of an established incorrect belief or any of a host of affective reasons including low confidence, poor self-belief and fear of mathematics for the 'clearest' instruction to be heard as a word salad.

As much as I wanted them to be, my study outcomes were not a simple body of evidence displaying the benefits of progressive against conventional pedagogies. Along with greater rates of positive emotional experiences, more instances of boredom were reported during rich lessons compared to routine lessons. Some boredom was chronic in nature, from students who were expressing their disdain for all mathematics. Boredom could also be attributed to an extent to students who were attached to conventional teaching. They were used to the familiar rhythm and order of direct instruction and were hesitant to engage in less predictable forms of learning, particularly working with minimal levels of teacher guidance.

The study was not complete without some analysis of the learning that was achieved through both modes of teaching. Unsurprisingly, explicit instruction delivered the scheduled outcomes and the learning intentions were met. Skill sets, drawn from the Victorian curriculum, were directly taught and directly assessed. Students were highly familiar with the drill. They were explicitly shown standard solution procedures and algorithms and given clear success criteria like, 'this is the standard you need to reach for the test'.

Students' summary books were stuffed with notes and examples and students were filled with confidence that the test questions would not surprise. This was not the type of mathematics education promoted by expert advocates. Far from it. In routine lessons, students learnt that academic success in mathematics came from organisation, rote transcription, compliance and a little bit of rehearsal. Hopefully, there was some development of conceptual knowledge amidst the orgy of procedural content, but that was not the point of routine lessons.

Despite my criticisms, I would be shooting the messenger if I blamed direct instruction for the limitations of conventional mathematics teaching. Ultimately, it is about a funnelled educational vision that blunt explicit teaching serves well. If specific mathematical problem-solution skills and procedures are perceived as the foremost – or only – important elements of mathematics courses, then explicit teaching will almost always prevail. Direct instruction alone is a great way to develop a stunted form of numeracy.

School curricula, such as the Victorian State version, need to value and promote a mathematics that does not assume conceptual knowledge can only follow after foundational skills are established. Instead, conceptual development should be considered as giving impetus and meaning to the acquisition of skills. It should be a preliminary goal or at least a concurrent aim as topics are taught. This would require a much more judicious and curated use of direct instructional methods than commonly occurs.

Work done during rich lessons was not formally assessed through tests. Learning was evaluated through analysis of written responses and observations of students responding to task demands during the lessons. The evidence showed students grappling with new ideas, forming original understandings of mathematical concepts including game-related probability, non-linear geometrical relationships and statistical modelling. There were no scripts to be followed: students had to identify the demands of given situations and create their own responses. It was challenging and unfamiliar work but importantly, it tended to be inherently more satisfying, interesting and enjoyable than routine tasks.

Rich tasks offered many more situations in which students could develop the mathematical attributes promoted by academic experts, as ill-defined and beyond exact measurement as they may be. Students were faced with types of academic demands and levels of challenge that were never encountered in routine lessons. By necessity, they were obliged to develop higher orders of thinking – such as creating, analysing and evaluating – to succeed. They had to work hard and there were never any answers at the back of a book: they had to check those for themselves as well.

Finally, in response to the question, 'where is the fun?', opportunities to experience mathematics-related happiness, enjoyment and interest were far more plentiful when students stepped off the conventional teaching and learning treadmill. I recorded moments when students high-fived after obtaining an elusive solution, shrieked in delight as highly unexpected sequences of cards were dealt and smiled broadly when they realised the success of their long lines of number crunching. It is likely that as adults, they would recall their rich task experiences and learning more completely and fondly than most other things they did in mathematics.

The beneficial cognitive and affective outcomes generated through the use of rich tasks in my study achieve even more value when considered against current worrying global trends in mathematics as identified through the 2022 PISA survey[93]. It revealed close to one in four students giving up as often as persevering when faced with challenging mathematics. 30–40% rarely participated in group mathematics discussions or asked

93 OECD, "PISA 2022 Results (Volume I and II) – Country Notes: Australia," Australia, 2022.

questions when they became stuck. Levels of interest, motivation and enjoyment continued long term declines while rates of mathematics anxiety increased. Lack of perceived meaningfulness also appeared as a growing concern for students.

We educators should really do something about this list of issues. They are as bad here in Australia as they are anywhere else in the world. We need mathematics pedagogies that reach well beyond the stark transmission of information from teacher to student, often enough a problematic process anyway. My PhD study added to the large body of knowledge about teaching mathematics in ways that reach students more deeply and impactfully than tends to occur with traditional instruction. This is the direction in which we need to move.

LEARNING FROM FINLAND

TRANSFORMING EDUCATION IN NEW ZEALAND AND AUSTRALIA.

THOUGHTS FROM DR SARAH AIONO

The Finnish education system is often celebrated for its remarkable success, which can be attributed to several foundational principles that transcend cultural and geographical boundaries. By examining these principles and their implementation, we can draw valuable lessons for improving the education systems in New Zealand and Australia, making schools places where both students and teachers want to be.

Universal Educational Principles

Finland's success is grounded in principles that transcend cultural and geographical boundaries. Trust, autonomy, and a holistic approach to education are the bedrock of the Finnish system. Finnish educators are highly respected and given the freedom to exercise their professional judgement. This stands in stark contrast to the current climate in New Zealand and Australia, where there is a notable lack of trust in teachers as professionals. This distrust is manifested in increasingly prescriptive mandates that undermine the value of teachers in the wider community. Consequently, this erosion of professional autonomy hinders the environment needed for both teachers and students to thrive.

Broader Societal Framework

Finland's educational triumphs cannot be viewed in isolation from its societal framework. There is a deep-rooted belief in the collective responsibility for education, beginning at home with strong parental leave policies and extending to community institutions like libraries. These institutions are not merely for book lending but serve as communal hubs for lifelong learning. In contrast, the disconnect between our communities and our schools in New Zealand and Australia often stems from a lack of trust, exacerbated by media narratives and the politicisation of education policy. The reintroduction of the GERM (Global Education Reform Movement) in Australia and New Zealand, along with increasing calls for a knowledge-rich curriculum that is highly prescriptive and levelled, further widens this disconnect. Such approaches fly in the face of what we know about individualised, responsive teaching. Instead of fostering trust and collaboration, they create an environment where teachers are seen more as implementers of rigid policies rather than as professionals capable of tailoring education to meet the needs of their students. This distrust undermines the value of teachers and creates barriers to effective educational reform. By adopting a more integrated approach, recognising that education involves the whole society and not just the schools, New Zealand and Australia could foster a more supportive and cohesive educational environment.

Evaluation Over Standardisation

In Finland, standardised testing exists but is used internally to tailor educational experiences rather than as a public measure of achievement. This reduces the pressure on students and teachers alike and allows for a more supportive and constructive use of assessment data. Moving towards this model could help New Zealand

and Australian schools focus on individual growth rather than competition, creating a more supportive educational environment.

The current trend in Australia and New Zealand towards a prescriptive, knowledge-rich curriculum, driven by the GERM movement, contrasts sharply with this approach. Instead of empowering teachers to address the unique needs of their students, it imposes a one-size-fits-all methodology that can stifle creativity and responsiveness in the classroom. Shifting the focus to a more evaluative and supportive use of assessments, as seen in Finland, could help mitigate these issues and promote a more holistic and effective educational system.

Respecting and Integrating Cultural Values

Moreover, Finland's commitment to linguistic and cultural pride, particularly in revitalising the Finnish language and integrating national minorities into the educational framework, provides a powerful example. New Zealand, with its bicultural foundations, can draw valuable lessons here. Continuing the progress that has occurred over the last six years to revitalise, decolonise and strengthen Māori educational practices and perspectives within the mainstream system will enrich the learning environment for all students, fostering a sense of cultural identity and inclusion. Similarly, Australia would do well to ensure learning environments and teaching practices align with Indigenous learning principles, empowering students to have a sense of belonging at school. Having a deep sense of connection, and seeing themselves reflected in the learning materials, practices, and relationships in school will ensure our most at-risk learners want to come to school.

Holistic Approach to Early Education

Finland's approach to early childhood development, supported by robust parental leave policies, lays a strong foundation for lifelong learning. In stark contrast, recent budget announcements in New Zealand have largely ignored the early years sector, providing little to no funding for crucial policy implementation. The privatisation of early childhood education in New Zealand has resulted in a wide continuum of quality within the sector, sparking ongoing debates about the qualifications required of teachers working in this area. Despite overwhelming evidence that the early years are among the most critical in human development, both the Australian and New Zealand governments continue to prioritise high stakes testing and examinations in the high school and college sectors, viewing the early years as less important. This misplaced focus overlooks the foundational importance of early childhood education and its impact on long-term educational outcomes. Investing in early childhood education similar to Finland's model is essential to ensure that learning begins well before a child enters the classroom, setting them up for future success.

Addressing Student Disengagement

In the wake of COVID-19, attendance rates in New Zealand have continued to decline, sparking widespread debate among policymakers, school leaders, and parents about how to re-engage students. Unfortunately, these conversations have largely excluded the voices of the students themselves. Rather than seeking to understand why students are disengaged, the responses have been punitive, including proposals to fine parents, mandate daily attendance reporting by schools, and publicise attendance records. These measures do little to address the underlying reasons why students do not want to attend school and fail to create a supportive environment for re-engagement. Perhaps it is time to ask the students themselves why they are disengaged. By listening to their perspectives and learning from systems like Finland, which boasts high attendance rates, New Zealand could develop more effective strategies to re-engage students and foster a positive school experience.

Balancing Knowledge and Skills

Lastly, in the push to raise literacy and numeracy achievement levels, there has been a significant shift towards a knowledge-centric curriculum in New Zealand and Australia. This focus on a one-size-fits-all approach often comes at the expense of the arts, social sciences, and experiential learning, which provide meaningful and relevant experiences for students. In contrast, Finland balances knowledge acquisition with skill development, ensuring that students receive a well-rounded education that includes creative and practical subjects. The Finnish model recognises the importance of cultivating skills such as critical thinking, problem solving, and collaboration, which are essential for students to thrive in a rapidly changing world. By adopting a more balanced approach that values both knowledge and skills, New Zealand and Australia can create an education system that better prepares students for the future.

By adopting the principles and practices that have contributed to Finland's educational success – trust, autonomy, societal integration, and a strong focus on early childhood development – New Zealand and Australia can create more effective, supportive, and cohesive education systems. Recognising the vital role of early education, valuing student voices, balancing knowledge and skills, and fostering a culture of trust and respect for educators are essential steps towards achieving these goals.

— Dr Sarah Aiono is the CEO of Longworth Education in Napier, New Zealand, an organisation that works to bridge the gap between practise and research in the education field.

FLIPPED LEARNING

When we deprive children of the power to make decisions about their own learning, we indicate how little trust we place in them. Flipped learning (not flipped classroom!) is still in the developmental stages in Finland. We have seen it applied in a university setting, but it is still uncommon in primary and secondary schools. We recommend texts written by Marika Toivola, Pekka Peura and Markus Humaloja whose work with flipped learning in the primary setting is world leading. As such, flipped learning is a fascinating look at just what is possible with cooperative learning and the development of student autonomy ... and a glimpse into the future of education.

Flipped learning is where the teacher accustoms learners to unprompted and self-motivated learning, and it also supports learners' freedom of choice in pedagogical matters. It approaches learning with respect to the needs of individual learners rather than taking the same approach for all. A flipped classroom, in contrast, typically involves learners studying theory at home and doing their work at school.

> *'I regularly had to talk about the fundamental skills for learning: self-regulation, persistence, and enjoying success.*

Discussions about freedoms, which my students had taken as rewards for shouldering responsibility in the autumn, soon got on the right track and they unanimously agreed that class was now significantly more motivating than routine teacher-led activity.'

– *Pekka Peura,* from Flipped Learning in Finland, 2020

Flipped learning is about long-term efforts to create a learner-centred learning culture, which requires respect and trust between teacher and learner.[94] One approach to flipped learning[95] involves the teacher first choosing a number of possible learning exercises. These exercises will contain those aspects of what the learner currently needs to practice. The learner will choose their preferred learning tasks from this selection and begin work. The teacher will gradually reduce the amount of support given, until the learner acquires self-regulation skills.

Videos are another common way of providing flipped learning. Although the flipped classroom can be said to have started from teaching videos shared on the internet, they are not at the core of flipped learning. Ready-made theory videos still only reproduce the lecturer's thoughts. However, the clear benefit over live teaching is that the learner can watch the video at the optimal time for their learning. If needed the learner can watch the video several times or skip over sections they have already mastered.

We learn to walk by crawling, and to speak by babbling. Learning these skills is not an externally led process – children themselves are active learners, and independently take responsibility for their

---

94 M Toivola, P Peura & M Humaloja, *Flipped Learning in Finland* (Helsinki: Edita Publishing, 2020)

95 Jeroen van Merrienboer & Paul Krischner, *Ten Steps to Complex Learning* (New York: Routledge, 2017).

learning. Taking responsibility for your learning is an instinctive reaction. The parents' role is to provide their child with an inspiring atmosphere that will support intrinsically motivated learning.[96] Each infant tenaciously develops strength and coordination, navigating numerous attempts and errors to discern which movements lead to stumbling and which propel them forward. It falls upon parents to nurture, bolster, and establish a secure environment for these explorations.

When a child feels secure and safe they will take responsibility for their own learning. However, our educational institutions and learning environments often lack this essential confidence in a child's innate drive and curiosity to acquire new knowledge, and fail to provide them with a safe environment for exploration.

> ***'Students must be given options for their own learning. These options can be content-related** (**what I learn and in what depth**) **and activity related** (**how I learn, with whom, and how do I demonstrate to myself and my teacher that I have learnt**).'*
>
> – *Pekka Peura, from* Flipped Learning, 2020.

Flipped learning is about long-term efforts to create a learner-centred learning culture, and this requires respect and trust between student and teacher. The teacher's task is not to get students to mimic the teacher's actions and eventually internalise instruction. Instead, teachers seek to create opportunities for learning, and support their students' commitment to agent-oriented learning.

When learning is examined with respect to the needs of individual learners, you inevitably end up with a situation in which

---

96 Toivola et. al. *Flipped Learning.*

the learners will not all learn the same things. This should also be noted when designing your assessment culture.

Do we want students to become responsible citizens and active producers of information, or should they settle for being tourists in the teacher's pre-planned world? If the goal is the former – supporting the student's overall growth – then teaching should be based on active participation, not teacher led information transfer.

Pekka Peura on flipped learning

'As a subject teacher', Pekka Peura explains, 'I still choose learning tasks that are in line with the curriculum, but, understandably, not all my students have intrinsic motivation for the subjects or themes in question. I support them by defining concrete minimum goals for learning that everyone needs to achieve. I also attempt to give everyone sufficient guided opportunities to influence the organisation of their own learning, so they get some sense of responsibility and self-direction. This also enables their autonomous motivation to increase.'

He adds, 'Some students have previously been able to get away with token learning requiring minimal effort and the illusion that their studies automatically progressed when the teacher explained theory and they wrote notes. They had become used to passive attendance as the teacher moved their studies forward, so their self-regulation and self-direction skills had remained undeveloped. Poor self-regulation skills lead to problems with self-paced learning, as students do not progress unless learning occurs.

'When I taught in the traditional manner, I kept tight control of my students' progress, and pushed and shoved every student across the line. Or, at least, that's what I imagined. Although I made sure that everyone took good notes, not everyone's exam results were entirely complimentary. I was living under the illusion that everyone would learn at least the fundamentals, but when reading through the exams, I noticed that some students had learnt next to nothing, and their understanding of broader data structures was next to zero...

'When I launched self-paced learning, I immediately began feeling inadequate. The students no longer progressed at the rate dictated by me and quickly began working at their own pace at the limits of their abilities. Suddenly, almost every student had something to ask me ... my sense of inadequacy was overwhelming.

'I found I had much more time for personal interaction with students. I was able to create custom learning paths for students at an early stage in accordance with their abilities, and guide learning towards each students' personal goals. Active discussion in small groups helped the students to advise each other and solve minor problems among themselves, thereby reducing both their need for assistance and my workload.'

While flipped learning students have been shown to perform slightly better in tests than those in control groups, teachers are not motivated by the search for better results, but rather to make learning more meaningful and humane.[97]

A social constructivist approach

Visible learning and teaching occurs when teachers see learning through the eyes of students and help them become their own teachers.[98] In Hattie's opinion, self-regulation is the most important characteristic in a learner, and the learners that will learn best are those that are able to assess their own competence level in relation to targets.

The social constructivist approach to education views the learner not merely as a passive recipient of information, but as an active participant. This process involves the learner's logical

---

97 Toivola et. al. *Flipped Learning.*

98 Hattie, *Visible Learning.*

utilisation, organisation, and integration of new information with previously acquired knowledge. Meaningful learning, from the learner's perspective, establishes a solid foundation for sustained motivation, prioritising profound comprehension over mere memorisation.

The 'social' part of the name comes from the importance of social discourse in learning and because the usefulness of information is revealed through its use. Learners must have the opportunity to examine their own ideas and ensure that their understanding is developing in the correct direction. The teacher's actions are based on understanding how the student thinks. Interaction and dialogue are used to foster the student's intrinsic motivation.[99]

Extrinsic motivation is when the task is carried out for the sake of external incentives, such as grades or glory (examples of this include exams, grades, awards, family, competition). Intrinsic motivation is doing something for its own sake. It is not possible to have everything at school happening for intrinsic motivations alone. The teacher holds great responsibility for creating an environment that is conductive to learning, and this responsibility is further emphasised when sources of extrinsic motivation are removed.

It is desired (sometimes known as 'identified regulation') that the students value the goal of the activity and find the process of working towards it to be worthwhile.

An informal learning environment that provides challenges and inspiration promotes the formation of intrinsic motivation. Teaching that supports autonomous motivation strengthens the learner's sense of self-determination, sense of competence and sense of social relatedness. [100]

The zone of proximal development is the area in which learning

---

99 R Kauppila, *The way people learn: socio-constructivist learning* (Jyväskylä: PS-Kustannus, 2007).

100 Richard Ryan & Edward Deci, "Self-Determination Theory and the Facilitation of Intrinsic Motivation, Social Development and Wel-Being," *American Psychologist* vol. 55, no. 1, 2000.

is possible, and in which the teacher plays a significant role in the student's learning. In flipped learning, heterogeneity is seen as a resource to support self-regulation. There is no justification for forming more homogenous groups of students. The teacher gives students the freedom to study at their own pace and level and ensures that teaching materials of all levels are available. It should be remembered that the key objectives of flipped learning are, in addition to knowledge transfer, supporting self-regulation and learning how to learn.

When the teacher's robotic actions are automated with technology such as videos, the teacher is left with considerably more time to move around the classroom and give students help when they need it. A well-functioning learning community is full of mutual tutors. If a student does not achieve the target level, they are given support and extra exercises with the assistance of either the teacher or a student who has reached the target level.

Flipped learning sets out with the idea that you simply cannot progress in a cumulative subject unless you have mastered the things that come before. If time is limited, this means that not all students will have attempted to learn all the same things.

It is not a question of teachers no longer being allowed to teach, but rather that they do not primarily spend time lecturing everyone at once.

Mason, Shuman and Cook[101] noted that students in a flipped learning culture spent less time studying outside school than those in traditional teaching, yet still performed better in exams than the control group.

---

101 G. S Mason, T. R. Shuman & K. E. Cook, "Comparing the effectiveness of an inverted classroom to a traditional classroom in an upper-division engineering course," *IEEE Transactions on education*, vol. 55, 2013.

Social skills

Flipped learning promotes the development of students' social skills, which has a clear connection to school satisfaction.

> *'Some parents and students did not understand why we "no longer taught". They did not understand that well-copied notes do not necessarily mean that a student has actively processed the subject matter. There are no shortcuts. Copying pre-chewed ideas, or even repeated reading and memorising, still does not mean that the learner has turned either the topic in question or its importance in the greater scheme of things into intellectual capital.'* [102]
>
> — *Pekka Pura, in* Flipped Learning 2020.

Collaborative learning is where two or more people learn together. There may be collective output, but not necessarily. Students are encouraged to share what they have learnt with others. It is learning how to direct your own learning. Discussion enables you to learn from others and to question both your own thought processes and the things people consider self-evident. Discussion thereby leads to deeper understanding and has a positive impact on both the quality and quantity of learning. [103]

When students are asked what is important to them at school, the answer that crops up time and again is 'friends'.[104] In order to increase school satisfaction, collaborative working methods must

---

102 Trivola et. al., *Flipped Learning.*

103 N. Webb, "The teacher's role in promoting collaborative dialogue in the classroom," *British Journal of Educational Psychology* vol. 79, 2009; N. Webb, "Peer interaction and learning in cooperative small groups," *Journal of Education Psychology* vol. 74, no. 5, 1982.

104 Ian Shochet, Mark Dadds, David Ham & Roslyn Montague, "School connectedness is an underemphasized parameter in adolescent mental health: results of a community prediction study," *Journal of Clinical Child and Adolescent Psychology* vol. 35, no. 2, 2006.

be an integral part of the school day, and students must be given the opportunity to develop relationships and self-esteem along with their learning.

One teacher used the entire first lesson with a new group of students working on a sense of psychological safety for every student. Five-person teams complete the following:

- Students write, 'I learn best when...' at the top of an empty page and then continue the sentence in silence for five minutes. They then discuss these with the team.
- Discuss and list things that a) increase mutual trust and security within a team, and b) weaken mutual trust and security within a team. Based on this, the team writes a set of rules for themselves for the module.
- Give each student a learning diary in which they write down their own personal goals. The teams then discuss everyone's personal goals and the learning approaches that have successfully served and supported learning in the past.

This takes an entire seventy-five-minute lesson. While the teams started to investigate the subject over the next few lessons, the teacher talked with every team separately about the rules they had set, their notes on things that promote trust and the learning targets they had set for themselves. As the module progressed, the teacher came back to these on a regular basis.[105]

While an informal learning environment suits most students, for some it is not the best option. In these cases, the teacher must take a hands-on approach and share responsibility for the students' self-regulation. This often means that these students are subject to stricter rules and have less room to manoeuvre than students with more developed self-regulation skills.

---

105 Toivola et. al., *Flipped Learning.*

Those students who can plan their time well and study efficiently will be left with either time to move onto tasks for the following week or to focus on personal projects.

Ultimately, student self-regulation is not a teaching methodology, nor is it tied to one, but it is related to the teacher's concept of humanity, concepts of knowledge and learning, and a way of regarding learners as complete human beings.

From the Finland National Curriculum: 'A learner's interests, values, working methods and emotions, and their experiences and notions of themselves as a learner, guide both the learning process and motivation. The learner's self-image, self-confidence, and sense of capability affect the kind of targets they will set for themselves. Encouraging advice received during the learning process will strengthen a learner's confidence...'

THE FUTURE

WHERE ARE WE GOING? INTELLECTUAL OR PRODUCTION LINE

There are a number of relatively recent developments in the education sector which suggest future directions. Most appear to be well-intentioned, with the goal of improving educational outcomes (though these 'outcomes' seldom include anything beyond results on standardised tests) and increasing the number of teachers available. None address the issue of students walking away from education.

Most solutions to the teacher shortage involve continuing the 'dumbing down' of the profession and the occasional reference to reducing workloads or increasing wages. New Zealand recently announced a plan to move teacher training to a more 'on-the-job' format, akin to an apprenticeship, where teachers are trained while based in a school and might attend to studies one day per week.

Here in Australia, it appears obvious that the dumbing down of the profession will continue, as shown by the push towards 'direct instruction' which is the only teaching method which could possibly be implemented with a scripted format, and an on-the-job apprenticeship-like training scheme being 'trialled' in New South Wales. Indeed, there were actually sanctions against administrators who publicly (and rightly so!) questioned the direct instruction push. This is a disturbing development akin to the shutting down of free speech in countries under dictatorships.

Some states in the United States have stepped around the shortage of mathematics teachers by implementing an online program in the classroom with a supervising teacher who may not be qualified as a mathematics teacher, or perhaps one mathematics teacher is among a number of supervisors for a group of classes all using the online system at the same time.

It goes without saying that while both of the above practices provide a 'solution' of sorts to the teacher shortage, neither is preferable to a well-trained, intelligent, professional teacher. The New Zealand model omits the presence of a standard university education in conjunction with a teaching qualification, and – like an apprenticeship – it is easy to lower the entrance levels required for this program, stepping around any concerns about university 'standards'.

A number of Australian schools have combined subject areas (English/Humanities/Religious Studies or Mathematics/Science) in a move which increases standardisation of curriculum and reduces teacher autonomy. For example, an English teacher can then be expected to 'teach' Humanities and Religion as well as English, with the aid of pre-prepared PowerPoint presentations. These presentations supposedly remove the requirement for the teacher to be qualified in the other areas as they simply lead the students through that day's PowerPoint. Ironically, these schools have found these positions hard to fill as understandably few teachers are willing to take on the responsibility for subjects outside their field of expertise.

Both the teacher and the students are reduced to playing a predetermined role in a scripted 'lesson' which will (supposedly) lead to a positive result on a test closely tied to the material in the PowerPoints. Any less-than-ideal result can be put down to either the teacher or the student not fulfilling their expected role. Needless to say, many students find it unsatisfying listening to a teacher (likely uninspired and unqualified) read from a pre-prepared lesson while exactly the same lesson is delivered to another 100 students at that year level.

Parents are able to access the day's PowerPoints and question both students and teachers if they feel that the prescribed material has not been 'covered'.

Where once 'teacher' was considered an intellectual role with the goal of encouraging deep thinking and creativity, they are now reduced to reading from a PowerPoint. This dumbing down of the profession has led to many of the best teachers leaving the profession, and those comfortable viewing students and content as data now thrive.

As for the students? Their opinions are superfluous to the greater goal of checking off content and gathering data. Unlike the music teacher analogy mentioned earlier in this text, questions about student enjoyment or future interest are never asked. The book is closed once the examination result is in. Like student wellbeing, it seems there is no price we're not prepared to pay for grades.

If scores and rankings remain the main driver of Australian educational systems into the future, we will be stuck with the inefficiencies and stagnation of today. We need to develop forms of recognition that encompass attitudes, skills, abilities, strengths and talents beyond the narrow forms of intellectual growth that we typically measure. There are some promising trials, green shoots of alternative structures to university entrance exams, but these need to be envisaged and supported by a broader range of educational authorities.

Future forms and functions of Australian schools are difficult to predict but perhaps the way forward can be informed by looking back. The schools in which we began teaching some four decades ago were very different and yet very similar to the schools of today. The affective nature of children and their academic strengths and challenges appear as constant throughlines. Students are as diverse as ever, positioned throughout the intellectual, developmental, social and demographic spectrums. A teacher who could develop strong working relationships with students in 1985 could still do the same with their students' children and grandchildren today.

It is the organisational structures, classroom technologies and resources, set curricula, assessment approaches and teacher workforce that have changed greatly. Teacher pay, unfortunately, remains at its long-standing modest professional level. Despite the fuss currently made about 'new' pedagogies such as direct instruction, most ways of teaching today are closely related versions of approaches that have been practiced for a long time.

We accept a content-based education system, but argue little about whether that content should be fact-based or something more.

Kenyan Olympic runner Abel Mutai was just a few feet from the finish line when he became confused with the signage and stopped, thinking he had completed the race. A Spanish runner, Ivan Fernandez, was right behind him and, realising what was happening, started shouting at the Kenyan to continue running. Mutai didn't know Spanish and didn't understand. Realising what was taking place, Fernandez pushed Mutai to victory.

A journalist asked Ivan, 'Why did you do that?' Ivan replied, 'My dream is that someday we can have a kind of community life where we push and help each other to win.'

The journalist insisted, 'But why did you let the Kenyan win?' Ivan replied, 'I didn't let him win, he was going to win. The race was his.' The journalist insisted again, 'But you could have won!' Ivan looked at him and replied, 'But what would be the merit of my victory? What would be the honour in that medal? What would my mother think of that?'

Values are passed on from generation to generation.

What values are we teaching our children? Let us not teach our kids the wrong ways and means to win. Instead, let us pass on the beauty and humanity of a helping hand. Because honesty and ethics are winning!

Similarly, most children are involved in organised team sports, but participation numbers drop considerably as they move into the teen years, often due to the competitive nature of many sports. All accolades are directed towards the winners, and others are by default, 'losers'. The same can be said for our education system, which assumes that its own competitive nature is enough to motivate all students. Just like in the sports scenario, only a small number of students are winners, and in many cases (selective schools might be an exception) the majority accept 'loser' status and 'quietly quit' as they are not able to just drop out as they can in competitive sports.

PREPARING FOR WORK IN THE TWENTY-FIRST CENTURY

Yuval Noah Harari, in his book *21 Lessons for the 21st Century*, describes our production line theory of education as 'bankrupt'. He adds, 'To stay relevant [in the twenty-first century] you will need the ability to constantly learn and reinvent yourself ... Humans ... will increasingly have to deal with things nobody ever encountered before, such as super-intelligent machines, engineered bodies, algorithms that can manipulate your emotions with uncanny precision, rapid man-made climate cataclysms and the need to change your profession every decade.'

He continues: 'How should you act when you are flooded by enormous amounts of information and there is absolutely no way you can absorb and analyse it all?

'To flourish in such a world, you will need a lot of mental flexibility and great reserves of emotional balance. You will have to repeatedly let go of some of what you know best and feel at home with the unknown. Unfortunately, teaching kids to embrace the unknown and to keep their mental balance is far more difficult than teaching them an equation in physics or the causes of the First World War.'[106]

This repeated changing of careers, particularly as AI continues to improve, brings its own challenges as we have to learn new skills. Harari believes that, 'Governments will have to step in, both by subsidising a lifelong education sector, and by providing a safety net for the inevitable periods of transition. If a forty-year-old ex-drone pilot takes three years to reinvent herself as a designer of virtual worlds, she may well need a lot of government help to sustain herself and her family ... (This kind of scheme is currently being pioneered in Scandinavia where governments follow the motto 'protect workers, not jobs).'

In what should be a huge challenge to twenty-first century century educators: 'It is far from clear whether billions of people could repeatedly reinvent themselves without losing their mental balance.'

The teenage brain is witnessing constant change as the body and relationships change faster than ever, but as we get to our 'middle years' the appetite for change is lost, and neuroscience tells us that the adult brain is a lot less flexible and malleable than the teenage brain. But if we try to hold onto some form of stable identity, job or world view, we risk being left behind by the faster-than-ever changing world.

How does today's fact-based, direct instruction focused education ('sit down and be quiet!') serve children who will be active in the working world (and possibly involved in their third or fourth career change) in 2070? It is tricky to even name a profession we can be certain will still exist in 2070. And what becomes of the large numbers who cannot transition to a new career? They may find that they are completely irrelevant.

---

106 Y. N. Harari, *21 Lessons for the 21st Century* (London: Vintage, 2019).

Many experts believe we should be concentrating on 'The Four Cs' – critical thinking, communication, collaboration and creativity. These will help to deal with the immense change to come.

THE NAPLAN OF THE FUTURE

The yearly implementation of the national assessment scheme, NAPLAN, has probably been the biggest change in the last few decades of Australian education. It is difficult to identify its benefits, let alone its purpose and justification of cost and effort. Notionally, NAPLAN provides a snapshot of educational achievement and schools cannot and should not prepare their students for the tests. The generated data is supposed to be used by schools to improve the quality of their educational outcomes.

Nice in theory: too bad the overall outcomes for Australian schools since NAPLAN was introduced have drifted in the opposite direction. Yet the program appears to still be part of the future for Australian education. How NAPLAN may suddenly change in character and usage to actually drive the strengthening of educational outcomes is completely unexplained and unknown. If NAPLAN is to remain as a major item on the educational agenda, we wonder what purpose it is serving. If NAPLAN primarily exists to generate league performance tables, pitting schools against schools, it needs to disappear.

CONTINUING INEQUALITIES

Possibly the most enduring trait of Australian education is the chronic unevenness of the system. This is not going away any time soon. A 2023 PISA report stated that Australian schooling was one of the most unequal systems in the world and increasingly polarised since their previous report in 2019.[107] We have toured

---

107 See Pasi Sahlberg, "The good news is bad news when it comes to Australian pupils' Pisa scores. But there's no need to panic," *The Guardian*, Dec 6 2023.

this inequality through our own experiences within most sectors of primary and secondary schooling. It is stark and entrenched.

The gap between the highest and lowest resourced schools in Australia is immense, and we keep coming back to this as it is simply impossible to ignore. It is worse outside of cities and within some demographics such as our Indigenous population. Resourcing differentials drive a raft of disparate outcomes for students, none more so than the contrasting jobs and lifetime earnings that are available to privileged versus disadvantaged students. The belief that it is appropriate to divide students into 'intellectual' or 'production line' categories should not exist in a decent future Australian education system.

The issue is not only about material resourcing. We saw many modestly housed and equipped Finnish schools and yet saw quality teaching and learning occurring within them. All students had access to good schooling. Effective approaches to teaching, learning and everything else a school may offer are a big part of preparing all students for any future role that their abilities and skill sets may take them. Descriptions of what that might look like fill the pages of this book. Educational outcomes determined by postcodes and demographics do not have to be an ongoing burden for future Australians.

DIRECT INSTRUCTION

The most immediate threat to the quality of future Australian education is the ubiquitous promotion of direct instructional methods as superior to all other teaching approaches. Among the many flaws of this campaign is the unsupported assumption that teaching of any form of knowledge in all contexts is best done through direct instruction. Kuhn details the inadequacies of direct instruction if education is to be considered more than standard knowledge acquisition and retention.[108] We believe quality learning should go a lot further than this starting point.

The push heralds a move towards scripted lessons of a type which can be 'taught' by a less qualified teacher. Telling something simple is a lot easier than teaching something valuable. We are already seeing low-grade direct instructional processes substituting for richer forms of teaching in some schools through the mandating of bulk sets of notes. Teachers can passively flick through sequences of supplied PowerPoint slides and claim to have taught a topic. It is claimed by proponents to be based on learning science, but the trend displays the hallmarks of a cynical ideology, a strategy to roll out a hidden political agenda.

The non-university degree teaching qualification will open teaching up to people who may not have previously been able to gain university entry and the 'profession' will be reduced to the reading of a script to perplexed students, who will find themselves as the meat in a data sandwich. Between the script and the poorly qualified teacher, all opportunities to recognise individuality in students will be removed. Political gains for educational administrators include easier provisioning of teacher workforces – no more teacher shortages – and decreased pressure to increase wages. Low-qualified workers deserve low-level pay.

This would be a devastating outcome for students who are on the outside of the intellectual, financial and demographic nirvanas of elite private education. As has always been the case in Australia: the wealthiest education sectors would be immune from the degradation of teaching and learning occurring in the mainstream. The best teachers, best pay, best resources and best environments would continue to be a bulwark between the fantastic education of the privileged and the modest education of the rest.

---

108 Kuhn, D., 2007. Is direct instruction an answer to the right question? *Educational psychologist*, 42(2), pp.109-113.

CREATING A SCHOOL WHERE STUDENTS AND TEACHERS WANT TO BE

'People who say it cannot be done should not interrupt those who are doing it.'

— *George Bernard Shaw*

'I alone cannot change the world, but I can cast a stone across the waters to create many ripples.'

'The less autonomy the child is given, the more they will try to assert control over every little thing in order to get it back.

And the reverse is also true. The more autonomy a child is given, the more easily they'll be willing to give up control when necessary, because it doesn't threaten their autonomy.'

— *Blimey Heller*

Why the resistance to change?

There is a strange reluctance to adopt any change in Australian schools (and the same can be said about the USA and UK) and we have had countless conversations with school leaders who admit that they understand that the practices they have employed have not brought positive outcomes – often the opposite has been the case – yet they have continued.

The bar seems to be set extremely high for any alternative practice, despite the fact that the same bar is virtually non-existent for the 'standard' practice.

> ***'In the subordination of teachers, research is pre-digested into easy-to-read summaries for teachers to know the practices being prescribed are 'evidence-based'. Such pre-digestion of research is selective presentation of evidence to promote desired practices. It further removes teachers from engagement with research evidence.'***
>
> – *Prof. Nicole Brunker, from* Escape Oppression Now, 2024.

The aforementioned countries all work with a top-down system where control is concentrated at the department and government levels, though this is often not specifically stated. Countries known for innovation often have considerably less government interference in their systems. Many governments clearly see education as a form of indoctrination (we always point to the fights surrounding any review of the history curriculum regarding relationships between the early settlers and the Indigenous people, or slavery in the US system, as an example of this) believing that teachers are teaching children *what* to think rather than *how* to think.

We are reminded of Terry Wrigley, 'Capitalism needs workers

who are clever enough to be profitable, but not wise enough to know what is really going on.'[109]

On the other side of this coin is John Taylor Gatto who asks: 'Should we continue to teach people that they can buy happiness in the face of a tidal wave of evidence that they cannot?'[110]

Depressingly, it is possible that current educational trends are promoted by neoliberal perspectives that monopolise narratives, shaping agendas to serve unfettered free-market capitalism. We are reminded of Southlake, Texas – the community that turned out to be the cutting edge of harnessing culture panic for political gains. It is, among other things, the district where the administrator famously told teachers to cover 'both sides' of the Holocaust. Schooling is viewed as a highly regulated industry that devalues democratic and egalitarian ideals and exists to produce cheap units of labour for a profit-obsessed corporate economy. Schools are places where Social Darwinism deems the less capable as weak and a Hobbesian 'war of all against all' replaces any vestige of shared responsibilities or compassion for others.[111]

Within this bankrupt vision, teachers need no real pedagogical skills and can be omitted from decision making in relation to what is learnt and how it is taught. Teachers are no longer asked to be creative or to think critically. On the contrary, they have been reduced to the keeper of methods, implementers of an audit culture, and removed from assuming autonomy in their classrooms.

---

109 Terry Wrigley, "Learning in a Time of Cholera: Imagining a Future for Public Education," European Education Research Journal 21, no. 1 (Dec 2020)

110 J.T Gatto, *Dumbing Us Down, The Hidden Curriculum of Compulsory Schooling* (Canada: new Society Publisher, 1992).

111 "Global Education Magazine: School Day of Non-Violence and Peace (January 30th 2013)," Global Education Magazine.

> ***Reducing pedagogy to the teaching of methods and data-driven performance indicators that allegedly measure scholastic ability and improve student achievement is nothing short of scandalous.***
>
> *—Henry Giroux*

The bleak perspective reaches into teacher training. Neoliberals want teacher preparation to focus on 'practical' methods in order to drive an 'outcome-based' education system, which is code for pedagogical methods that are as anti-intellectual as they are politically convenient. This is a useful approach for creating armies of number crunchers and for downgrading teachers to supervising the administration of standardised tests, but not much more. The reduction of teaching into a skill set that services data-driven performance indicators, only loosely associated with scholastic ability and academic improvement, would be nothing short of scandalous.[112]

What becomes of children for whom the biggest life influence outside of their own family has now been downgraded from a successful, intellectual role model to a 'on-the-job' trained supervisor who was unable to gain university entry?

> ***'... there is an attempt to deskill teachers ... Teachers are no longer asked to be creative, to think critically, or to be creative ... they have been reduced to the keepers of methods, implementers of an audit culture, and removed from assuming autonomy in their classrooms.'***
>
> *— Henry Giroux*

112 Giroux, "School Day of Non-Violence and Peace".

And there are always the essential elements of the GERM, mentioned earlier (in the opening chapter) in this text, where schools need to be doing the same things in order for the required rankings and comparisons to be seen as 'relevant'. The overseeing bodies here undoubtedly believe that one or two 'rogue' schools could lead to a domino effect and the 'power' of the ranking (shaming!) system could be lost.

Another handbrake on change within a system can be that those who have the greatest influence and voice to bring about change are usually those who are doing well within the existing system. It's always worth asking what these voices against change may be gaining from the system as it is. Money (school funding)? A desire to indoctrinate? Power?

Dean Ashendon from the Melbourne Graduate School of Education believes that, 'The overhaul must come from the ground up, from the organisation of the daily work of students and teachers to the structure of the system and its governance.'

He continues: 'There is no entity, national or other, no government, state/territory or federal, and no stakeholder or combination of stakeholders with a span of responsibility and authority and a relationship between brain and body close enough to conceive and drive change of the kind and scale required.'[113]

Some insights are provided by Professor Richard Teese, in his 2003 book, *Undemocratic Schooling.*[114] He outlines a disturbing picture of systemic bias and structural inequality in Australian senior secondary education, driven by state curriculum policies, resourcing levels and university entrance practices. Teese's data suggests a pronounced early twenty-first century skew in advantages towards

---

113 Dean Ashenden, *Unbleaching the Whale: Can Australia's Schooling be Reformed?* (Centre for Strategic Education, 2024).

114 John Polesel and Richard Teese, Undemocratic Schooling (Melbourne: Melbourne University Press, 1990.

demographically privileged students. There is no reason to believe that anything has changed in the decades since.

Australian education is characterised by an entrenched system of winners and losers. The extreme polarity in outcomes between the wealthiest and most disadvantaged sectors of education is a source of considerable shame. Which end of this spectrum do those most resistant to change represent?

The most disadvantaged by the current system are usually those with the least influence or voice to actually bring about any change.

Where are the voices of those students (and the thousands of teachers) who have dropped out of school?

We have encountered many arguments against changing, though further examination of these always leads to a dead-end. Our standardised system of supposedly monitoring and motivating schools by ranking and comparing them against each other is dependent on them all doing as close to the same things as possible (we're always bemused that somehow the fact that the enormous differences in the facilities in which these things are done is apparently not an issue!) so this is certainly one reason why they fail to support any alternative methods. This system also assumes that all students are motivated to learn whilst simultaneously doing nothing to encourage this motivation. It also ignores the fact that many children – particularly those from less-than-ideal family circumstances – are repulsed by the competitive nature of the system (and many have avoided or dropped out of competitive sports for the same reason) and are triggered by many of the controlling compliance rules and regulations in place.

With estimates that we could be short 23,000 teachers in the next decade[115], it is clear that government schools (and some private schools) will not be able to afford the sort of wage increases

115 Simon Kuestenmacher, "A Growing Problem Looms for Australian Schools as Teachers Flee," *InDaily* published April 15 2024.

required to fill this gap. Some of those schools that will be able to retain and attract good teachers promote the very practices which have been driving teachers away.

CREATING CHANGE – PRIORITIES

As to whether change can be achieved in Australia, we have visited schools such as Croydon Community School and Assumption College Kilmore (and there are dozens of other examples, although the lack of media coverage given to these would make you think otherwise and leads us to ask why the media only covers traditional models?) where the standard, old-fashioned program has been shaken up and redesigned with enormous success proving that Australian students, teachers and society are no different to those of the countries where such practices are standard.

Pasi Sahlberg was a huge part of the creation of Finland's successful system. Now residing in Australia, he told us that he is often contacted by principals wanting to know who they have to ask about making changes to their school; he simply tells them 'If it is the right thing to do then just do it, you don't need anyone's permission.'

If there is one secret to the success of countries such as Estonia and Finland, it is that they do exactly what is required and do not persist with practices which are not in the best interests of teachers or students. Waiting for the government departments to suggest change is not being an education leader. If school leaders and teachers do not create change in the best interests of students and the profession, then others will and their interests may lay elsewhere.

One of the first things we suggest any school to do when re-evaluating their practices (and shouldn't every school, like any organisation, be doing this?) is to list in order of importance their priorities, practices and goals. Indeed, the conversation might begin with the question, 'What is the purpose of school?'

Ideally this process would involve school administrations and staff. Some of the entries on this list are randomly shown below, but they may vary from school to school:

- Teacher professional development
- School camp
- Student and career counsellors
- Homework
- Teacher/staff wellbeing
- Academic grades
- Standardised test results (NAPLAN etc)
- Student wellbeing
- Buildings and classrooms (would you spend money on these ahead of the other things listed?)
- Student voice/autonomy
- Teacher voice/autonomy
- Ranking and comparing students
- Evidence-based practice
- Parent voice/involvement
- School uniform
- Discipline/behaviour
- Technology/computers
- Teacher-student relationships
- Enjoyment/love of learning and school (school satisfaction)
- Student attendance
- Critical thinking
- Importance of each subject
- Curriculum
- Inclusion
- Student independence
- Creativity
- Learning Management System (LMS)
- Break times (how much time is needed for lunch? Other breaks?)
- Retain and attract great teachers
- School traditions

Once the school staff have completed the priorities list, it should be shown to students and parents. It is essential that these groups are on board and have a clear understanding of the whys and goals involved in this change. Presenting this to students could be done at a class level. It is essential that at this stage it is clear that there is no 'correct' order for this list to take, and it is likely that no two people will agree on every position on the list. The reason for the activity is to generate thought and discussion.

We stress that in this discussion the priorities can and will change over time, as the needs of the students and greater society change.

LIST WITH DISCUSSION POINTS

> ***'Whatever an education is, it should make you a unique individual, not a conformist: it should furnish you with an original spirit with which to tackle the big challenges: it should allow you to find values which will be your road map through life; it should make you spiritually rich, a person who loves whatever you are doing, wherever you are, whomever you are with; it should teach you what is important: how to live and how to die.'***
>
> *— John Taylor Gatto*

The above list is repeated on the next few pages along with notes, arguments and considerations on each point which may help to clarify our thinking. As you work through this list, consider which elements are dependent on others; for instance, is it possible to achieve (and are you satisfied to have) academic results without wellbeing? Is either of these possible without student attendance? Indeed, it will become obvious as you work through the list that nearly everything is in some way dependent on other parts of the list.

Are any being done just because 'that's what we've always done'?

Avoid the temptation of having 'non-negotiables'. There will be a few of these that appear later as a result of government regulations – curriculum is a good example – but these vary from state to state. Have literally everything 'on the table' at the beginning of this discussion. Research into organisational change suggests that its success is dependent on around 80% 'buy-in' from those in the organisation. It cannot be done just with a shift of administrative attitude. This 'buy-in' will come from giving staff a sense of autonomy and ownership of what is proposed.

All staff do not have to agree on the list (and it would be very surprising if this was to occur), but all will be in a better position for having spent time considering it and discussing it with colleagues. With the top-down nature of Australian education it's very easy to just go through the motions as though we have no choice; but the truth is that we do have a choice in nearly all of these, and being aware of this is in itself empowering.

It also helps to be aware that those things we don't make a conscious choice on are still present in our practices and can only be removed or moved down the list with a conscious effort.

Teacher Professional Development

All of the research tells us that the teacher is the most important element in the education chain. Studies tell us that some 50% of teachers plan to exit the profession in the next five years. Any school which fails to monitor how they interact with their teachers is simply being negligent. With 80% of those teachers who leave the profession maintaining their registration for at least a couple of years, there is always the possibility that some may be tempted to return – but they certainly will not be doing so if the working conditions have not changed.[116]

---

116 Sharon McDonough, Robyn Brandenburg and Wendy Moran, "A Study of Teacher Educator's

If we treat our teachers as genuine professionals, then we should be encouraging them to develop their professional knowledge and experience in every way possible. Teachers in the world's leading education systems usually have experience with the education systems of at least one other country, and often are encouraged to study or work overseas and funded to do so. This is part and parcel of being a 'professional'.

A key reason for the enormous trust and autonomy given to teachers in these systems is the breadth of professional knowledge and experience they possess. This autonomy and trust also leads to a desire for greater professional knowledge as it builds the intrinsic motivation of the professional to excel in their occupation.

Australian and New Zealand teachers are often criticised for failing to follow the latest research or practices, yet they are discouraged from exploring research or practices other than the status quo. Every practice used in our schools should stand up to critical examination.

Australian teachers do a remarkable job in the old-style 'industrial model' classroom environment, but micromanagement can be found throughout Australian classrooms in the form of external curriculum, assessment and, often enough, ill-considered pedagogical directives. This tends to discourage any form of genuine professional development as individual responses and initiatives are unlikely to be encouraged in everyday practice here. Be open to teacher ideas for professional learning – anything related to education will bring its own benefits, and trusting the teacher with this is part of teacher professional autonomy.

School Camp

School camps are an invaluable opportunity for staff and students to meet and interact with each other beyond what is usually

---

Work: Complexity and Confrontation," *Educational Forum* vol. 87, no. 4 (2023): 334 – 346.

possible within the classroom. Camps can be seen as a staging area for building the positive relationships that may generate huge benefits if brought back to the classroom. Any number of potential classroom issues may be headed off if staff and students enjoy strong, mutually respectful understandings of each other.

Much of the groundwork for building this brand of social capital can be done through the agency of an environment and sets of activities that are far removed from school classroom settings. Individual benefits to students include the development of a sense of belonging, leadership qualities, independence and resourcefulness. Camps should be seen as a win-win for the entire school community, generating benefits for pastoral, wellbeing and academic programs. Administrations should encourage, facilitate and reward participation from as many teachers and students as possible.

The viability of school camps has come into question most recently and teacher workloads have been rejigged to ensure those volunteering for such extra-curricular activities are fairly compensated. This is vital to ensuring the future of this precious school activity.

Student/Career Counsellors

Schools in Finland and Estonia place a high priority on support staff including counsellors. Helping students find their passion and direction is considered as important as any of the learning aspects of school. Students who understand why they are studying are well on the way to developing intrinsic motivation and the creation of this isn't all up to the teacher. Once a student has an idea of what inspires them and how this might create their future, they are no longer asking why they are at school.

The Finnish careers counsellor might see every student once a year. A 2024 study on early school leavers by the Smith Family found a 24% increase in the likelihood of a student staying at school until Year 12 when they have had careers advice that they can recall.[117]

Students with issues in their lives outside of school will have access to counsellors who can offer support, a calming word or encouragement as required. For many students, the school environment may be far more secure than their home environment.

Homework

Countries such as Finland and Estonia rarely give compulsory homework (whereas many Asian countries do so on an almost absurd scale), though students in these countries frequently study outside of school hours as they are interested in their studies and want to do so. There is also an understanding that play, socialising and sports are important aspects of the development of the child/young person and that these are usually more important than academic grades.

Research related to the academic benefits of homework has revealed mixed outcomes.[118] Homework directions should be carefully considered. The setting of homework can be justified when it is meaningful to students, it is accessible and there exists the after-school time resource in which it can be comfortably accommodated. If any of these conditions are not met, homework can do more harm than good. Homework tasks ideally support classroom learning and students need to be aware of the academic benefit. Students should be able to independently perform the tasks, and the work should not impact on their (reasonable amount of) recreational time.

We encourage teachers to adopt the neuroscientific finding

---

117 "Pathways, Engagement and Transitions: Experience of Early School Leavers," The Smith Family, published March 26, 2024.

118 "Key Lessons: What Research Says About the Value of Homework," Reading Pockets.

that engagement with academic content at a high frequency is a more effective learning strategy than for a lengthy duration. The existence of active homework sanctions regimes indicate that homework setting is problematic. The last thing any school needs is for homework to be associated with punishment – this completely derails the point of homework.

Interestingly, some prominent education researchers, such as John Hattie, have called for a complete ban on homework in primary schools. We find it interesting how some research is embraced when it fits the desired narrative and ignored when it does not.

Teacher/Staff Wellbeing

Studies suggest that attempting to improve staff wellbeing without actually looking into the conditions that created a wellbeing problem is fruitless.

Companies around the world spent $61.2 billion on wellness interventions in 2021. That amount is projected to grow to $94.6 billion in 2026. The problem is that most workplace wellbeing interventions cost money and take up time, but have little or no impact on employee wellbeing. In some cases, they may actually undermine workplace wellbeing. It turns out the most effective way to improve employee mental health is by reducing stress, rather than adding new ways to cope with it.[119]

Wellbeing programs tend to be less effective if implemented as stand-alone initiatives, as if once the meeting or session or activity has been attended, wellbeing is achieved. Practices and interactions that promote true wellbeing should infuse all aspects of school endeavours. Courtesy, respect, supportiveness, understanding and

---

119 William J. Fleming, "Employee Well-Being Outcomes From Individual-Level Mental Health Interventions: Cross-Sectional Evidence from the United Kingdom," *Industrial Relations Journal* vol. 55, no. 2 (March 2024): 162 – 182.

empathy are all qualities in any area of school activity that will build and sustain wellbeing for all participants.

Academic Grades

A substantial amount of schooling consists of the rote transfer of facts from students' short-term memory to long-term memory. This is an unspoken reason behind the push for direct instruction. When such retention is the major focus of assessment, students come to understand that their learning is equivalent to recall, regurgitation and good grades.

Knowledge is less likely to be retained if acquired for the sole purpose of performing well on a test, as opposed to learning in the context of pursuing projects and solving problems that are personally meaningful. Students who manage to remember some of the factual material they were taught are not necessarily able to make sense of those bits of knowledge, to understand the connections among them, or to apply them in inventive and persuasive ways to real-life problems.[120]

Psychoanalyst Erich Fromm put it this way: 'Hundreds of scattered and unrelated facts are dumped into the heads of students; their time and energy are taken up by learning more and more facts so that there is little left for thinking.'[121]

The question a school needs to consider is whether you are happy, as a school community, to accept academic grades and test results as your only success criteria. If we put the grades first, we are saying that all else – including student wellbeing – is an acceptable cost to pay for achieving grades.

We also encourage schools to consider whether they need to use a percentage grade for everything. There's a wealth of research showing that the use of a percentage number – or a letter grade

120 Alfie Kohn, *Feel-Bad Education* (Beacon Press, 2018).

121 Erich Fromm, *Escape From Freedom* (Discus Books, 1965).

– reduces the likelihood of students even bothering to read the comments made by the teacher. For this reason, many schools decide to avoid grading and opt for the comments alone. There is no problem with teachers deciding whether they think a grade or comment is appropriate for a particular task.

> *'Competition is appropriate in some arenas, but in education it is a repugnant motivator that will alienate teachers from one another and decrease the chances of all students succeeding. Competition is about winners and losers among teachers and their students. A Darwinian survival of the fittest, applied to education, cannot be healthy for an education system in a democracy.'*
>
> *— David C. Berliner*

Unspoken in all of the above is the assumption that all students are aiming to achieve high grades. One of the goals in establishing intrinsic motivation is creating a desire to learn, to be involved in school, that is not driven by the chasing of grades. The message that everything is a competition is unhealthy, and young children involved in free play rarely make it a contest – indeed, if they want others to continue playing with them, they have to ensure that all participants are enjoying the experience.

Once we have removed the necessity to rank and compare each student to others, the options are wide for assessment styles which give students productive feedback to assist them to improve on their own standards.

Collecting data on things like school satisfaction from students (avoid doing this with individual subjects or teacher's classes) is a worth-while exercise, as these numbers are as valuable as attendance data – the two, when put together, paint a much more holistic picture than attendance rates alone.

Standardised Test Results/ 'Data' (**NAPLAN etc**)

We are always sceptical of standardised tests which parachute into schools, labelled as a means to diagnose problems, but then disappear without any action to offer on 'findings'. If we were a mechanics service who did this, customers would be furious at us for charging a lot of money, taking a lot of your time, and then not doing anything about the problems we claim to see in your vehicle.

The average Australian student would not be able to count the number of standardised tests they have taken to identify learning gaps. They would also be unlikely to name a time when they took part in any form of tuition to assist with bridging this learning gap.

When I (Michael) explained how frequently NAPLAN tests are administered in Australian schools, Finnish educators asked incredulously, 'So your students have five lots of matriculation-type exams by the time they finish school?... Starting at *eight years old?!'* They stared at me as though I were an evil supervillain. In Finland children don't start school until the age of seven. They do not do any form of standardised testing until they are in their late teens.

Up until that point I had been ambivalent about these tests. This changed dramatically when, in a discussion with one of my Year 8 classes about growth mindset thinking – the belief that basic abilities can be developed through dedication and hard work – a third of students admitted that the experience of taking the Grade 3 NAPLAN test (as eight- or nine-year-olds) had made them decide that they were 'no good' at mathematics. Some said they could remember making that decision.

I couldn't help but wonder whether they'd had similar experiences in other NAPLAN-tested subjects.

But a standardised test does not and cannot measure creativity, critical thinking, curiosity, compassion, courage, cooperation, empathy, enthusiasm, humility, flexibility, humour, honesty, leadership, motivation, persistence, integrity, resilience, resourcefulness, reliability, initiative, taste, initiative, self-awareness, courtesy, or friendliness – things we should all want for the children of today.

Standardised tests only look at current students, yet surely the more important question is where students are at five or ten years after school? As a parent looking for a school, would you prefer a school obtaining impressive results on standardised tests, or a school where 95% of the students report life success and happiness a decade after graduating?

> ***'If you run an education system based on standardisation and conformity that suppresses individuality, imagination and creativity, don't be surprised if that is what it does.'***
>
> *— Sir Ken Robinson*

Among the many issues that have long plagued the NAPLAN program, the integral question of student care/effort has festered throughout. A recent study involved offering Year 7 students financial incentives to outperform their previous Year 5 NAPLAN outcomes.[122] It worked. What does this finding suggest about the average student investment of effort in NAPLAN? We believe that, like anybody, students with no motivation to expend energy on an endeavour won't, in fact, expend that energy. Maybe NAPLAN has been a waste of time if many students don't believe it has helped them in any way. It wasn't supposed to be like this.

Student Wellbeing (see also The Break)

Some education influencers believe that academic success alone

---

122 Jayanta Sarkar and Dipanwita Sarkar, "What Happens When You Pay Year 7 Students to do Better on NAPLAN? We Found Out," *The Conversation*, July 19, 2024.

can be the answer to the wellbeing crisis.[123] If this were the case, then the suggestion seems to be that a few good grades will be the cure to your anxiety, depression, or whatever issues may be impacting your wellbeing. We would certainly agree that positive life events might make one feel better than they were before, but to suggest that school grades can have this effect on all students seems rather unrealistic to us (and it assumes that their studies have a sense of genuine meaning to them – not all students come from backgrounds that value educational achievement) and indeed a somewhat shallow way of looking at the world. History is strewn with successful people who have taken their own lives, despite having successful films, hit songs, books, works of art, businesses, and good grades.

We tend to agree with the research showing that, like employee wellbeing (see above), wellbeing programs are of little value unless adjustments are made to the very circumstances which have led to the wellbeing issues. There is a wealth of research telling us that autonomy, control, choice, a sense of purpose and human relationships all contribute to an improved sense of wellbeing and general life-satisfaction.

Of particular concern with student wellbeing are negative peer relationships. Student wellbeing is compromised by the existence of bullying, manipulation, exclusion, belittling, coercive interactions, aggressive and threatening subcultures and intolerance. Over-competitiveness and unrealistic academic goals can also lead to stress and anxieties. About 90% of Singaporean secondary students experienced stress in relation to academic activity in 2022, despite Singapore ranking very highly in international academic achievement surveys.[124] What hidden wellbeing costs lie behind that brand of success?

---

123 Nathaniel Swain et al., "What We Want to Say Right Now to Sahlberg and Goldfeld," *EduResearch Matters*, published May 29, 2023.

124 Tan Chee Soon, "Test Anxiety," *Nanyang Technological University*, published September 16, 2024.

Further sources of wellbeing issues include environments and circumstances outside of the school. Teachers and administrators who are sensitive and empathetic in relation to student feelings, or who can 'read' beyond appearances, should be best placed to offer support or diffuse harmful situations. Creating and maintaining inclusive and non-threatening cultures and environments within schools should be standing items of administrative business. Of course, students who are happily engaged in their academic work – not fixated on performance rankings and who feel valued and cared for by their teachers – will be less vulnerable to suffering from wellbeing issues.

Schools in Estonia and Finland ensure that students have regular access to counsellors, and a Finnish student can expect to see a careers counsellor once a year from quite an early age. A student who can answer the question "Why am I here at school studying...?" is more likely to feel a sense of positive wellbeing than one who has never been asked to consider these questions.

Buildings and Classrooms

We are frequently bemused at the insistence from the powers-that-be on inspecting a school's curriculum documentation to ensure that all are onboard with the current policies, and that all students country-wide are receiving instruction on the same material – while at the same time ignoring the fact that some are being taught in buildings and grounds worth hundreds of millions of dollars (some have performing arts facilities with orchestra pits and heated swimming pools far superior to the nearest public pools and art centres), while others are in portable classrooms sited on dusty paddocks.

Why do we not see a push for the standardisation of educational resources, even in principle if not practicality? After all, we are endlessly told about the desirability of academic standardisation.

Classroom buildings and academic facilities such as libraries that don't leak, are temperature-controlled, hygienic, sound-proofed, spacious, equipped with contemporary IT technology, furnished with comfortable seating and appropriate working spaces ... these should be givens. Where specialised infrastructure doesn't exist (particularly in state systems), pools, theatres, gymnasiums and indoor sports venues should be planned and funding sought. No less is needed to give all Australian students a fair shot at a materially standardised education.

Of course, quality infrastructure does make a difference, but it alone will not make up for standardised curriculums that ignore the individual characteristics of students.

And even if we insist on viewing learning as a contest: we would never see it as reasonable to have the AFL club Collingwood playing against South Wagga Wagga, even if both utilised standardised training drills and activities.

Student Voice/Autonomy

> ***'To truly transform the educational experience, school leaders must actively involve students in the decision-making process. By creating platforms for student voice, such as student councils, advisory boards, or regular feedback sessions, leaders empower students to contribute their perspectives, ideas and aspirations. This not only fosters a sense of ownership and engagement, but also ensures that decisions are made with a deep understanding of student needs and aspirations.'***
>
> — *Dr Mary Hemphill, from* What Makes a Great Principal: The Five Pillars of Effective School Leadership

If choice is related to interest, and interest is related to achievement, then it's not much of a stretch to suggest that learning environments in which kids get to participate in making decisions about what they're doing are likely to be most effective, all else being equal. Students are less interested in whatever they're forced to do and more enthusiastic when they have some say.

The more pressure students feel to succeed, the more likely they'll be to choose easy tasks.[125]

Finland and Estonia actively encourage student independence by asking parents to allow children to walk to school (and we saw many catching trams and buses) unaccompanied by adults from the age of seven. We have seen this even during a snowstorm; come recess, all children were outside playing. The school has drying cabinets in the corridors to ensure that all damp outer garments are ready to go again at the next break. Children learn about responsibility by being *given* responsibility, unlike the method used by most Australian schools of removing all possible risks.

As long-serving teachers, we have heard of many ex-students of ours losing their lives in an unexplainable auto accident (or similar) where it appears that the student was engaging in risky behaviours for no reason other than because they could. Bubble wrapping our children and removing all possible risks does nothing to help them learn about decision making in risky situations. When they turn eighteen, they have access to cars, alcohol and many more dangerous opportunities. Keeping them away from all risk in the previous eighteen years is a terrible preparation for this time.

Secondary school students in Finland (Year 9 and above) are free to come and go between classes, visiting coffee shops or other campuses. We saw schools where students created their own timetables and decided when they wished to take examinations

125 Kohn, *Feel-Bad Education.*

or other assessments, and could postpone these if they felt they were not sufficiently prepared. We were impressed with the level of maturity and self-discipline displayed by the students in these schools which had removed every area where a student might choose to 'rebel': it is hard to rebel against your own choices.

Student views and preferences are generally much less evident or influential within Australian schools. This is an area of opportunity if we want to develop both the quality of learning and the levels of wellbeing in our schools. According to the Student Wellbeing Hub, 'Student Voice is one of the five elements of the Australian Student Wellbeing Framework. When students have authentic opportunities to be active participants in their own learning, they feel connected and are able to use their social and emotional skills to be respectful, resilient and safe'.[126]

As it stands in most Australian schools, students are currently as disempowered as teachers in relation to how education is controlled. A glimpse of how the voices of participants in Australian education may be heard was offered by the 2023 Royal Commission into people with disability.[127] The powerful individual stories of many disabled people were told and underpinned a strong set of recommendations for future improvements in the sector. The stories of students and teachers currently in the Australian education system would also make for a very interesting hearing. Is a Royal Commission into the state of Australian education needed?

(Mandated) Evidence-Based Practice

'Evidence-based' practice should come with the word 'mandated' before it, as this is often the accompanying condition. Supposedly, the practice is so water-tight in its effectiveness that all argument

---

126 "Australian Student Wellbeing Framework," Student Wellbeing Hub.

127 "Final Report," Royal Commissions, published September 29, 2023.

or questioning is to be removed. In effect, it is an attack on teacher professional autonomy and a means of micromanaging teachers.

Sydney University researcher Nicole Brunker noted: 'In the subordination of teachers, research is pre-digested into easy-to-read summaries for teachers to know the practices being prescribed are 'evidence-based'. Such pre-digestion of research is selective presentation of evidence to promote desired practices. It further removes teachers from engagement with research evidence.'[128]

Evidence-based practice is one of the buzzword phrases in contemporary education. It's used in resumes, curriculum documents and school mission statements. We've always been inclined to ask about this evidence, which usually draws a blank response. We're wary of evidence drawn from one class at an advantaged school, and more so of 'meta studies' where evidence is drawn from an ocean of learning environments, and studies where data and findings from a university engineering course might be applied to a class of five-year-olds. We're always asking about the control group, and comparisons using alternative methods – important questions to ask when analysing *any* research!

When someone says that science conclusively proves that this instructional strategy is more effective than that one, we want to ask what exactly is meant by 'effective'? As we discuss elsewhere, that question is so obvious, so foundational to any claim, that it's astonishing to realise how rarely it's asked. Often it turns out that 'effective' – along with other terms of approbation such as 'higher achievement', 'positive outcomes' and 'better results' – signifies nothing more than scoring well on a standardised test. Or having successfully memorised a list of facts. Or producing correct answers in a math class (without grasping the underlying principles). Or being able to recognise and pronounce words correctly (without necessarily understanding their meaning).[129]

128 Brunker, "Escape Oppression Now".

129 Alfie Kohn, "The Siren Song of 'Evidence-Based' Instruction," published May 23, 2024.

Evidence is always open to 'cherry picking' as required to support current educational trends. There's also a huge body of evidence on topics such as standardised testing and curriculum which are ignored. A recent UK study (evidence-based, we would hope!) suggests that using research to improve learning outcomes in schools is simply not working. The study draws upon data from a large qualitative analysis of interviews with 167 school staff and a survey of 285 schools. In addition, it reports on a review of 100 school policy documents, a review of the evidence, and a study of examination data and teacher attitudes at one school. It argues that the mechanisms to put research into practice are failing. A wide variety of practices are being justified by a small number of studies of questionable relevance. In some schools, attempts to be guided by research have not had the expected positive impact, which has caused weariness and frustration. It also presents evidence that, in some contexts, certain kinds of improvements to teaching may widen attainment gaps (the difference between the lowest and highest levels of performance).[130]

The study's author clarified her findings: 'It is also becoming apparent that the gains in education are usually very small, perhaps because learning is the sum total of trillions of interactions ... It seems that evidence is much harder to tame and to apply sensibly in education than elsewhere ... But we now need to think harder about the peculiarities of how evidence works in education. Right now, we don't have enough evidence to be confident that evidence should always be our first port of call.'[131]

To quote Dr Jared Cooney Horvath, 'Matters of practice can

---

130 Sally Riordan, "Improving Teaching Quality to Compensate For Socio-Economic Disadvantages: A Study of Research Dissemination Across Secondary Schools in England," *Review of Education* vol. 10, no. 2 (August 2022).

131 Sally Riordan, "Schools are Using Research to Try to Improve Children's Learning – But It's Not Working," *The Conversation*, published April 3, 2024.

never be decided by deferring to theory; the latter will always be too general to address the former.'

Whilst we would always encourage the use of evidence-based practices, it should always be at the discretion of the teachers and not as an approach imposed on an entire school. The gains from many such evidence-based approaches are usually very small and likely to be cancelled by the losses as a result of reduced teacher autonomy and control in the classroom environment.

Allow well-trained teachers to apply their professional autonomy and judgement to make the most appropriate decisions for the needs of their students. Cooney Horvath concurs: 'Although drawing on educational research is worthwhile ... pedagogical decisions must always be ceded to the experts in pedagogy: namely, teachers.'[132]

We believe individual teachers should not simply be expected to accept the label of 'evidence-based' as a catch-all justification for adopting any classroom initiative. The evidence base for any pedagogical change and circumstances related to the data gathering should be disclosed to teachers. Teachers should then evaluate the data in relation to the characteristics of the classes in which they intend to implement the initiative. Schools should allow teachers the freedom to make their own reasoned decisions, and give justifications if necessary, about what will best serve the learning interests of their own students. See the chapter *'Looking Under the Bonnet of Learning Science and Direct Instruction'* for more observations on evidence-based practices.

We have always loved the mantra given to the student teacher in Finland. It conveys trust, autonomy and respect for professional knowledge: 'Study best practice and then see if you can improve on it'.

---

132 Jared Cooney Horvath, "Why You're Probably Wrong About the Science of Learning," *Tes Magazine*, published May 1, 2024.

Teacher Voice/Autonomy

How we treat and support our teachers in the education system becomes the lens through which our students receive and view education, and then the lens through which they view the world outside of education.

It can be one of trust, innovation, creativity, autonomy, critical thinking, collaboration and inspiration - or one of compliance, control, micromanaging, standardisation, competition, ranking and judgement.

We are creating society.

> ***'High burnout cultures say, "If they don't like it at this school, they should go somewhere else." The problem with this culture model is that teachers are - going somewhere else.'***
>
> *— Sue Webb, author, Teachers Cry Too*

One journalist did some numbers recently and found that, if we grow the population aged under eighteen by just 6%, we must increase the schoolteacher cohort by 6% just to maintain current teacher to student ratios. This means we must add 23,000 workers to reach 414,000 teachers by 2034.[133]

If we want to entice the best and brightest young people to the teaching profession, then we must provide them with the trust and autonomy given to other professions. A survey of teachers in Finland asked what it would take for teachers there to leave the profession: loss of autonomy was one of the top responses.

Pasi Sahlberg: 'In my country we want to have teachers with self-esteem, that they feel that they are professionals just like medical doctors and lawyers and others.'

133 Kuestenmacher, "A Growing Problem".

The best young people looking to enter professional life now have the option of professions which offer flexibility to work from home or work part-time, enormous independence and autonomy, and the chance to be innovative and creative. We have to ensure that the teaching profession is an attractive option in this field.

Ranking and Comparing Students

> ***'Children from difficult beginnings often cannot tolerate failure or being wrong. The sense of failure subconsciously often reminds them of deeper losses and triggers embodied memories deep in their core.'***
>
> — *Dr Lori Desautels*

'What it (ranking) does is make it very obvious to everyone who is struggling and who isn't,' Dr Naomi Fisher, Clinical Psychologist and Writer, observes. 'It's a public shaming of those at the bottom, who are often those with special needs or who have other difficulties in their lives. And its anxiety provoking for many. Those at the top worry about losing their spot and about no longer being seen to be "good at maths". Those at the bottom are told to "try harder" even when they are trying their best and quickly become despondent. Sometimes the ranking uses reaction times - doing your times tables super-fast is what gets the most points, so those who need more processing time quickly start to panic. Some start to freeze when they are asked questions, which is never going to be helpful for doing maths.

'Ranking focuses everyone on points rather than learning,' she continues. 'Parents tell me that their children say they know they are stupid, because everyone else is doing better. There's no way for parents to deny this, it's literally written on the whiteboard.

They can tell them that other things matter too, but that's not what they see at school. Removing a child from the ranking doesn't solve the problem, because everyone can see that they aren't there and they'll ask why.

'Is anyone doing the risk assessments of the effect of this on the most vulnerable? When you rank a class of children, someone is always going to be at the bottom. Often the same, most vulnerable kids. There's no way for them all to succeed. If you do this often, some kids are being told again and again that they are the losers. In front of the whole class.'[134]

Similarly, we suggest that keeping the students unaware of this ranking – a commonly presented solution to these issues – does not make it appropriate. What is the purpose? Identifying weaknesses of any kind is a pointless pursuit unless there is a concrete strategy in place to assist with such weaknesses.

We refer to the Finnish policy of asking, 'Is this good for students or teachers?'

Parent Voice/Involvement

We were amazed at the great respect and trust given to the teaching profession by all levels of society in countries such as Estonia and Finland. This can be attributed to the non-political nature of education and the equity in the system. The fact that these countries also personalise education and have a focus on student independence and wellbeing are also important factors.

When I (Michael) explained to Australian parents that I was using practices borrowed from or influenced by what I had seen in Finland, the most common response was a huge 'thank you' for seeing their child as more than just a standardised student. Not a single parent asked me to forget about considering the needs of their child and just concentrate on getting academic results.

134 Naomi Fisher, "I am still hearing from parents," LinkedIn, posted April 7, 2024.

Parent-teacher interviews are an effective way to sample parental concerns and sources of satisfaction. Between us, we have conducted thousands of interviews and can report that the desire for their children to be happy at school is by far the highest priority for parents. It is incongruous to note that despite our schools typically implementing so many academic, behavioural and pastoral care goals and policies, possibly the most fundamental aim, 'foster student happiness', is rarely expressed.

Jane Louise Hunter, Associate Professor, Teacher Education at the University of Technology, Sydney supports our findings.[135] She describes typical parental perspectives succinctly:

'For parents, it may help to remember the most important things have not changed: your child is progressing at school, they are engaged in what they are learning, and they are happy to go.'

School Uniform

This is an area which we have, in the past, chosen not to engage with as we have seen the attachment many Australian schools have to controlling the clothing students wear. If uniform tops your list of priorities, can we suggest a career in the clothing industry, or the military?

We are always concerned about the message a school sends when it places a uniform at the top of the list, as it does when it refuses to include any student without a uniform. What does this tell students about our real priorities? Does it suggest to them that standing your ground at all costs on a matter not directly related to your goals is acceptable? It can be argued that school systems are about creating compliant, uncritical populations. As dedicated educators we abhor this idea and therefore find the idea of 'uniform' or any other practice which supports this idea as

---

135 Jane Louise Hunter, "Is There a 'Right Way' to Teach? Recent Debates Suggests Yes, but Students and Schools are Much More Complex," *The Conversation*, published July 25, 2024.

something to be avoided.

Is there an association between military-style student regulations and issues of intimidation/bullying like we have seen in some Australian Defence organisations? When we hear stories of female teachers having to cope with (and many ending their careers because of) Andrew Tate–influenced sexual harassment[136], we have to question the military style organisation, discipline and even military uniform (we think most schools have moved away from the marching!) that many schools operate within. Particularly when so many of the traditional practices are justified by the phrase 'they have to get used to it in the real world'. Unless we are preparing children for a future in the military, most of the above is from the 'that's the way we've always done it' file. Indeed, educators in countries that do not have school uniforms are quite bemused at our inability to trust our students to dress themselves!

School uniforms can be part of a school culture that instils in students respect for their school and respect for themselves. This is certainly desirable. However, it is even more desirable that student respect is sourced from strong teacher relationships, caring and effective teaching practices, love of being at school and love of learning. Rather than issuing punishments for hair out of place or the wrong-coloured socks, any school would be better served by focusing on making their classrooms places where students want to be.

Perhaps our schools are too caught up in the idea of 'looking the part'. Sometimes it's more important to be actually doing the right thing rather than being concerned with being seen to be doing the right thing. We are always open to any neuroscience explaining how wearing certain clothing or hairstyles can increase or hinder the ability to learn.

---

136 Norman Hermant and Ahmed Yussuf, "Andrew Tate's Ideology Driving Sexual Harassment, Sexism and Misogyny in Australian Classrooms," *ABC News*, published April 2, 2024.

Discipline/Behaviour (see also Student Independence)
'What if our square pegs aren't the problem?' Morgan, Costello and Gilbert ask us to consider. 'What if they are actually the canaries in the coalmine, alerting us to the mounting problems in our education system?

'The child who deviates, who refuses to behave like everybody else, may be telling us – loudly, visibly and memorably – that the arrangements of our schools are harmful to human beings. Something toxic is in the air and these children refuse to inhale it. It is dangerous to exclude these children and their warnings.'[137]

As we moved from school to school on our last Finland tour, we made a point of asking each teacher, principal and administrator about how they dealt with issues around discipline in their school, particularly the current Australian scourge – poor classroom behaviours. When we saw calm, composed and focused students at one school after another, we could not help but wonder what created this level of serenity. The response was always a slightly bemused look, perhaps of pity that Australian educators were preoccupied with this theme, and a comment about the self-regulating influence of student autonomy or choice within the school.

Education writer Amanda Ripley queried Kim, an American exchange student in Finland (who had obviously seen both sides of the equation) about this phenomenon. Kim told her: '... there just seemed to be something in the air here. Whatever it was, it made everyone more serious about learning, even the kids who had not bought into other adult dictates.' Kim's reference to 'other adult dictates' referred to the fact that these students were still rebelling against the adult society around them, but neglecting their education

137 Ellie Costello and Fran Morgan, *Square Pegs: Inclusivity, Compassion and Fitting In – A Guide for Schools* (Independent Thinking Press, 2023).

did not appear to be among their choices for this rebellion.[138]

Kim was surprised to find she could come and go freely from her Finnish school, visit nearby shops or just take a break with other students at a coffee shop. She also noted that teenagers were treated more like adults: there were no regularly scheduled parent-teacher conferences. If teachers had a problem with a student, they usually just got together with the student.

Indeed, this reflects the idea that all students want to learn, and we believe this to be true, with the caveat that they want to learn certain things in certain ways. Essentially, they want to have some input into these fields. Once they have this input, their work then goes on to matter to them. I (Michael) remember during the COVID pandemic when schools went to remote learning, I asked a Finnish colleague how her students had been coping with this. She responded, 'They have been trying to ensure that it does not impact on their learning.'

My students had been doing exactly the opposite, presenting constant computer, camera and wi-fi problems as excuses for less-than-regular input into their studies. The difference was that the Finnish students were working on 'their' learning, whereas my students were part of a system where they had little if any choice; essentially nothing about it was 'theirs'.

Technology/Computers

The rush to one-to-one computer use in schools has proven to be misguided with a wealth of research suggesting that they are linked with a drop in reading skills, academic grades and more. We agree wholeheartedly with the advice of neuroscientist Dr Jared Cooney Horvath who stresses that computers should only be present in the room if they are essential for the particular lesson. In countries

---

138 Ripley, *The Smartest Kids.*

such as Finland, many schools have a class set of devices shared between a number of classrooms. We feel certain that students will have appropriate computer skills without using them all day, every day at school.

Australian schools were inundated with classroom technology, in the forms of laptops and tablets, about twenty years ago. Australia was a world leader in pushing digital technology out to students. Unfortunately, the potential for enhancing educational outcomes has been largely unrealised. Teachers have been challenged in positioning computers to support student learning, often utilising software or accessing internet material for no better reason than because it was now possible.

Digital technology too often acts as a source of individual distraction and blunts productive social interactions.[139] Many schools *mandated* the classroom use of computers by teachers and in hindsight this was an excessive policy. There needed to be greater understanding of how computers could add to what was of value in classrooms rather than replace it. This is an ongoing challenge, and any school should actively monitor the classroom impacts of technology and keep options open, even encouraging teachers to make some classes free of computers or devices at times.

Given the ambivalence (at best) around whether computers have actually enhanced the quality of education, the ignorance about possible outcomes associated with classroom AI is unsettling.

To pretend AI can be kept out would be a forlorn position. One opinion is that wholesale, unbridled use of AI will probably not help. Another is that the distraction effect, so prevalent with computers, must be much more deeply considered. Genuine research programs should be implemented and conducted in schools that truly represent the broad spectrum of education in Australia, not just in niche environments such as selective entry schools.

---

139 "Impact of Technology on Kids Today and Tomorrow," Western Governors University, published October 3, 2019.

In the meantime, schools must monitor and evaluate the impact of AI within their classrooms. This needs to be done without the fake pressures to deploy and utilise that were so evident when computers first arrived. How is AI enhancing the quality of our students' learning? What are they gaining? What are they losing? Do the benefits outweigh the burdens? What do we have to do for AI to be a valuable addition to our teaching? Again, it is teachers who are best placed to address such questions. Administrations should be wary of imposing tight blanket policies for the use of AI in their schools until teachers have had opportunities to investigate its impact in their own subject areas.

A compelling early appraisal of the possible impacts of AI technology was performed by Cooney Horvath[140] in 2024. Chief among several identified issues and limitations was the loss of teacher-student empathy in learning interactions with AI systems. Cooney Horvath warns that strong empathy is a significant driver of cognitive brain functioning: a sobering thought for the growing numbers of people advocating for the replacement of teachers with AI technology.

Teacher-Student Relationships

We recently talked to a couple of teachers of the same subject for two senior high school classes that obtained far superior final course results to all other classes taught at the same year level. We asked them what it was that lay behind their success. Unequivocally, it was their relationships with students. It was an unsurprising response given we have observed the same powerful factor in play during all of our teaching lives, everywhere we have taught. Positive relationships with students are possibly the strongest force in the educational universe.

---

140 See Jared Cooney Horvath, "The Limits of GenAI Educations," *The Harvard Business Review* July 16, 2024.

In terms of student cooperation, motivation, interest and investment of effort, a strong teacher-student relationship exercises enormous leverage. An ability to bond with their students is almost always central to the practice of the most successful teachers. Schools should encourage all teachers to develop the levels of social skills, understanding, rapport, empathy and care that are needed for healthy relationships to develop with students. This is often easier said than done as such attributes generally need to be deeply rooted in any individual's psyche. The immense rewards on offer make the effort worthwhile.

One of Professor John Hattie's less publicised but possibly most important findings is acknowledgement of the significance of teacher-student relationships.[141] He promotes acceptance, warmth, empathy and nurturing as elements of care. Coupled with high expectations, the relationship can lead a student towards academic success.

Enjoyment/Love of Learning and Intrinsic Motivation

Research from the Smith Family found that the most common reason for students dropping out of school was 'not liking school', an answer given by 32% of those who had dropped out.[142]

Extrinsic motivation tends to reduce long-term interest and effort in the topic at hand and reduce creativity, as well.[143] Research has found that motivation driven by extrinsic factors tends to lead

---

141 See Shaun Patrick Killian, "What Everyone Needs to Know About High-Performance, Teacher Student Relationships," *Evidence-Based Teaching*, accessed July 23, 2024.

142 "Pathways, Engagement and Transitions: Experience of Early School Leavers," The Smith Family, published March 2024.

143 Edward Deci, R Koestner & Richard Ryan, "A meta-analytic review of experiments examining the effects of extrinsic rewards on intrinsic motivation," *Psychological Bulletin* vol. 125, no. 6, 1999; Kohn, *Feel-Bad Education*; Hillary Wehe, Matthew Rhodes & Carol Seger, "Evidence for the negative impact of reward on self-regulated learning," *Quarterly Journal of Experimental Psychology* vol. 68, no. 11, 2015; Beth Hennessey, "Rewards and Creativity" in *Intrinsic and Extrinsic Motivation* (Academic Press, 2000).

to 'decreased wellbeing'.[144] Experiments using student rewards to improve academic achievement have failed repeatedly.[145] If and when incentives have resulted in very limited short-term 'success,' researchers have found they tend to increase participants' focus on the reward itself, not on the task. Work quality then suffers, and task interest tends to decline to previous levels – or below them – after the reward is given.[146] If a student has learnt to play a musical instrument in order to impress others or to win awards, it is unlikely that student will continue to play that instrument when awards or people to impress are not present.

Researchers have identified four general areas that can contribute to creating the conditions where intrinsic motivation can be supported:

- Autonomy: having a degree of control over what needs to happen and how it can be done
- Competence: feeling that one has the ability to be successful in doing it
- Relatedness: doing the activity helps the student feel more connected to others, and feel cared about by people whom they respect
- Relevance: the work must be seen by students as interesting and valuable to them, and useful to their present lives and/or hopes and dreams for the future[147]

The research on this is unequivocal, yet creating intrinsic motivation is a rarity in our system. If we invite you to try a new type of food, you may do so quite happily if that form of cuisine has

---

144 Joshua Howard et. al., "Student motivation and associated outcomes: a meta-analysis from self-determination theory," *Perspect Psychological Science* vol. 16, no. 6, 2021

145 Adams, 2024; Jens Dietrichson et. al., "Targeted school based interventions for improving reading and mathematics for students with, or at risk of, academic difficulties in Grades 7–12: A systematic review," *Campbell Systematic Reviews* vol. 16, no. 2, 2020; Larry Ferlazzo, "Resources for Starting a New School Year Strong," Larry Ferlazzo's Websites of the Day, posted July 31, 2016.

146 Larry Ferlazzo, *The Student Motivation Handbook: 50 ways to boost an intrinsic desire to learn*, (London: Routledge, 2023); Kohn, 2016.

147 Ferlazzo, *The Student Motivation Handbook.*

some interest, but if we offer you a sum of money to eat something we have created, it is an entirely different scenario. Certainly, eating the food for its own good qualities is virtually off the table (sorry about the pun) and now, simply getting through the food in order to receive the reward is the goal. What does it say about this food if we have to bribe you to eat it?

An analogy we often use is that of a racehorse that loves to run, versus one whose jockey frequently resorts to the whip. The whipped horse may occasionally win a race, but the horse that loves to run will likely win more, and it will frequently be running even when there isn't a race. And education is not a race.

Perhaps part of the problem is that intrinsic motivation is difficult to measure. If a student learns something and it is not measured by a test, did the student actually learn anything?

In the horse racing analogy above, the running done by the horse that isn't officially in a race is not measured and recorded. Do we place a value on running fast alone?

Do we place a value on students using their learning in the real world, even though it may not be part of an official test there and a grade given and recorded for posterity?

Finnish teacher Saara Tahtela sees it thus: 'Talking about results in the same sentence with teaching is a little complicated since the results are not always immediately visible or noticeable, but they may come later on in the life of a student.'

In Finland and Estonia, lessons do not commence until the teacher is satisfied that a positive classroom culture has been achieved, conscious of the fact that learning is most effective in this environment. In Australia we seem to commence the lessons as soon as we have established complete compliance in all aspects.

> *'We destroy the love of learning, which is so strong when they are small, by compelling them to work for petty*

> ***rewards, gold stars, or papers marked 100 and tacked on the wall ... In short, for the ignoble satisfaction that they are better than somebody else.'***
>
> — *Alfie Kohn*

Enjoyment generated through doing schoolwork can be associated with enhanced levels of academic engagement in students.[148]. A common attribute of many successful teachers is the instinctive ability to design tasks and implement lessons which foster the experience of enjoyment. Yet, it is rare in teacher training, professional development or pedagogical initiatives to find any promotion of the beneficial effects that academic enjoyment can exert. The influence is dreadfully undervalued.

The student experience of enjoyment within the context of academic activity fosters several deeply positive outcomes. Hernik and Jaworska[149] report that students benefit by '... feeling safe, feeling valued and a necessary part ... of a learning community'. My (Fabio) research identified orientations of students towards academically valuable states and behaviours through the experience of enjoyment. These included heightened levels of engagement and perseverance, greater attentiveness towards tasks and enhanced collaborative activity. All of this is without even touching on the teacher gains to be made through their students enjoying themselves. That would fill another book.

> ***'From a child's perspective, everyday school life often takes on meaning through friends: going to school is nice when you have friends there. Friends and belonging to a group***

148 D'Agostin, "Task-Related Emotions," 2020.

149 J Hernik and E Jaworska, "The effect of enjoyment on learning," in *INTED2018 proceedings* 2018. IATED.

> ***are important to every child. A child should be able to feel like an important, full-fledged member of the classroom and school community. Belonging to a group increases comfort and safety at school and has been found to improve students' learning performance.'***
>
> — *From* Welcome to Lower Secondary School *by The Finnish Parents League*

Professor Maija Aksela of the University of Helsinki is one of the planet's foremost STEM educators. She leverages the power of student enjoyment as a central element in her approach towards teaching and learning. Her guidance contributed to Finnish science student outcomes ranking among the best in the world. One of Aksela's appealing slogans well expresses the spirit of her understanding: 'The fun of math is for everyone'.[150]

I (Fabio) was recently at a local professional seminar with about 300 other teachers. A successful business entrepreneur was asked how he managed the teams of people he led. His response should have been obvious to all: 'If people enjoy themselves at work, you get the most out of them'. I looked around the room and did not see the slightest hint of recognition from anyone that what had just been said should be a cornerstone principle of our own teaching profession.

> ***'We want our teachers to focus on learning, not testing. We do not, at all, believe in ranking students and ranking schools ... In Finland, having happy children is the most important thing, we want to bring back the joy of learning.***

---

150 See Maija Aksela, Jan Lundell & Topias Ikävalko (eds), *LUMA Finland – Together We Are More*, online book (LUMA Finland, December 2020).

When you go to schools here, you see happy, active and engaged pupils.'

— Kristiina Volmari from the Finnish National Agency for Education

Student Attendance

Attendance has not returned to pre-COVID levels in most countries. The UK has even introduced a system of fines for the parents of chronically absent students, with little real success. Some US states have made truancy a crime. To our astonishment, we hardly ever hear about changing the schools that these students are avoiding, or even making them a place where these students might actually want to be.

Some schools have started to take data on school satisfaction levels among students, and this was the catalyst for Assumption College in Victoria to introduce their vertical curriculum model. The resulting choice and autonomy it gave students saw school satisfaction move from one of the lowest in the state to one of the highest in the country. Academic improvement has also taken place.

Attendance sanctions prioritise adherence to system, structure and process above human need, connection and belonging. So often we hear that poor attendance is an issue primarily about the student. If a student was afraid to go home, we would ask what was wrong there and the police may even be called! We need to address non-attendance by striving to make schools places where all students know they belong.

Critical Thinking

Recent pushes for more direct instruction suggest that critical thinking is not highly valued in our system, though it is undoubtedly more important in today's world than at any time in history. The effective teaching of critical thinking could be problematic in schools where many practices are in place because 'that's the way we've always done them'. We know that students model and learn from their environment; what messages are we sending if this environment does not stand up for critical thinking?

The Australian Curriculum lists 'critical and creative thinking' as one of seven general capabilities. A New South Wales government education department team explored how such thinking was fostered in primary and secondary schools.[151] They reported, 'There is compelling evidence that inquiry-based pedagogies (that typically include a component of direct instruction) facilitate the cultivation of the general capabilities'. This would seem to not align well with recent trends towards a preponderance of mandated direct instruction: another example of how our desire to micromanage teachers often conflicts with research and best practice.

A tour of critical thinking definitions suggests the skill involves the dispassionate questioning and evaluation of evidence, ideas, events, assumptions, propositions and theories through processes of reasoning, reflection, self-awareness, creativity (or imagination) and logic and drawing from an adequate knowledge base. Direct instruction can offer students guidance and modelling in how critical thinking may be developed but consolidation of the ability requires extensive opportunities for deeper individual and collaborative engagement.

As Stevens and Ructtinger found, schools that offer multiple forms of pedagogy, ranging through the spectrum from teacher to student centred, may be best placed to promote the development of critical thinking skills. Interpretations of state curricula that frame content in terms of conjectures to be questioned, open-ended problems and unfamiliar contexts would also facilitate critical thinking.

---

151 Robert Stevens & Liliana Ructtinger, *Cultivating Critical and Creative Thinking*, (NSW: NSW Department of Education, 2018).

Importance of Each Subject (see also Curriculum)

You may wish to try and list subjects in order of importance, or perhaps you consider them all to be of equal importance?

Should some subjects receive more class time than others, and if so, why? Many schools and school systems have allocated equal class time to all subjects and found academic success with this model; there are advantages from a timetabling perspective as the equal time creates increased possibilities for student choice and staffing flexibility. It also allows for a form of natural streaming to occur as students select the appropriate 'level' of a subject that they feel suits their abilities and interest. There is an immense body of research supporting the arts as assisting academic and social emotional development.

Curriculum

Is the curriculum a list of things and facts to be learnt to prepare for assessment, or does it include deeper learning, application of knowledge and critical analysis of knowledge and concepts? If it is the latter, then an emphasis on direct instruction and testing should be avoided.

Stanford University is a great example of an education institution which places a strong emphasis on 'intellectual vitality' in its educational approach. Unlike the rote memorisation and standardised testing often prevalent in mass schooling, Stanford encourages a focus on depth, individual growth, and the unique contributions each student can make. This perspective aligns with the idea that true learning goes beyond mere achievement checklists. Intellectual vitality involves seeking out the unknown, forging new paths, and telling personal stories that reflect one's passions and experiences. It's not just about following a prescribed curriculum; it's about nurturing intellectual curiosity and fostering a love for learning.

There are many aspects of the curriculum that are non-negotiable as they are part of the government requirements for a school. These vary somewhat from state to state. For instance, in Victoria the minimum requirements at Year 7 are that schools must 'report on' certain subject areas and elements of those. Many of these compulsory areas can be covered in one semester, as we have seen at Victoria's Assumption College, thereby freeing up students and teachers to study and teach in areas of interest. For instance, at Assumption, a history teacher with qualifications in this field was able to offer an Archaeology subject, creating a rare option for students interested in history.

For decades, members of elite (and not-so-elite) sports teams all followed the same training regimes, hewing to the same warm-up activities, dietary requirements, fitness standards, skill sets, recovery routines and so on. In fact, catchphrases such as 'There's no I in TEAM' were commonly bandied about as subtle reminders that this idea should not be questioned. Attend an elite sports team's training session today and you will see perhaps a dozen different warm-up exercises; a different diet regime for every player; and individual fitness, skills and recovery routines for each team member based on their age, previous injuries, existing skills and so on. The modern sports coach knows that the best outcome for the team comes from optimising conditions for each individual on that team. No two players are the same, and no one would want them to be. It's their unique individual characteristics that, when combined, create the champion team.

While an Australian might argue that the classroom is not a team situation, the Finn would take a broader outlook and say students are being prepared to take their place in the outside world where they will form part of a much larger team.

Many students from less-than-ideal backgrounds will happily self-sabotage their own success rather than risk seeing more failure in their lives. They will more readily do this if we have not taken the time to ensure that their studies are in fact 'their studies' rather than a cookie-cutter curriculum in which they have no vested interest.

We are concerned by the often-heard suggestion that teacher workloads can be considerably reduced by the provision of one-size-fits-all lesson plans. Teachers are trained to prepare lessons and any interference with this undermines teacher autonomy, trust, and the profession itself. Such suggestions as prefabricated lesson plans may be well-meaning but they are not in the best interests of teachers or students.

Ironically, many of the short-term solutions to the 'teacher shortage' are in fact contributors to the very problem they seek to redress. There is a fine line between helping and micromanaging.

The question remains: will we prioritise each student's unique potential, or succumb to the allure of a one-size-fits-all education system driven by market forces?

Additionally, implementing an expert-level curriculum requires expert level knowledge. Not only do we need expertise in the content area, but expertise in teaching, and expertise in the audience for the instruction. The standards movement skips past all three, assuming that if one sets certain standards, the content takes care of itself, the specific audience doesn't matter, and the actual teaching is where you blame educators for faulty implementation. The curriculum/materials industry (sometimes referred to as 'knowledge brokers', treating content as equivalent to stocks and shares) has limited expertise in the first two and assumes that its actual audience is the people who make purchasing decisions in schools, not the people in the classroom who have to deal with it.[152]

152 Peter Greene, *Curmudgecation.*

Inclusion

Inclusion is a new frontier for Australian education, and it presents schools with an enormous future challenge. An NDS factsheet[153] provides the following statement on inclusion:

> *Inclusive education recognises the right of every child and young person – without exception – to be included in general education settings. It involves adapting the environment and teaching approaches to ensure genuine and valued full participation of all children and young people. It embraces human diversity and welcomes all as equal members of an educational community.*

Nobody can dispute that the provision of equal educational opportunities for all children regardless of their personal challenges is a noble principle. The concern is how this vision can be brought about within an Australian school education system that already struggles with some of the most inequitable outcomes in the world.[154] We cannot even deal with postcodes being the best determinant of student outcomes. How can we possibly meet the added challenge of offering a fair education to students who present with greater disadvantages than we currently fail to accommodate?

The PISA outcomes for Finnish education, one of the world's stronger systems, have fallen in recent years. Finnish educators have identified the challenges of implementing inclusive policies as one of several major influences in the decline. This does not augur well for us. For inclusion to work, it seems clear that Australian educators will need to reconsider a lot about what we presently accept as routine.

---

153 Australian Coalition for Inclusive Education, *Driving change: A roadmap for achieving inclusive education in Australia* (Australia: CYDA, 2020).

154 See Larissa Mavros, "Tonight: leaders to explain the Gonski 2.0 education revolution," *UNSW Sydney Newsroom*, 24 May 2018.

This will include definitions of academic success, pedagogies and curriculums, average class sizes, disciplinary policies, student wellbeing approaches, physical classroom environments and ability grouping. This is not an exhaustive list.

To give inclusion policies the best chance of working in Australia, we need to extend the principle to the teaching workforce. Inclusion has been heralded by various government and private agencies but – as is so common in Australian education – the voice of teachers is so far absent. The goodwill, upskilling and vocational drive of teachers are crucial elements if inclusion is to become a successful reality in our schools. Teachers must be a major part of the consultancy and decision making that will need to occur.

In mid-2024, the Australian Government did not adopt the NDS policy of integrating all students into mainstream schools. However, pressure for this process to ultimately occur continues to build.

Student Independence

> *'When you want to teach children to think, you begin by treating them seriously when they are little, giving them responsibilities, talking to them candidly, providing privacy and solitude for them, and making them readers and thinkers of significant thoughts from the beginning. That's if you want to teach them to think.'*
>
> — *Bertrand Russell*

Imagine that your boss at work controlled you the way a teacher controls children at school. You are reprimanded even if you are a minute late. You are not allowed to leave your seat while at work except at specified breaks. You are not allowed to compare notes with, or even talk to, your co-workers except at specified times when you are given permission. To go to the bathroom, you must ask permission. You are told minute by minute what you must do and how, and everything you do is judged and ranked in comparison to the work of your co-workers. And suppose your employer also required you to do more work at home, every day, and encouraged your loving spouse (or friend) to be sure you do that work. And you are told exactly what to wear, and how to do your hair and personal grooming, every day.[155]

The modern sports coach is aware that the players must be 'on side' with the coach: the old style of loud, brash delivery bordering on verbal abuse common in the seventies and eighties has been replaced by emphasis on understanding the players, empathising with them and working with them to build a trust-based relationship.

Michael Poulton, who specialises in sports coach development having previously worked for the AFL and several of its clubs, has watched the shift occur. 'We've matured as an industry. The notion of, "Do as I say and don't ever question it" and "Don't think, just do" is not contemporary thinking,' Poulton said. 'People aren't striving to be their best when they're just being told, "This is the way to do it, everyone does it that way so shut up and keep going".'

Montessori educator Blimie Heller summed up the essence of student independence:

> ***'The less autonomy a child is given, the more they will try to assert control over every tiny little thing, in an attempt to get it back. And the reverse is also true. The more***

155 Peter Gray, "Letter #41."

autonomy a child is granted, the less they feel the need to assert control over every detail."[156]

Creativity

Creativity, frequently lost in all the business of a school chasing 'real' academic results – such as those generated by NAPLAN – is a key requirement in the world of the twenty-first century. The fact that it is hard to measure and ignored by most standardised tests should not be a reason to avoid it. I (Michael) once heard a CEO for a major company state that when sorting through resumes in employment applications, he first selected the players of musical instruments as this was evidence of creative, disciplined and persistent people. Teaching is a creative profession, but it is not so when we standardise it.

The role of creativity is more visible in the arts but less recognised in many aspects of valuable learning. It is an important element of both critical thinking and problem solving, allowing students to generate useful strategies, approaches and perspectives.[157] Creativity can be modelled by teachers, but it is a difficult attribute to develop more explicitly. Setting tasks and challenges that leave students with no choice but to be inventive in their negotiation may be effective in stimulating creative thinking. Activities that encourage risk-taking and playful exploration are also associated with growth in creativity.

Hennessey and Amibile[158] provide a neat summary of some circumstances that inhibit the development of creativity in

---

156 Blimie Heller, 'The less autonomy a child is given, the more they will try to assert control over every tiny little thing, in an attempt to get it back. And the reverse is also true. The more autonomy a child is granted, the less they feel the need to assert control over every detail,' Facebook, November 2021.

157 See "Critical and Creative Thinking (Version 8.4)," Australian Curriculum, Assessment and Reporting Authority, accessed August 12, 2024.

158 Beth Hennessey & Teresa Amabile, *Creativity and Learning: What Research Says to the Teacher* (Washington DC: National Education Association of the United States, 1987).

students. These include setting up competitive situations, focusing on expected assessment, having students work towards extrinsic rewards and setting tasks with single response success criteria. Such items are fairly commonplace in Australian schools, suggesting that we have plenty of space in which to enhance our fostering of creativity.

Learning Management System (LMS)

All schools, both primary and secondary, now work with computer programs known as Learning Management Systems (LMSs) which we refer to as the 'altar of standardisation'. These systems are an online repository where the entire standardised curriculum can be uploaded with lessons, resources, rubrics and assignment tasks stored and shared easily. These programs are costly, and it is made clear to teachers – who in most cases get no say in selecting these – that they are expected to use them.

Many LMS platforms are custom-made for the distribution, collection and grading of assignments. They can be an ideal platform for the bulk delivery of highly scripted lessons, supporting the trend towards learning being made to fit the system rather than being tailored by teachers to suit the needs of individual students and classes. Left unsaid in all this is that the work is, of course, identical for every student. So are the evaluation standards, making it difficult to assure a failing but trying student that there is any worth to their efforts. The rubric is the same for all – too often a cut and dried instrument of standardisation, with its blunt insensitivity to individual achievement.

The LMS has become the conveyor belt of this education system. The material submitted by students cannot be handwritten (authenticity checking is one reason for this condition), despite research in this area telling us that handwriting significantly increases memory and understanding[159].

If increased understanding isn't a core objective of any education system, what's the point of learning at all?

The conveyor belt was critical to the success of the assembly line during the Industrial Revolution. It was important that every participant did exactly the same thing in exactly the same way, to exactly the same standard. But that was more than a century ago, and was for manufacturing, not learning.

An LMS can also make the curriculum visible to parents, the implication being that they can expect their child to be learning the particular set curriculum specified for that particular date. This would serve to constrain a teacher's scope to interpret and implement content in ways and according to schedules that they know will best serve their students. So, in a perverse way, parents are conscripted into supporting a system for which there is no evidence that it improves the educational experience.

And what becomes of the teacher? Much autonomy, creativity and professional judgment has been replaced by a computerised system of curriculum dispersal, retrieval and assessment that treats every student (and teacher) with inflexible uniformity. This is not to say LMSs should be banned. The Finns use them as much as we do, but they fit their systems to support rather than set their educational approaches.

As Professor Allen Reid, Professor Emeritus of Education at the University of South Australia, points out, the LMSs have 'been a financial bonanza' for private technology companies such as Summit [Learning], owned by Facebook founder Mark Zuckerberg. These companies have developed online tests and learning resources capable of tracking the progress of, and devising programs for, individual students.

---

159 S Bouriga & T Olive, "Is typewriting more resources-demanding than handwriting in undergraduate students?" *Read Writ* 34, 2227–2255 (2021).

With such programs, students become automatons moving through standardised progression levels. Creativity and critical thinking are stifled as students are steered down a predetermined path. And teachers are increasingly excluded from the process, as planning and decision making are done by algorithms.

The version of personalised learning Australia promotes should be one that nurtures a love and passion for learning, not one that reduces it to a checklist.

Break Times

Finnish schools take a break approximately every forty-five minutes. The neuroscience is clear that students will learn more in a ninety-minute session with a fifteen-minute break in the middle than in the same session with no break. It is particularly powerful if, after the break, you can revisit the skills being taught in the session before the break.

I (Michael) have used this technique with Year 8 students doing double periods of English (in the middle of a 100-minute class) and the improvements in outcomes such as concentration, positive classroom energy and the amount of material covered are noticeable compared to the same 100 minutes of tuition without the break.

This goes against our idea that more is always more, but it is easily tested. Finnish educators take it for granted that all teachers do this and were shocked when I told them that it is not done in Australia.

We ran the Teacher Trust program (the precursor to Creating Schools Where Teachers and Students Want To Be) with several schools around Orange in New South Wales, which tested implementing these breaks. The schools that made this timetable change reported immediate success with both students and teachers reporting improvements in all areas. One school told me that some pushback they had from a small group of parents was withdrawn within a month when they noticed the difference in their children.

When I used the fifteen-minute break – unofficially – in my own teaching, an unexpected improvement came from the students understanding that they had a break coming up very soon and they would be able to chat with friends, run around and burn off excess energy, and have a bathroom break: this removed all of these potential interruptions from the learning part of the session.

The respect for a teacher who recognises that students are not machines is also obvious, and it can be the beginning of the disappearance of the 'us vs them' mentality that the military style of so much of the standardised GERM system encourages. It is another step in recognising the 'more is not necessarily more' principle in relation to face to face teaching.[160] A September 2024 presentation by Pasi Sahlberg showed that by the end of primary school, Australian children had spent more classroom hours than students in many other countries had spent in their entire Years K-12 schooling. Our academic outcomes are certainly not proportional to face-to-face time being taught.

Retain and Attract Great Teachers

Studies and personal experiences have shown that, if we place an emphasis on teacher autonomy, trust and professional development, we will create higher levels of job satisfaction, increase the likelihood of teachers remaining in the profession for the long term, and improve the chances of attracting good teachers to this school environment.

A Year 12 graduate with a healthy final year score will be able to choose (if she hasn't been headhunted already) professions offering autonomy, innovation and creativity, flexible working

---

160 T. D. Walker, *Teach Like Finland* (New York & London: W.W.Norton & Company, 2017).

hours and wages that a teacher can never achieve. We are unlikely to ever be able to match some of these, but professional autonomy, trust and respect are all available with minimal dents to the budget.

But are we prepared to stop trying to control all that teachers do? Standardised curriculum and teaching to the test ensure micromanaging of teachers. If we have to allow students to sit compulsory standardised tests then it will be done, but what does it say about trust and respect for the profession when more than 70% of teachers have said that they are not happy about it and we continue to ignore this?

Education unions are calling for cuts to teacher's administration and compliance work, more time for lesson planning, extra system-wide support for higher needs students, a focus on wellbeing for teachers and principals, more support personnel in class, access to specialist staff and consultation with teachers regarding proposed policies and reforms.[161]

School Traditions

Practices, customs, events and cultures that are sustained over time contribute to any set of school traditions. Traditions can be incorporated in formal policies and protocols or can find expression in behaviours, beliefs and attitudes that are independent of school administrations.[162] School identity is largely formulated through its associated traditions.

The older a tradition, the more precious it tends to be considered. Although school traditions are often viewed as fixed, not needing to be changed or not changeable, they should always be monitored in relation to educational benefit. While enduring traditions are often a significant factor in any school's appeal, some types of tradition

---

161 The Australian Education Union, "Summer 2023," *The Australian Educator Magazine* Issue 120, 2023.

162 John Spacey, "94 Examples of School Traditions," *Simplicable*, April 14, 2024.

can be problematic. In particular, pedagogical traditions that do not serve contemporary educational needs well should be identified.

Teaching traditions that have surpassed their 'use by' dates can stifle the development of creative and effective educational practices. These include the indiscriminate use of technology (such as the 'we are a laptop school' mass rollout of computers in the early 2000s), rigid assessment policies, stale curriculum content, insensitive student management, blunt ability grouping processes and unfair teacher class allocation practices. No sentiment should be lost on retaining pedagogical traditions that function against the learning interests of students.

THE NEXT STEPS: TRUST, HOPE, AND COMPETENCE

Keeping conversations as open as possible is essential: research into change management has found that something close to 80% of staff need to be 'onboard' in order for the changes to be given the greatest chance of succeeding on their own merits. Those involved will either have ownership of the change and feel some responsibility to ensure the greatest chance of success, or they will feel that it is something being imposed on them and while they may not oppose it, they will not be adding to any efforts to ensure success and may in fact discreetly sabotage it.

It is not enough to simply tell teachers, 'This is what we are going to do'. This will ensure failure, regardless of the merits of any change being implemented.

Most schools and teachers do not discuss the goals and reasoning behind their operation. Just doing so will make an enormous difference to all aspects of your school's operations.

We took great inspiration from the Finnish educators' professional oath. It ensures that the students' interests come before anything else, similar to the oath sworn in professions such as medicine. It doesn't mean that the school cannot have religious or other affiliations, but it does mean that the educators are obliged to put the interest of the child ahead of others. If this is problematic for a school, then they have bigger issues to work on.

There is also a tendency to apply rigorous standards to any change, often placing the bar higher than would be the case if the status quo were being maintained.

It is worth deciding what success will look like, and the priorities list earlier in this chapter will inform this.

- Is it just academic results?
- Standardised test results?
- Student satisfaction data? (Is it reasonable to have any of the above without this?)
- Teacher satisfaction data? (Even if the above goals are achieved, without this a school will not last long as staff turnover takes its toll)
- Student/teacher retention data?
- Pathway success (have students successfully moved on to university, work or other targeted pathways when they leave school?)

How long will it take? Improvement in general satisfaction will be obvious as quickly as in a few weeks' time. Given that we have had the current program (the GERM) in place for some two decades and we've continued despite no obvious improvement, we should not feel any great pressure to achieve dramatic gains in a short time. This would be unfair to all involved.

We don't mean to omit parents from this discussion, however it is a rarity for parents to be unhappy if a number of the above criteria are present. In our experience (and we are both parents as well as experienced teachers), all parents really want is for their children to be enjoying learning and developing at school. It is important for parents to have an understanding of how we are building independence and trust in students.

Working on priorities with the above list will help to clarify future directions and the timing of these. Once the list is 'ordered' the next discussion should look at the relationship between the priorities, as they are all intertwined, and it can be difficult to work on one or two without looking at others at the same time.

For instance, student wellbeing cannot be a priority without also prioritising student counsellors. And student attendance cannot be a priority if wellbeing and counsellors are not.

Any decision should be preceded with the question: Is this good for students and teachers? If the answer to this question is not an immediate 'yes', then we should not go ahead with the practice.

Step One:

One of the simplest changes to implement as a starting point is the fifteen or twenty-minute break after every forty-five-minute session. It is an excellent starting point as it immediately sends the message that we are invested in improving the student experience of school. It is also a good introduction to letting go of the 'more is more' idea of instruction time, replacing it with an emphasis on quality time.

What does this look like? One school in Orange, NSW gave each break a name – so the first break, at 9:45 in the morning might be called *Early Morning Break*, *Rooster Time* (more appropriate for younger children) or just *Break One*. The students exit the room and go to the playground. Teachers are assigned with yard duty, or those teachers may work together to decide how best to supervise that particular area. This will vary with each school.

The Finns are always trying to build student responsibility, and do so by *giving* students responsibility. Students are in the playground even when there is a snowstorm and it's twenty below zero. They know that the students have walked to school (without parent accompaniment) in these conditions, so why would they not allow them to play in the same conditions?

Teachers will notice an improvement in student engagement and the general quality of class time immediately, in recognition of the fact that we are now acknowledging the students' needs for a break for social time/exercise/drink/bathroom.

Indeed, these breaks are closer to what we would have in an adult workplace situation, where listening to someone speak for 100–120 minutes while sitting in one place would be rare. Surely it is ludicrous to expect this repeatedly, nearly every day, from children and teenagers?

Try to avoid using this time to detain a student or catch them up on some extra tuition as this is contrary to the purpose of the break. We love the fact that the break has a positive impact on all areas of school from engagement, to wellbeing, to academic performance – all by actually taking some time to do nothing. The message we are giving is that wellbeing is more important than everything else, with the understanding that everything else will be better for us taking the time to ensure our wellbeing.

There is a wealth of neuroscience and evidence to support this practice, and you will notice a difference immediately.

> ***'You need to understand that humans form attachments to ideas, people and other things. When the attachments are threatened, we tend to lash out in ways that don't reflect our best selves. That's why whenever we set out to make an impact there will always be those who will hate what we're trying to achieve, not for any rational logic necessarily, just because for whatever reason, it offends their dignity, their identity, their sense of self. It's not your job to convince people of things that they don't want to be convinced about... As you gain traction, your most irrational opponents will lash out, overreach and help your cause.'***
>
> *— Greg Satell, Change Expert*

Step Two:

Encourage independence in students and teachers. Encourage parents to allow their children to walk to school unaccompanied. If distance makes this impossible, ask that they drop the student a block or more from school rather than at the gate. The goal is to develop a sense of independence; a sense that they are trusted to be responsible for themselves.

Other possible changes in future could include allowing senior students (or all!) to dress themselves rather than wearing a uniform (Australian schools have formed an obsessive attachment to uniforms, but we must ask ourselves about the military 'uniformness' of it and why we do not trust our students to dress themselves), and allowing secondary students to leave the school grounds during 'spare' periods (we have seen schools where senior students are trusted to go for a coffee when they do not have a scheduled class).

Senior students will have complete freedom to move, attend whatever classes they wish and organise their own schedule when they attend university in the near future, so controlling their movements in the latter years of secondary school does nothing to prepare them for this.

This second point is particularly important in the building of a sense of trust and responsibility in students. Senior students can be just months from university, where they are completely responsible for all areas of their studies. Outside of school they have access to cars, alcohol, (and so much more) and may have children and/or marry. This is how to prepare them for the 'real' world, rather than removing all their autonomy and responsibility.

Be sure to treat teachers like the professionals they are and omit any micromanaging, such as hour counting. Setting times when teachers can come and go only leads to clock watching and mistrust.

Make wellbeing a priority by creating an environment which

does not lead to wellbeing issues. There's research making it clear (see earlier in this book) that immense amounts of money spent on wellbeing programs are of no impact if the conditions which brought about the welfare problems are not changed.

The first step to changing the system is to stop complying with it.

Step Three:

Removing all standardised curriculum is a logical next step. Like the break, it has broad implications across our entire list, emphasising the individual interests of the student and the skills (and trust) of the teacher. A strong message is sent that these values are more important than ranking or comparing students to each other or the rest of the country. This also conveys the message that the student (and the teacher!) is more important than the content: something most schools agree to in principle but do not follow in practice. There will always be mandatory curriculum which must be reported on (and this varies from state to state), but aside from this, schools and teachers have a relatively free hand to create courses and interpret content.

This will also remove the need for lessons to be placed on the LMS as teachers are being trusted to shape and design content most suitable to the needs of their students – this will differ from class to class, and sometimes from student to student. Obviously, the teacher will now be designing assessment materials for their classes. This increase in autonomy (it is not necessarily less work, though teachers are encouraged to collaborate) creates ownership of the content and increased work satisfaction for teachers, particularly if it doesn't come with pressure to achieve grades. In fact, all we have done is return to the non-standardised situation schools were in twenty years ago before the GERM was implemented.

The only standardised test will be the NAPLAN (if it is still being done), and it will be completed in the spirit that it was intended: a snapshot of some things. If the school has decided that the broader education and development of the individual is the goal, NAPLAN scores may improve, but they are not a representation of all that your students have learnt.

For some great lesson ideas encouraging creativity and intrinsic motivation, see the '*appendices*' section of this book.

Other curriculum possibilities include creating a vertical curriculum (this applies more to a secondary school setting) where students may select and share classes with peers from up to three other year levels. The autonomy, independence and sense of responsibility generated through such a structure is something special to see. Some schools, such as Assumption College in Kilmore, have shown how vertical classroom compositions can be successfully established.

Step Four:

Create a love of school and learning by encouraging student input in the creation of assessments and curriculum materials. At the start of the school year, begin with a positive experience (rather than ending the year with an excursion or celebration as many do) and start the teaching phase when you are sure that students are enjoying school. At all times keep in mind that, whenever we push a child away from school or learning, we are shaping their attitudes to these for the rest of their lives. There is no point in obtaining good grades in any area if the student no longer enjoys that subject. No matter how good you are at something, that skill is of no use if you don't enjoy doing it and avoid it.

We are now well on the way to creating a school where students and teachers will be thriving in an environment they are constantly creating and building. Allow variation in assessment methods from class to class. This refers to more than just different assignments or tests, but in the use of measurement modes. Rather than a percentage grade, some teachers may wish to use numbered systems, perhaps from one to six, with a few words to describe each. The rubric can be very restricting as it creates a recipe for a preconceived outcome, encouraging standardised assignments and standardised work from the students. If the task is individualised, a discussion between the student/s and teacher could centre on what the completed work might look like, and a few notes taken on this, rather than issuing a standardised rubric.

> ***'When students cheat on exams it's because our system values grades more than students value learning.'***
>
> *— Neil deGrasse Tyson*

Once the need to rank and compare is removed, possibilities for innovation appear, and students having a say in creating and shaping their tasks is what creates the intrinsic motivation, as it becomes *their* thing rather than something the teacher requires them to do. Every student has areas in which they have a passion and specialist knowledge, and the more we tap into these the greater the chance of bridging the gap between their world and that of school and learning. This is where the gold can be found: intrinsic motivation and responsibility for their own learning.

Any visualisation of an excellent school should not overlook the characteristics of our elite institutions. Throughout Australia, we have many examples of fine school education and we owe it to all Australian children, not just a small minority, to aspire for the same high quality and opportunities. The universal provisioning of magnificent playing fields, sports complexes, concert halls, libraries, arts facilities and learning spaces is an obvious challenge. But the ideal should never be abandoned.

In a shorter term, there are other, more accessible measures that can enrich and add appeal to the school experiences of our students. Teachers play a highly significant role in the lives of students who enjoy school and are successful. This should be a self-evident foundation principle for any place wanting to become a great school. A standing question for administrations should always be, 'how do we foster the circumstances that allow our teachers to be the brokers of student happiness and success in our school?'.

> *'When you want to teach children to think, you begin by treating them seriously when they are little, giving them responsibilities, talking to them candidly, providing privacy and solitude for them, and making them readers and thinkers of significant thoughts from the beginning. That's if you want to teach them to think.'*
>
> — *Bertrand Russell, from* Philosophical Totems of Bertrand Russell.

Step Five:

Our final suggested step is a restructuring of rules and discipline through increased student ownership, responsibility and control of their own learning. If we have created a sense of ownership for school and learning in general, issues with 'behaviour' will be reduced to a minimum as students are reluctant to rebel against something they have had a hand in creating and have a shared ownership of. In the '*Flipped Learning*' chapter – may we suggest you have a close read of this – a classroom teacher said that one of their disciplinary rules was that they allowed students the freedom to move around the room and the adjoining corridor, but restricted this for any student who did not respect the rights of others.

We love the idea of one classroom rule: if what you are doing interferes with learning, hurts someone, or prevents you (or others) from being your best self, you shouldn't be doing it!

Think carefully about any 'sanctions' or punishments. If we have created intrinsic motivation in the class, then there will be peer pressure to allow the group to continue with the activity, which may be sufficient. If we are creating a love of learning and school, we must consider the impact of any sanctions on this. Why is this student not motivated to participate in a positive way in this activity? If they do not have any ownership of it, did they have an opportunity to participate in its creation?

Unlike a direct instruction situation where the students are expected to predominantly show respect and deference to the teacher, other pedagogies require that students are able to respect each other and work together in teams. This models the expectations of most modern workplace scenarios and these skills can be included on any assessments (and are particularly powerful when implemented as self-reflective assessments).

We need to avoid an 'us vs them' situation with teachers and students. We are all on the learning journey together, and maintaining enthusiasm for this journey should always outweigh the desire to gain grades or standardised test results. If a particular activity requires a different way of operating to the usual, such as an excursion or a particular project, a class discussion could clarify what everyone (not just the teacher!) requires.

Many students react negatively to the controlling, compliance-based approaches of traditional schooling. However, if they actively participate in determining the modus operandi, the likelihood of this negative reaction diminishes. We were impressed by Finnish schools that explicitly communicated to students that their educational experiences were the top priority. A student could not respond by pointing to the uniform, or other regulations unrelated to learning, as there were none of these.

> *'To truly transform the educational experience, school leaders must actively involve students in the decision-making process ...This not only fosters a sense of ownership and engagement but also ensures that decisions are made with a deep understanding of student needs and aspirations.'*
>
> — *Dr Mary Hemphill, from* What Makes a great Principal: The Five Pillars of Effective School Leadership

The issue of intrinsic motivation lies at the heart of many poorly behaved students. There are many causes of misbehaviour, including external situations and influences that no school can hope to control. Motivation, however, is a student attribute that teachers can foster. An important element of motivation is meaningfulness, a student is more likely to behave in ways that support academic development if they know why their effort matters.

Creating an unforced willingness in students to negotiate classroom tasks and behave appropriately can be a teacher's greatest challenge. Compliance backed by sanction regimes is always a poor substitute for compliance driven by intrinsic motivation. Overhanging threats of punishment or more commonly termed 'consequences' may be necessary in the absence of other strategies, but they can never replace intrinsic motivation. Teachers should always pursue approaches that reach towards what a student may find meaningful to them.

For students who have long been disaffected with academic experiences, the pursuit of meaningfulness can be difficult. A strategy that may find traction is to share with students the teacher's own motivation for teaching a topic and deliberations for selecting teaching methods that could work. Educators are all aware of state and national curriculums from which our lesson-by-lesson content is drawn. But do students know this? If they could be informed of the broader value attached to their proposed learning, a form of relevance may be fostered.

The ACARA Australian Curriculum site offers an excellent source of content elaboration for F-10 and senior studies in all academic areas. Relevant content lines and phrases could be presented to students and put to them as a collaborative challenge. This is a little like the HITS 'learning intentions', but without the blunt, intractable 'non-negotiable' tone. Students could be offered a certain level of buy-in, an opportunity to stir the beginnings of intrinsic motivation. How can this material be best taught, learnt and appraised? What do we need to do?

Actual work samples, drawn from students at different levels of proficiency at all year levels and in each subject topic, are perhaps the most valuable items on the ACARA site. The real work products could be shown to a class and used as motivational challenges. What did it take for these other students to reach such a stage of learning? Why did they think it was important? What will it take for us to do likewise? Such a shared, transparent and responsive approach could support a common sense of learning ownership between teachers and students.

Even students most hardened in their disregard for academic study can be reached when presented with unending opportunities to make their schooling about them rather than done to them. We know of schools, such as Croydon Community School, where similar practices flourish, along with their appreciative students. The principle of inviting students to exert greater control over their learning should not be restricted to the margins: it is relevant anywhere. We are dealing with emerging adults, whether they are ten years from adulthood or less than five years from that status. To give students a glimpse of adult decision making, responsibility and self-determination is nothing less than what they are owed.

We have worked extensively with students who struggle to see the relevance in schooling. These are the students for whom rules and disciplinary procedures are primarily written. I (Fabio) once had a junior high school mathematics class who were streamed for their modest performance histories in the subject – they found mathematics hard and did not enjoy it. At the start of a challenging topic – Index Laws – I discussed with the class different ways that the content may be taught and invited them to join in an experiment.

I proposed that the topic be taught in a traditional direct instructional manner and then again in a more progressive style, incorporating manipulatives and collaborative activities. The aim was to investigate which approach was more successful with this class. Students were free to adopt the proposal or reject it and they had a say in proceedings: this was the key point of the exercise. The realisation that they could determine an important aspect of their learning was transformative for these students. They decided to participate.

They now had buy-in, a motivation to try. The class had agreed with their teacher that learning the topic was going to generate interesting outcomes. It became intrinsically worth studying. Students found meaning and applied themselves like anyone who believes in their work does. For the record, most students performed best when the learning was not explicitly driven but textured, with a series of self-directed guiding activities, prompts and summarising sessions.

The initiative was also based on neuroscientific learning principles that had been advertised to the whole year level. The students saw themselves as genuine candidates for an enhanced teaching and learning trial. The teacher's learning intentions had become the students' learning desires, invigorating the teaching process. When students were powered by their own intrinsic motivation, their attitude, behaviours and ultimately academic outcomes improved seamlessly.

The idea of student voice as a means of enhancing learning and minimising poor behaviour has research support. Leading education researcher and author Robert Marzano advocates that the considered offering to students of real choices related to academic activities can reap valuable rewards. He writes:

> ***Research has shown that providing choices to students of all age levels often increases their intrinsic motivation. Choice in the classroom has also been linked to increases in student effort, task performance, and subsequent learning. However, to reap these benefits, a teacher should create choices that are robust enough for students to feel that their decision has an impact on their learning.*** [163]

Marzano's advocacy is entirely based on classroom approaches and actions centred on improving academic engagement. Such a focus is the ultimate key to dealing with student misbehaviours and ill-discipline, so rampant currently in Australian schools. Sanctions regimes, proposed good behaviour courses and other band aid measures to gain student attention, respect and composure may enforce a degree of compliance. Genuine affiliation and engagement can only arise from the employment of quality pedagogies.

---

163 "Tips from Dr Marzano," Marzano Resources, (updated 2024).

LOOKING FOR A SCHOOL?

FOR TEACHERS

Teachers and parents can, and should, have a huge influence on the future of education, particularly in the current Australian system which often sees itself as part of a commercially competitive 'business' market. While leaders in these institutions might be content to maintain the status quo as regards practice – the system is working as a business model, with enrolments and government funding both healthy (particularly for private schools) – there are 'market forces' that they have to acknowledge.

Currently, with the 'shortage' of teachers, it is undoubtedly an employee's market. We have heard, and applaud the idea, of teachers actually doing CRT work in schools in a particular area in order to get a feel for the cultures of particular schools before deciding which ones to approach for more permanent work.

Join LinkedIn. It's a great way to communicate with the broader teaching/education community to gain an insight into current trends and thinking. It's also a great way to find out about educational and neuroscience research, particularly as we have seen attempts made to restrict Australian teacher's access to a wide range of research outside of the mandated practices.

We suggest that a teacher looking to work at a particular school (this applies for any school, not just a school following the ideas suggested in these pages) should be looking out for the very practices (these are the red flags) which are causing teachers to leave the profession in such great numbers. Whether at the interview or at the research level (asking a teacher or former teacher at this school), consider the following questions: they will reveal a lot about the culture you are potentially going to enter.

- Does the school use a standardised curriculum or scripted lessons? This is always a sign of micromanaging of teachers and little professional autonomy for them, both of which are key reasons for the teacher exodus we are seeing at the present time. Also, does the school specify hours that teachers have to stay at school? The very definition of a profession is that it is not a pay-by-the-hour role.
- Are there examples of innovative practices at the school? If the school has none of this it may be a 'closed shop' for ideas, working with archaic practices to create cookie-cutter students with teachers micromanaged in all aspects of their work.
- Is there a history of large staff turnover? This is a huge red flag. Unless there have been major changes recently, you can be sure that this will continue. We have heard horrifying stories of administrators who have dismissed concerns about staff turnover with the comment, 'We can replace them...'.
- Ask both the school administration and the union representative about the school's attitude to the teacher union. If it is dismissive or negative, this is indicative of a lack of concern for conditions and general morale in a school. The best principal we ever worked with attended union meetings and voted to strike with the statement,

'Anything which improves the working conditions of my staff is a good thing.'[164]

- Does the school judge its progress on standardised test results such as NAPLAN, or does it believe that its students are more than something able to be gauged by a standardised test? You may find your work judged solely on similar shallow criteria, with deeper learning, relationships, mental health and other aspects disregarded.
- How does the school deal with planning time lost due to school excursions, and other interruptions?
- How are decisions made at the school? Is there transparency and teacher voice in this decision making?
- Is there genuine consultation and a concern that support exists for the directions taken, or are decisions made at an administration level before staff are told (this may even be called 'consultation' although the decision has already been made) and basically expected to follow as directed?
- How often are there meetings and are they just for the dissemination of information or do staff have a say in decision making? We have heard of schools with 'meeting expectations' prohibiting questions which are not supportive of the agenda! We suggest that if practices do not stand up to a few questions then they really are questionable.
- Ask existing staff about the staff morale. Is there an 'us vs them' culture between staff and administration? Is there a consultative committee? Is it taken seriously and are the meeting minutes displayed for all to see?
- Is the school combining subjects to get around the shortage of teachers in particular areas? If you are an English teacher, you may find yourself obliged to 'teach' (we use the inverted commas here as

164 Brother Tony Smith, Chanel College, late 1980s.

it is likely to be little more than reading from a prepared PowerPoint script) subjects such as Religion and Humanities as the school has decided to timetable them as one. This will also severely restrict your autonomy as an English teacher, as invariably you will have to follow the same script as others. Similarly, the head of department for English and Humanities will often find their department's interests are often in conflict with those of the Religious Education faculty, particularly in a religiously affiliated school.

- Is there a merit and equity system in place for employment and promotions? If your background is in a government school (where it has been standard for decades) you may be surprised to find that this is rare in non-government schools. If decision making in this area is being done fairly (with 'merit and equity') why would a school not want to participate in such a program?
- How is professional development decided? Who decides exactly who attends a particular program? Does the program have to align directly with the school's current program or is there an openness to learning about other practices? I (Michael) recently spoke at a school which was holding a PD Day titled 'World Educational Trends'. The message to staff was that there is a world of educational thinking out there and we must always be looking to improve our thinking and practice. Unfortunately, many schools try to shut down any professional pedagogical thinking outside of the mandated practice currently in use at that school.
- Does the school track staff members' PD history and encourage them to regularly attend? Or are they happy to have staff training fall behind? One of the authors of this book spent nearly twenty years at a particular school where, after being turned down for a number of PDs, ceased applying for and attending external PD through the school for two decades. This was never considered an issue by the school, much to our concern. Unfortunately, many Australian schools have ceased to view themselves as active in evaluating and innovating practice and just follow the pack.

FOR PARENTS

As a parent considering a school for your child, it can be a daunting field to negotiate with underfunded government schools and non-government schools whose enrolments have benefited from public school neglect. Often this increased enrolment scenario is taken by the school as affirming of the practices of the school and a justification for the continuance of decades of antiquated ideas. Do you go with the under-funded government school (which is changing as we speak) or risk the conservative-leaning private system where little has changed since you attended school, and they like it that way? Often a private school experiences increased enrolments due to the lack of appropriate funding for nearby governments schools, creating a false sense that the former's practices are the reason behind the increase. If a school is experiencing a high demand, it's well worth investigating the general growth in nearby residential areas and the other schools servicing these areas.

During a tour of the school, consider asking the following questions to gain a clearer picture:

- Does the school use a standardised curriculum? We have yet to meet a parent who says they have a 'standard' child. Standardised curriculum means that all children in a particular grade level are taught the same thing at the same time, completely ignoring individual strengths and differences – and micromanaging teachers and students. We are amazed at the number of schools which claim to be 'child centred' while at the same time using a standardised curriculum. Invariably, a school with a standardised curriculum will require teachers to teach to the test, dismissing any students with interests or knowledge outside of that test. And invariably a student's worth will be judged on their results on these tests. Every student wants to be acknowledged as an individual.
- Does the school use 'scripted' lessons? Scripted lessons are

literally the assembly line version of education. They remove any opportunity for individual interest and open the door to the school using less qualified teaching staff (they may not be qualified to teach math, or in the near future may not be university qualified teachers). Scripted lessons also ensure that students receive nothing but direct instruction all day, meaning a focus on surface-level learning and a lack of any attempt to create intrinsic motivation or enjoyment of learning. A school cannot be claiming that they are focused on the individual student – or student wellbeing, critical thinking, developing intrinsic motivation or deeper learning – while using scripted lessons.

- Does the school have specialist subjects such as Music and Drama, subjects which are often sacrificed by primary schools as they are not present in NAPLAN tests? Obviously, if a school has less than 100 students, specialist teachers might not be an option, and the advantages of such a small school might outweigh the absence of these specialists. There's a large body of research showing the benefits of Arts subjects, but much of it has fallen on deaf ears, often the ears of the same people who claim their practice is 'evidence-based'. The absence of these subjects indicates a school where NAPLAN results take precedence above the wellbeing and real learning of students.
- Does the school have counsellors and careers counsellors, and what are the ratios of these to students? A lack of these (one careers counsellor can do very little for a thousand students!) is sometimes indicative of a lack of concern about student behavioural motivation and motivations for their studies. We saw schools in Finland where an unmotivated student was viewed as a student with other things going on in the background of their lives, rather than labelling the student as a troublemaker. A student with a clear vision of what their future career or study path might entail is a lot more likely to be motivated than one with little idea as to why they are at school.

- Ask about the school's priorities. If the students appear to be very 'well-behaved' and polite, is this due to a heavy-handed discipline regime (dictatorships have excellently behaved citizens) or is it due to content students who believe they are listened to and cared for? Are there any examples of individuality among the students at the school - for instance different hairstyles - or is there a military standard? The last thing you want is for your child to be in a school that cares more about uniform than wellbeing.
- Have a browse through the list of priorities in the previous chapter and look for a school which aligns with the priorities of you and your child. In Australia we often hear about school choice being a big strength to the system, but this is lost if parents are not discerning or if all schools are offering the same things.
- Rather than asking about a school's NAPLAN results, ask what the school does with NAPLAN results. Is NAPLAN used as a marketing device, or is it used as a tool to facilitate extra tuition? Schools rarely have data on students after they graduate, but a parent should be more interested in long-term outcomes for students in areas such as life satisfaction, mental health and career satisfaction.
- How has the school been coping with the challenge of teacher retention? If there has been a large staff turnover, this is often an indicator of a toxic culture. Does the school often find itself understaffed on particular days and having to combine classes?
- If the school has large student numbers, how do they ensure that students feel their personal needs are met and they don't just become numbers? The research on larger schools indicates the benefits, perhaps a few extra subject choices and 'bigger' facilities, are rarely outweighed by the negatives, and the justification for their existence is almost always financial. Multiple campuses might be a positive in a particularly large school.

FOR PRINCIPALS: THE ROLE OF A LEADER IN A SCHOOL WHERE TEACHERS AND STUDENTS WANT TO BE

Written with Barbara J. Smith, retired Canadian Principal and education writer.

> ***'To truly transform the educational experience, school leaders must actively involve students in the decision-making process. By creating platforms for student voice, such as school councils, advisory boards, or regular feedback sessions, leaders empower students to contribute their perspectives, ideas and aspirations. This not only fosters a sense of ownership and engagement but also ensures that decisions are made with a deep understanding of student needs and aspirations.'***
>
> — *Dr Mary Hemphill from* What Makes a Great Principal: The Five Pillars of Effective School Leadership

In the current environment where it seems nearly every teacher is leaving or considering leaving the profession, and student disengagement and mental health issues are at record numbers (we have no memory of school counsellors and psychologists when we started teaching or were students), maintaining the status quo is simply not an option and cannot be justified. If you are not prepared to make a stand for students, teachers and the profession, then why are you working in education?

A recent study from Federation University found that a key reason for many teachers leaving the profession was dissatisfaction with education leadership. One participant, Paul, a former secondary teacher who had nearly twenty years of experience, indicated that teachers were treated 'like an infant' by school leaders who simultaneously demanded professionalism from their staff.

He said he felt 'greatly undervalued and patronised by members of the leadership team' and got 'no sense of personal satisfaction from classroom teaching nor recognition from leadership for the amount of time and energy put into teaching'.

Researcher Robyn Brandenburg told Education HQ Magazine that it was devastating to read through participants' responses.

'Honestly ... it was gut wrenching, heartbreaking, because a lot of them didn't want to go. They just felt pushed,' she says.

'And often it was a self-protection mechanism, like, "if I don't go, my wellbeing will continue to suffer."'

Often the demands and administration pressures placed on teachers came 'from the top down', Brandenburg says.[165]

These pressures include great demand to maintain standardised curriculum – as it is very difficult to rank and compare one school with another if they are doing different things – and obtain improved NAPLAN results. This places immense pressure on leaders to run a 'tight ship', and any deviance from the standardised program is seen as a problem which can lead to poor outcomes. Like the students, the teachers become pawns in the contest of chasing impressive academic data. It is rare for schools to collect data on student satisfaction, and those that collect data on teacher wellbeing often keep the data hidden or implement programs such as yoga or mindfulness without actually addressing the causes of the dissatisfaction.

These conditions are not good for administrators either. More than half (56%) of school leaders surveyed agreed or strongly agreed that 'I often seriously consider leaving my current job'. Those with six to ten years of experience were most likely to say they were thinking about quitting.

---

165 R Brandenburg et. al., 'I left the teaching profession ... and this is what I am doing now': a national study of teacher attrition. *Aust. Educ. Res.* (2024).

As one survey respondent with a decade of experience as a principal noted:

> ***I don't feel ready for retirement but can no longer sustain my work as a principal.***

Another said:

> ***Most nights when I am awake, I will count how much longer I have to work before I retire or think about what else I could do instead of this job.***[166]

A recent study comparing principals' autonomy in Australia, Jamaica and Finland found[167] that in Australia, 'principals are located as business-oriented entrepreneurs, competing in an environment oriented to the success of the enterprising individual leader and school. Surviving and thriving is the primary telos of individual principals and schools.

'... a praxis orientation in which principals may operate not only as enterprising individuals maximising their own good but also as "moral and professional agents with the collective moral and professional agency, autonomy and responsibility to practise their profession ..."' However, whether they can do so in ways that move beyond a market orientation to autonomy is debatable.

In contrast the Finnish principal knows that 'a market orientation towards autonomy in Finnish education is not a driving force. Rather than being concerned about their competitiveness in a quasi-market, schools are allocated direct funding by the municipalities ... In Finland, as a manifestation of the high professional autonomy

166 Australian Catholic University, 2024

167 S Kemmis, J Wilkinson, C. Edwards-Groves, I Hardy, P Grootenboer & L Bristol (eds) *Changing Practices, Changing Education* (Singapore: Springer, 2014).

of teachers there is no inspection system, public accountability mechanisms or any other kinds of hierarchical control. Teachers and principals carry out their work relatively unimpeded ... Importantly, however, the good for teachers in terms of maintaining their professional and pedagogical freedom has been regarded as an important value in Finland, in contrast to Australia. Therefore, in summary, it can be said that in Finland we may distinguish features typical of both the professional and praxis orientation. The emphasis on market orientation remains low.'

Findings from Heikkinen et. al.[168] concluded that, 'if a culture of teacher autonomy is not encouraged, principals will have to inspect, control and survey practitioners in order to preserve aspirations of educational quality. On the other hand, if teachers are nurtured as autonomous agents the principal's role will evolve into one of nurturing, facilitating and enabling equal educational outcomes, promoting an agenda of quality and inclusive education for all.

We have seen many schools where there is very much an 'us vs them' relationship between the administration and teachers. The principal of a school we both worked at would vote to strike at a union meeting before leaving the meeting to put together a roster to cover the classes impacted by the strike. The school had a highly democratic method of decision making which saw staff meetings often going until 6 pm as we untangled the pros and cons of new proposals.

In the above scenario, an enormous amount of time and energy is saved when the trust between the staff and administration enables them to concentrate on the education issues. This trust relationship is impossible to replicate with students and staff if it is not present in other areas of the school.

---

168 Hannu L. T. Heikkinen, Jane Wilkinson & Laurette Bristol, "Three orientations for understanding educational autonomy: school principals' voices from Australia and Finland," *Journal of Education Administration and History* vol. 53, No4, 2021.

To make matters worse – and Australia is certainly no different – Renee Owen, from Southern Oregon University explains:

'Administrator licensure programs primarily train new leaders to comply with current laws and systems; they aren't training administrators to be revolutionary! So not only are our public school systems not designed for second-order change – which requires changes in beliefs and behaviours – but our leaders are not trained for transformative change.'[169]

Disruptive change is rarely expected from district level supervisors or 'higher ups', but it is exactly what is required to make teaching more fulfilling and learning more engaging. The gatekeepers may frown upon systematic restructuring, but that doesn't mean that teachers should be apathetic and give up on schools. Teacher education institutions can develop lab schools to demonstrate how peer-reviewed research can inform practice, and how practice can inform theory. Educational experts should lead educational change, not follow a faulty system.

> ***'Whether you've just become a principal or you've been in that role for years, try looking at everything with fresh eyes: don't become numb to the little things in your school that might be old to you but new to people entering your building. Everything sends a message of who you are as a community, whether you pay attention or not.'***
>
> — *George Couros, from* What Makes a Great Principal

Teachers and bold school leaders can make room for more leadership roles and make sound arguments for adding more bodies in schools that can free up teacher-leaders to support teachers. There are so many ways to be a school leader, beyond

169 Renee Owen, "Can we make real transformative change in education?" *Greater Good Magazine*, Berkeley University of California, April 21, 2022.

publishing in peer-reviewed journals. Teachers can present at conferences as well as host and organise them. Such opportunities provide excellent growth experiences.

An inspired culture can be built with people whose imaginations, creativity and capacity to innovate are not constrained. How often is a new school opened that replicates another school? Too often. For each new school that is approved, there should be hundreds of new offers to meet the varied needs of students, teachers and communities. More laboratory schools should inform the budgets, curricula, staffing and physical plants of new schools. Educational innovation needs more spaces to thrive. According to Nordengren:

> *'We believe a professional culture built around teachers as leaders is optimal for attracting, developing, and retaining the best kindergarten–12 teachers. Leadership is expected from beginning teachers, argues Nathan Bond in the Educational Forum, as novice teachers "are expected to function at the same level as veterans in terms of instruction in the classroom and engagement in the activities in the larger school community".'*[170]

Teacher-leaders can coordinate action research and book clubs; they do not simply go to conferences, but present at them, or better yet, organise them. Teachers-leaders can coordinate social events and school spirit in a valued role as VP of School Culture. Teacher-leaders can keep a pulse on school wellness; they can coordinate professional learning activities with other schools. They can share engaging teaching and learning experiences in a TedTalk. They can become Habits of Mind consultants; they can teach continuing education courses. They can write curriculum resources – and

170 C Nordengren, "New educators want opportunities for teacher-leadership, too." (online: ASCD, 2016).

publish them![171]

Certain teachers may be committed to improving different areas of a school, so it is important for school leaders to develop opportunities for shared leadership, honouring the varied voices and initiatives of teacher-leaders. The school leader may determine some key goals for the school, but must be careful not to project a vision that all must 'jump on board or get out of the way'.

> ***'Administrators should embody a professionally irreverent mindset themselves, demonstrating a willingness to challenge the status quo and embrace innovative ideas. Show where you have changed your mind, changed course, or decided to pause based on what others have shared with you. Make that thinking visible by creating an open space to question and challenge ideas, inside of being clear how decisions are made and where influence or change possibilities exist.'***
>
> *— Dr Sarah Sirgo*

A realistic school leader will invite input from teachers. Innovators will know that some teachers will be inspired by change right away, while others may need more convincing that students will truly benefit from new ways of doing things in the school.

> ***'Build positive relationships, listen, hear, seek to understand, ask clarifying questions, be kind, be kind, be kind. Then maintain positive relationships, keep listening and asking, check that what you heard is what they meant, be kind, be kind, be kind.'***
>
> *— Bronwyn Harcourt, Principal Croydon Community School*

171 B. J Smith, *Teacher Shortages and the Challenge of Retention* (Maryland: Rowman & Littlefield, 2023).

Some administrative points we like:

- Your title makes you a manager, your people make you a leader.
- Don't preach teamwork then play favourites. Hypocrisy kills culture.
- Don't micromanage. Trust your team or don't trust your team, but micromanaging is never the answer.
- If you are not developing your team, you are diminishing them. The world's leading education systems are always looking outward for areas to improve, rather than applying blinkers to restrict focus.
- If your team is reluctant to 'speak up' then you've already failed.
- If you're not accountable, you're not credible. Everyone makes mistakes and a leader taking responsibility for their mistakes shows a wonderful example for others.
- Be the change you want to see. One of the best principals we worked with would routinely free up teachers by taking their classes for them in a process which also allowed that leader to gain valuable experience teaching the students in the school.
- Try and maintain the idea that you work for your staff rather than the other way around. If you lose them, you really are nothing.
- Celebrate success but don't make it the reason for doing things. Intrinsic motivation should always be a focus.

LOOKING UNDER THE BONNET OF LEARNING SCIENCE AND DIRECT INSTRUCTION

Australian education in 2025 is in the grip of a concerted push towards a pedagogy drawn from a contemporary version of learning science. Direct instruction is positioned at the centre of the initiative and is being promoted by a broad collection of private institutions and public agencies. The vigour and relative suddenness of the direct instruction campaign raises the question of interests. Is this pedagogy and our current state of learning science such an obvious fix for our Australian students' decades-long academic decline? Or are there other agendas at play?

We look at the current configuration of Australian learning science and the advocacy for its central pedagogical approach – direct instruction. We also refer to this pedagogy as explicit instruction. Our considerations include examining the celebrated work of Professor John Hattie and a critical look at the description of learning science written by Trisha Jha from the Centre for Independent Studies. The approach we have used is to evaluate the works against related research, theory, knowledge and our own extensive experience as school educators. We don't claim to prove or disprove anything, but simply raise several glaring problems with what is lauded by some of its more excitable proponents as the 'holy grail' of education.

John Hattie – HITS

Professor John Hattie has been a highly influential figure in Australian education for nearly two decades. His giant meta-analysis of Australian and international studies investigating what teaching methods work best in generating quality learning identified a list of promising strategies, along with their quantified impacts (effect sizes). These approaches were presented as High Impact Teaching Strategies, or HITS[172], and have been promoted by educational authorities around Australia for over fifteen years. The teaching in most Australian schools, to different degrees, has been influenced by HITS, making it one of the most widespread educational initiatives of this century.

We asked John Hattie in the early stages of the HITS release about the nature of the data that had been used in his meta-analysis. We were particularly interested in the incorporation of affective data such as student motivational levels, interest, happiness, self-efficacy, confidence and so on. It was a simple answer. No data of this type had been considered at all. The HITS were based on academic pre- and post-testing results. In Australia, HITS became the cornerstone of the newly emerged 'learning science', a set of classroom principles which supporters maintain has a strong evidentiary basis.

The limited nature of the evidence upon which HITS are predicated is of major concern. An assumption appears to be that correlations can be drawn between specific classroom interventions and academic performance differentials and

---

172 See "High Impact Teaching Strategies (HITS)," Victoria State Government Department of Education, updated April 2023.

referenced against control group data: notoriously challenging to organise in education research. This statistical exercise is the basis for claiming that causal relationships exist between interventions and performance changes. It sounds something like science but, unlike real science, many experimental variables have not been controlled, just ignored. For a start, student affect matters. The same intervention with different affective settings can be associated with vastly different changes in performance.

Perhaps the understanding is that HITS effect sizes are averages that cover a wide range of student feelings, attitudes, dispositions, motivation and confidence levels, academic cultures (big difference between your average Singaporean and average Australian student for example) and orientations towards study. Were the calculated effects biased in any direction by skewed quantities of positive or negative affect? We don't know. That's a big reason why any teacher playing with HITS in their classroom should be prepared for the initiative to be unhelpful as much as it is advertised to be useful. It's not that HITS is a bad idea. It's just that it is far from a fail-safe resource for improved classroom teaching. After all, for as long as HITS has been around, Australian school academic performance has stagnated or gone backwards. Now *there* is an evidence-based caution.

An early indication that Hattie's findings were derived from a problematic data set was his conclusion that class size does not impact academic performance[173]. This idea was seized upon by people - whose interest in education was not based on any understanding of quality - as breakthrough research. Between the authors of this book, we have over seventy years of classroom experience, teaching hundreds of Australian primary and secondary classes ranging in sizes between ten and thirty-

173 J Hattie, *Visible learning: A synthesis of 800 meta-analyses on achievement* (London: Routledge, 2009).

nine. We find it unsettling for anyone to suggest that there is no difference in learning conditions and outcomes for a class of a dozen or so through to classes over triple that number in size. Hagemeister[174] shares our concerns, further pointing out uncontrolled demographic variability in Hattie's class size findings as a major issue. He also identifies a host of questionable statistical assumptions and procedures used to support Hattie's assertions.

The class size finding must have come from *somewhere*. For student numbers not to matter, a teaching approach needs to be highly effective and efficient. We can only imagine this happening if classes display unusually high levels of uniformity, ability, motivation, compliance and engagement, perhaps as may be found in Shanghai or Singapore, much less commonly in Australia. The outcome more likely could have been obtained if the academic content had low degrees of challenge and complexity, where the need for individual support, follow-up, repeat and remediation is minimised. Is that another flaw in HITS approaches?

Are the strategies based mainly on work that is easily digested and academic progress that is just as easily measured? We believe there is much valuable learning that is challenging for teachers to foster and assess and for students to master. Learning that cannot be crisply defined, taught explicitly or quantified but nonetheless distinguishes the master from the beginner. We are not always convinced that HITS was compiled with this type of learning in mind.

Professor Robert Hattam of the University of South Australia compiled a preliminary list of ten investigations[175] (conducted between 2003 and 2021) into research studies that heavily support the saturating phrase, 'evidence-based', in education. The reviews

---

174 Volker Hagemeister, "A critical analysis of the section on class size in Hattie's Visible Learning," *Open Journals*, 2020.

175 See the Bibliography under Robert Hattam for the full list of investigations.

express concerns including the use of coverall meta-analyses, simplistic definitions of 'learning' and invalid extrapolations in driving pedagogical initiatives such as direct instruction. Australian conceptualisations of 'learning science' would seem highly flawed in the light of Hattam's reading.

Trisha Jha – Learning Science According to the CIS

HITS are considered by some to not be actual elements of learning science but teaching principles derived from scientific evidence. Trisha Jha from the Centre for Independent Studies (CIS) outlined a set of guiding principles upon which the Australian version of learning science is based, at least in 2024[176] Her otherwise well-researched and comprehensive guide presents several contentious interpretations and perspectives that may help explain the issues that we have with the ubiquitous promotion of learning science throughout Australian education.

Jha declares that progressive approaches to school education have been discredited by twenty-first century research. John Dewey, seen as one of the earliest influential proponents of alternatives to Industrial Age educational pedagogies, has been proven 'wrong' according to Jha. It turns out, she states, that direct instructional methods have been superior to other forms of teaching all along. These are sweeping claims, presented with little compelling evidence and questionable in that it appears to have taken well over fifty years of research for such clear-cut, definitive and almost self-evident realisations to have been suddenly established.

Learning science is located by Jha in a narrow field that associates it strongly with cognitive principles but excludes affective and social influences. Jha references the concepts of 'biologically primary knowledge' and 'biologically secondary knowledge' (BPK

---

176 Trisha Jha, "What is the Science of Learning?" *Analysis Paper* 63, February 2024.

and BSK). BPK includes social interactions, emotional responses and other non-cognitive forms of affect. Jha notes that BPK is instinctively or autonomously learnt and has no place in learning science because teachers cannot teach or foster such knowledge. Wow. In all of our teaching we have missed a simple trick in not telling students to leave their emotions, attitudes, self-concepts and beliefs outside the door as they walked into our classrooms!

A learning science that excludes affect revisits a less enlightened era when emotions were regarded as psychological forms of softness or weakness, unfortunate distractions from serious thinking, more evident in less capable people. A substantial body of academic literature, including contemporary neuroscientific findings, does not support the assertion that affect is either redundant or beyond a teacher's influence in learning. This is a major flaw in Jha's science. Emotional responses can focus or divert attention, drive motivation and engagement and enhance creativity and imagination[177]. Student attitudes towards learning and beliefs are fed by feelings that arise during academic activity. Far from being secondary and incidental in relation to cognitive processes, all manner of affect must be considered for effective teaching to be done[178].

By hiving off affect, learning is reduced to a simple, mechanical transaction that is built around the transmission of knowledge. Completely optimised teaching practices only have to be sensitive to the cognitive limitations of working memory. BSK is the business of learning science for Jha. It includes knowledge that is not 'naturally' acquired through evolutionary needs and has to be deliberately uploaded to the brain. It is totally transferable from a

---

177 See R Pekrun, *Emotions and learning*, Educational Practises Series (Geneva, Switzerland: International Academy of Education (IAE), 2014).

178 R Pekrun, "Academic emotions," in T. Urdan (Ed.) *APA Educational Psychology Handbook, Vol. 2.* (Washington, DC: American Psychological Association, 2010).

teacher to a student and should be explicitly taught to achieve the greatest learning efficiency.

A bizarre example of BSK given by Jha is kicking a football. You can tell a student that kicking is when a ball and boot make contact, but nobody would claim to have learnt to kick by stopping there. A quick Google search on the aspects of kicking that need to be addressed through explicit instruction indicates six phases: the approach, support leg and pelvis, swing limb loading, hip flexion and knee extension, foot contact and follow through. We could add ball orientation, grip and release, kicking arc, accuracy, range, trajectory, kick type, wrong foot kicking and timing. This is a daunting instructional agenda for what should ultimately become a simple act of kicking a ball. We can report in our own extensive coaching experiences that we have never observed a strong association between explicit instruction and students learning how to kick a football.

In Jha's interpretation, the kicking skill has been taught by the teacher and learnt by the student. The rest is 'overlearning', where the student consolidates the learnt skill. We argue that the rest is the actual learning: the teacher demonstrated the skill and alerted students to what may be learnt. It is within the hundreds of playground hours and many sessions of sports field practice where the learning occurs. And for every student who learns how to kick well, their skill will be different from the ability described by the teacher. It will be the student's own developed concept.

One only needs to note the great diversity in kicking approaches of AFL footballers to realise they have learnt the art in their own way. For those who might think that this argument is only relevant to sports skills, consider learning to drive a car, or conducting a science experiment. Both are situations where being capable of performing the task is very different from being able to answer questions or understand direct instruction on the subject.

Trial and Error Learning

Trial and error experiences, as arise naturally through play-based activity, are powerful pathways for learning to occur (the activity of play itself is widely regarded as providing valuable learning opportunities, see Veraska et al, 2022, for a discussion of play-based learning according to Piaget and Vygotsky[179]). The novice kicker will stub their toe, kick with their shin, shank a football sideways and kick with a hook. They will try to adjust their kicking according to their own physiology, coordination, interpretation of instruction and contextual needs. This cycle may be spun through thousands of times. As for timing, that aspect of expert kicking defies simple explanation and starkly illustrates why direct instruction only initiates the learning process here. Timing is a mystery that every student has no choice but to work out for themselves through trial and error.

Does direct instruction do play-based learning, or trial and error? We are doubtful. The characteristic high levels of prescription, orchestration and control would inhibit the freedom needed for a student to encounter and deal with their own issues. If a teacher has tried to lay out all aspects of foundational knowledge and concepts and then tightly organised a learning activity timetable, the student does not need to perform trials, just follow instructions. Any mistakes are not prompts for self-evaluation, adjustment and repeat, they are indications that the instructions have not been correctly followed and should be revisited until the proper procedure has been implemented. Too bad if the instructions did not cover individually encountered issues.

Trial and error as a student learning approach is argued by some[180]

---

179 Piaget and Vygotsky, "Powerful Inspirators for Today's Students in Early Education and Developmental Psychology," in N Veraksa, & I Pramling Samuelsson (eds) *Piaget and Vygotsky in XXI Century* (Germany: Springer Cham, 2022).

180 See Greg Ashman, "Primary vs Secondary," Filling the Pail, August 16, 2015.

to be a BPK strategy: a primal response lacking in cognitive skill or deliberation and therefore out of place in any direct instructional teaching regime. There is no room for trial and error in problem-solving, the argument goes, only front-loading with knowledge via direct instruction. This perspective unfairly devalues the power of trial and error, as illustrated by its problem-solving use in learning how to kick a football.

'Means-end analysis' is a more formal term for trial-and-error learning and is employed extensively in AI design. The approach is typically not an uninformed random guessing game but a backwards and forwards refinement process, targeting an end outcome, that generates and evaluates interim solutions before feeding them back into problem-solving algorithms in cycles until success is achieved[181] . There is plenty of thinking that goes into trial and error.

True problem solving requires the application of an unknown method to an unfamiliar situation[182], not a known method to a familiar situation, which diminishes the role of direct instruction as the central learning pedagogy. Means-end analysis is a useful tool for initiating engagement with true problems. For it to be excluded from any learning science on the basis of a BPK tag diminishes the problem-solving reach of that science. From our teaching perspective, trial and error has always been a great starting point in problem solving, providing an invaluable level of access for students who may be otherwise challenged.

We would argue that turning problem solving into a primarily knowledge-building exercise through direct instruction is not the only or necessarily optimum way that individual ability may be gained. Students can easily develop highly teacher-

---

181 See *Britannia Online Dictionary*, s.v. "means-end analysis" accessed August 30, 2024.

182 See University of Waterloo, "Teaching Problem-Solving Skills," Centre for Teaching Excellence, accessed 2 September 2024.

dependent mannerisms with negative consequences for their own resourcefulness, ownership, strategising, lateral thinking and initiative in problem solving. For teaching allied higher cognitive skills, such as critical thinking, NSW Department of Education Research[183] identifies a variety of pedagogies, particularly inquiry-based, that may be useful. We believe this is also true in teaching problem solving.

There are no hard and fast recipes for success in problem-solving other than individual students working hard and making sense of their own situations in relation to content they have been tasked, perhaps through instruction, to master. They need to draw on inner resources, some developed through direct instruction and others gained through alternative forms of learning. There are many different roads, usually conceding some autonomy and responsibility to students, that may take them forward. Direct instruction may launch a learning voyage but as a pedagogical approach it often struggles to power the higher-level thinking journey. John Dewey was closer to the mark than Jha appreciates.

Clarity

Every advocate of direct instruction is preoccupied with being 'clear'. In Jha's learning science, a teacher being 'clear' is critical in doing explicit instruction and it is her most commonly employed directive. Who defines 'clear'? Not the student, it seems. We have incessantly found during decades of teaching that the spectrum of clarity within a typical mixed ability class – not streamed or selected for advantageous learning traits and with a competent teacher – ranges from crystal to mud. Many students find it unclear for a host of reasons, often unpredictable and covered in other parts of this book. And if it is not clear for students, it is a teacher's conceit to claim otherwise.

---

183 Stevens & Ructtinger, *Cultivating Critical and Creative Thinking.*

Moreover, the more challenging the content, the muddier for students that explicit instruction becomes. This can only add pressure on teachers to limit the depth of content that they aim to teach. The clarity issue is difficult for teachers to address. Often the reasons for students being confused or not understanding teacher talk can only be identified through individual questioning and interaction. Issues can range in extent from trivial to deep, requiring from a few seconds to several minutes or more to address, if they can be addressed at all within a lesson.

Regular stopping and checking for understanding, as is advised by direct instruction enthusiasts, can break the flow of descriptions and explanations and what does a teacher do anyway if they uncover an intractable block for some individuals? It tends to be the same students all of the time who encounter issues during direct instruction, and they often become wary of always being the ones to hold up the class. They usually learn after a while to keep their problems to themselves. It is not uncommon for many students to sit through seemingly clear, detailed teacher lectures and learn next to nothing.

Attention Spans

The matter of student attention span is completely absent within Jha's learning science. We have both employed explicit instruction to lesser or greater degrees throughout our teaching careers and have always found attention span to be a significant limiting factor on what may be achieved. The American Physiological Society reports that research in this field is scarce but a commonly accepted figure for optimum school student attention is about ten minutes[184]. TED talks are limited to eighteen minutes largely on the basis of adult viewers' average attention spans. Should this

184 See Neil A Bradbury, "Attention Span During Lectures: 8 seconds, 10 minutes, or more?" *Advances in Psychology Education* vol. 40, no 4, 2016.

issue not be addressed in the promotion of explicit instruction? Queensland researchers recently conducted local research related to attention spans, titled, "My brain leaves the room": what happens when teachers talk too much?"[185]. The report sounds a strong caution about the overuse of explicit instruction. It is also an excellent example of the importance of student voice in evaluating pedagogies.

So, for how long during an average fifty- or sixty-minute lesson can a teacher hold student attention? Probably less than is assumed by explicit instruction enthusiasts. Cutting teacher talk into short segments, interspersed with breaks of student activity should help. But breaks need to be of true durations, several minutes at least, if the teacher is to create genuine discontinuity between complete student attention phases. Can enough new content be explained in such a manner for gainful student activity to occur each time?

In our experience, the explicit explanation and demonstration of any set of skills or processes in most subjects regularly takes at least twenty minutes, well beyond the average attention span of a school student. If this was an issue for only a small minority of students, perhaps it could be tolerated. However, we fear the challenge of maintaining attention during prolonged explicit instruction is problematic for an unacceptably high proportion of students and a weakness of this pedagogy.

Is Student Interest Important?

A hint of the bias present in Jha's science of learning lies in her acknowledgement of an elite Victorian private school as a source of reference. The school self-describes itself as an open-entry school, usually meaning the opposite of academically selective entry schools such as the state Melbourne High School. Yet their 2023

---

185 See H. Tancredi, C Killingly & L. J Graham, "'My brain Leaves the Room': what happens when teachers talk too much?" *The Conversation* July 17, 2024.

median Year 12 study scores out of 50 were 39 and 36 respectively, the reverse of what may be expected given the nominal student enrolment policies. A median of 39 indicates that half of the school's Year 12 cohort were ranked in the top 10% of the state, while 36 is closer to the top 20%.

Jha would promote the elite school's educational alchemy as evidence of superior teaching according to her science of learning. However the difference, on the surface, is more a case of pedagogical magic, an outcome that sits among the planet's greatest educational value-adding performances. Is it really so? Is there more to the story? Some correspondence with an administrator from the elite school provided further insights.

An ardent advocate of direct instruction, he argued that situational interest or interest in particular lesson content was 'ephemeral' in nature and not an impactful element in student learning. In the thousand or more Australian classrooms that we have taught, there is not one in which student interest in content was not an invaluable learning ingredient. The administrator's school class compositions and student management policies must be very different to anything we have experienced in dozens of schools. No wonder that Jha can dismiss student affect as irrelevant to teaching. Her error lies in claiming validity for the conclusion across schooling in general.

My (Fabio) own PhD research, '*Task-Related Emotions in Mathematics Education*'[186], investigated associations between student interest and classroom content. Hidi and Renninger[187] provided a useful conceptual model for understanding student interest in the context of lessons. The researchers distinguished between situational and individual interest. Situational interest involves the immediate capture of student attention and stimulates

186 See Fabio D'Agostin, "Task-Related Emotions," 2020.

187 S Hidi & K.A Renninger "The four-phase model of interest development," *Educational Psychologist*, vol. 41, no.2 (2006), pp.111-127.

both cognitive and positive affective responses while individual interest results from longer term engagement, immersion, knowledge retention and/or valuing of academic study. Situational interest is often a necessary precursor to the development of enduring individual interest

Sources of individual interest may differ depending on the age of a student. Any student who highly prizes their education may exhibit individual interest in a subject independently of experienced content. Older students revisiting an area of study that they have previously known and enjoyed (and probably in which they have encountered situational interest) may be expected to display enhanced levels of individual interest.

I (Fabio) am guessing that the focus of the highly successful school is more on given individual interest, working with students who do not require the spark of situational interest. Great, if you get to only teach students who independently possess strong individual interest in academic material. It is highly unlikely that a truly open-entry admittance policy would generate such elite class compositions. This school's student cohort probably represents at best 10% of the Australian student population. To extrapolate findings based mainly on the attributes of a minority cohort is to ignore many formidable learning needs of a large proportion of Australian students.

At a conference once, I talked to a visiting high level Chinese mathematics education administrator, who reported directly to the national education minister. He may have had a million mathematics teachers under his watch. In remarks related to the strength of Chinese mathematics education, particularly in Shanghai, I commented that in Australia, I found much of my mathematics lesson planning time devoted to making my teaching interesting and relevant to students and asked if it was the same in China. He replied, 'In China this is not a problem, students have no choice. They know they must learn.' So, it is true: there are places where interest need not be indispensable to learning for many students. Australia is not one of them.

Teaching Concepts Through 'Manageable Parts'

Jha promotes the teaching of concepts through direct instruction. Her suggestion that complex concepts can be broken into 'manageable parts', reflecting a Lego brick perspective of conceptual knowledge, is problematic. Key theorists on the development of conceptual knowledge, such as Vygotsky, are adamant about the limitations of direct instruction. Blunden, interpreting Vygotsky, states that, 'direct instruction in a concept is impossible, and can only lead to the memorisation of a form of words'.[188] He also directly quotes from Vygotsky's writing:

> ***'The teacher who attempts to use [direct instruction] achieves nothing but a mindless learning of words, an empty verbalism that simulates or imitates the presence of concepts in the child. Under these conditions, the child learns not the concept but the word, and this word is taken over by the child through memory rather than thought.'***
>
> — *From* Thinking and Speech by Lev Vygotsky

Blunden elaborates that in early childhood, concepts are developed after phenomena or objects have been encountered, whereas in school learning based on direct instruction concepts tend to be given before or ultimately even without experience of the concept subject matter. This often leads to a lack of meaning and a hollow conceptual understanding. School students can find it challenging

188 See Andy Blunden, "Vygotsky on the Development of Concepts," in *Concepts: A Critical Approach* (Leiden: Brill, 2012).

to reverse the familiar ways in which they originally developed conceptual knowledge.

Greeno's four knowledge domains of an 'extended semantic model' illustrates the complex nature of conceptual development[189]. In the context of mathematics, a concept is an understanding of a system (such as Directional Bearings) that emerges from the associations and interplays of multiple skills and ideas, including pre-concepts, purposes, origins, algorithms, vocabulary, symbolism, sequences, incidental knowledge, applications, utility, strengths and limitations. Many of these elements come from experiencing the situations in which the concept is grounded[190]. Their assembly into an integrated, consolidated understanding usually defies the simplicity of ordered brick-by-brick construction.

A large body of academic literature in mathematics education supports Vygotsky's contention about the difficulty in teaching conceptual knowledge through direct instruction alone. Professor Jo Boaler's 2002[191] book, *Experiencing School Mathematics: Traditional and reform approaches to teaching and their impact on student learning*, reports on her research comparing the parallel academic outcomes in two schools, one utilising direct instruction as the main pedagogical form and the other employing more progressive, student-centred methods. Boaler's findings firmly suggest that the levels of conceptual understanding were superior when teaching went well beyond direct instruction.

A landmark observation by Skemp, *Relational Understanding and Instrumental Understanding*, essentially identifies the limitations of conventional instructional teaching, particularly in relation to

---

189 J. G Greeno, "Situations, mental models, and generative knowledge" in Klahr, D. and Kotovsky, K. (eds) *Complex information processing: The impact of Herbert A. Simon* (Lawrence Erlbaum Associates, 1989) pp. 285-318.

190 See Karen Sloan, "7 Strategies to Teach Conceptual Understanding in Math," *Carnegie Learning* (blog), April 17, 2023.

191 Jo Boaler, *Experiencing school mathematics: Traditional and reform approaches to teaching and their impact on student learning.* (London: Routledge, 2002).

establishing robust mathematical concepts.[192] Schoenfeld (1988) drives the point even harder in his study, *When Good Teaching Leads to Bad Results: The Disasters of 'Well-Taught' Mathematics Courses*[193]. He describes how the transmission model of knowledge, the cornerstone of direct instruction, can appear like efficient teaching but, used extensively, it actually fosters shallow, low-level understanding of mathematical concepts. Schoenfeld's warnings reverberate decades later as educational authorities seek to prescribe direct instruction as a panacea for Australia's struggling academic performance rates.

I (Fabio) have regularly received the same negative feedback from students who have encountered a test problem that is even slightly different from the routine practice found throughout direct instructional teaching. 'You didn't show us the steps!' Such complaints reflect the fragile conceptual hold on mathematics that is commonly generated by students who become reliant on instruction that emphasises high levels of content reductionism and problem-solving micromanagement. Another common reflection from students ill-served by excessive direct instruction is the forlorn post-test failure observation, 'but I got it when you did it'. For many mathematics students, explicit demonstrations and examples become a proxy for their own learning.

Schoenfeld goes further. He fears that mathematics taught solely or primarily through direct instructional methods generates harmful beliefs and attitudes among students. Mathematics is not learnt as a powerful, malleable and highly useful body of concepts, skills and abilities but as a dry, rigid set of rules and procedures, used for meaningless purposes. Ewing's 2004 study

---

192 See David Tall and Michael Thomas (eds.) *Intelligence, Learning and Understanding in Mathematics: A Tribute to Richard Skemp* (Post Press, 2002).

193 A. H Schoenfeld, "When good teaching leads to bad results: The disasters of 'well-taught' mathematics courses," *Educational psychologist* vol. 23, no.2 (1988), pp.145-166.

of mathematics classroom outcomes illustrates the futility of textbook-based direct instruction in teaching concepts bit-by-bit for some students and adds to Schoenfeld's concerns in relation to this form of pedagogy.[194]

Alfie Kohn, a US educational commentator, cites research illustrating the learning shallowness that can be an outcome of direct instruction. Students explicitly taught academic skills and processes often succeed when their ability is immediately assessed. However, even after relatively brief passages of time such as a few weeks, the same students will struggle to demonstrate their learning: a strong indication that conceptual understanding has not been achieved.

Kohn believes that proponents of direct instruction as the apex approach of all educational pedagogies are guided by research that is based on limited visions and measures of learning outcomes. This position is the same as that held by Professor Robert Hattam, mentioned earlier. Kohn quotes a finding from an overview of direct instruction research conducted by Schwartz et al (2009)[195]:

> ***'Studies favouring direct instruction tend to be small-scale, use limited measures and time horizons,*** [***and rely on***] ***'skill acquisition' or simple concepts as the learning goals...'***

Tampere University, one of the foremost Finnish teacher training institutions, went from Lego brick to more holistic approaches towards conceptual understanding at least a decade ago. Tampere academics moved away from the direct instruction of conceptual

---

194 B Ewing, 2004. 'Open Your Textbooks to Page blah, blah, blah':'So I Just Blocked Off,' In *Proceedings of the 27th Annual Conference of the Mathematics Education Research Group of Australasia Inc (MERGA). Mathematics Education for the Third Millennium, Towards 2010*] (Mathematics Education Research Group of Australasia, 2004).

195 Daniel L. Schwartz et al., "Constructivism in an Age of Non-Constructivist Assessments," in Sigmund Tobias & Thomas Duffy (eds) *Constructivist Instruction* (London: Routledge, 2009).

knowledge after tiring of the ineffectiveness. As one academic, Sami Suhonen, reported to us, 'We would teach things logically through lecture one day and when we asked students about it the next day, there was nothing there. It was as if we had taught nothing'.

The University turned to a more experiential approach, featuring trial and error as an important learning mechanism. Suhonen noted, 'It is difficult to see collaborative groups making obvious errors and not directly intervene, but allowing students to discover their mistakes and work out their own responses without much help is powerful learning'.

Jha's assertion that direct instruction can adequately teach conceptual understanding by breaking concepts into digestible components is highly contested[196]. The neuroscientist Jared Cooney Horvath states that the development of 'deep comprehension', is fostered by many informed educators through student-centred, constructivist approaches[197]. It is not good policy or good science to advocate the teaching of concepts in a piecemeal manner through direct instruction. Like with jigsaw puzzles, you can tip all of the jumbled pieces onto a table but that only starts building the picture.

The associations between explicit instruction and memory appear the strongest ground for Jha's learning science, although the definition of all learning as a form of long memory development seems simplistic in the context of teaching[198]. Ron Ritchhart, in his book *Creating Cultures of Thinking*[199] states that memory

---

196 The pro-direct instruction school administrator cited earlier on the topic of interest did not respond to our query about how concepts may be taught through a direct instructional approach.

197 See Jared Cooney Horvath, "Why you're probably wrong about the science of learning," *Tes Magazine* May 1, 2024.

198 Jarod Cooney Horvath, "Aside from nobody knowing what a 'memory' is, this definition counts forgetting (which is a change in memory) as learning. I don't think Alzheimer's should be lumped with learning," LinkedIn, July 2024.

199 Ron Ritchhart, *Creating Cultures of Thinking: The 8 Forces We Must Master to Truly Transform Our Schools* (Jossey-Bass, 2015) p 194.

and practice may build a knowledge and skills base but does not develop understanding. He uses the term 'impoverished learning' if memory is the only thinking students are required to perform. Yet Jha's learning supposedly is all about memory.

Jha's perspective invites checkbox lists of stages for effective learning to be achieved, such as *Rosenshine's Principles of Instruction*[200]. His item number seven, as presented by Jha, 'obtain high success rate', reads like going to the corner store for a litre of milk. It represents the style of statements that may be found in teaching advice that is little more than painting by numbers. Would it be deep conceptual understanding that item seven is referencing? A teacher better not go there in a lesson if they want to keep up their strike rate! Good teaching and learning does not always run like clockwork, it is a harder game than that. We believe quality teaching is more than a set sequence of straightforward acts, dealing with information storage and retrieval from long memory and guaranteeing success.

Further Inadequacies of Jha's Learning Science

There is more than one elephant in the Jha and Hattie room of learning science. Social interactions and relationships can greatly impact cognitive development. For example, it is well documented in neuroscientific literature that learning is significantly inhibited when a student experiences fear[201]. 'Fight or flight' dominates a scared student's thinking, significantly constricting their working memory, and is one of Jha's evolutionary BPK responses. But unlike her handwashing of BPK responsibility from the teaching playbook, a teacher is centrally placed to address the issue. 'Don't

---

200 B Rosenshine, "Principles of instruction: Research-based strategies that all teachers should know," *American Educator* vol. 36, no.1 (2012) 12–39.

201 See T.S Bledsoe & J.J Baskin, "Recognizing student fear: The elephant in the classroom," *College Teaching* vol. 62, no.1 (2014), pp.32-41.

frighten the children' at number one on Rosenshine's list would be a very helpful amendment, steeply based in cognitive science.

Science involves the systematic study of objects, systems and phenomena through empirical data gathering. Laws, principles and causal associations between factors are determined by measuring the behaviour of variables that may be dependent on selected influences. For causal associations to be asserted, it is crucial that all unselected possible influences are controlled or neutralised[202]. The scientific method can then generate understandings that are universal, or applicable anywhere that the same measured variables are solely in play. We believe that neither the HITS or Jha's learning science are drawn from this form of systematic inquiry. Jha's learning science reads more like an echo of Lysenko's Soviet potato science than a dispassionate catalogue of conclusions based on adequately considered experimental data.

Neither source of teaching principles incorporates the full range of factors that influence learning. The assumption that a few selected cognitive processes and outcomes form a complete set of relevant classroom-learning variables has not been demonstrated to be valid. The ignoring or downplay of psychocentric and social affective influences (Hattie's comments on student-teacher relationships, as discussed elsewhere in this book, while generally appropriate, contain several discordant statements) leads to an overly simplified classroom model of teaching and learning. In many Australian school situations, this model will not provide the basis for quality teaching. Instead, the glaring inadequacies of current learning 'science' will only deliver sub-optimal academic outcomes for many students and frustrations for many teachers.

Is the establishment of a true learning science achievable? At worst, the current learning science is somewhat akin to mixing

202 See Pritha Bhandari, "Control Variables: What are they and why do they matter?" Scribbr, published 1 March 2021.

vinegar and baking soda, observing the fizz and subsequently claiming to have mastered chemistry. At best, cognitive processes including important elements of brain functioning in relation to long, short and working forms of memory have been identified, providing valuable insights into the mechanical side of learning. But we should move on from the validation of direct or explicit instruction and dismissal of inquiry-based teaching approaches on the basis of a skeletal cognitive model of learning.

A More Impactful Learning Science

Rather than pushing and pulling between a dichotomy of opposing, incompatible pedagogies, can explicit instruction and more experiential, student-centred inquiry styles of teaching co-exist as complementary methods? We believe that a valuable property of any learning science should be an appreciation of the strengths and limitations of all available teaching approaches, without ranking based on frequently spurious effect sizes. Used judiciously, with an acute awareness of what can and cannot be achieved in relation to any given classroom circumstances, targeted outcomes and student cohort nature, explicit instruction can be a suitable approach, just like alternative methods[203].

Perhaps the starting point for a functioning learning science should be a comprehensive vision of what learning may be and how it may be fostered. Even if the focus is only academic learning, a vision should embrace influences and processes beyond the accumulation of knowledge in long-term memory. Where do student abilities, dispositions, and attitudes fit in? Indeed, where does a love of learning reside and how does it develop?

Professor Guy Claxton, a renowned cognitive scientist, frames the multiplicity of influences on academic learning in his observation, '[there are] neurodynamic, attitudinal, social, emotional, embodied

---

203 Hunter & Carter, "Is there a 'right way' to teach?".

and cultural factors that play a major, if often invisible and unsung, role in every moment in every classroom'[204]. Skourdoumbis and Rowe agree, stating, '...application of rigid positivistic principles and a mechanistic worldview cannot account for the multifaceted human actions that form the human experience'[205].

The vision should also include how learning is measured and valued. This subsequently requires principles for enhanced academic outcomes not to just carry the generic label, 'evidence-based', but to spell out what specific form of learning is applicable. Is it foundational skills, deep conceptual development, critical thinking or something else? All characteristics of settings in which data is generated should also be disclosed. A science that attends to each of these concerns is not going to be neat and streamlined. That is fine because it should serve a field of endeavour, teaching and learning, which is also not neat and streamlined. There are many approaches that should not be summarily dismissed because they cannot be tidily shoe-boxed or placed within a favoured ideology.

Terada and Merrill, reporting in *Edutopia*, present a mature, balanced and sensible advocacy for policies that may be embraced by a sound learning science:

> ***'Combine direct instruction, such as lectures, demonstrations, and closely guided practice, with inquiry-based approaches that promote deeper comprehension and transference, such as open-ended questions, self-directed research, and projects. Be flexible and let the needs of your students and your learning goals guide your decisions.'***[206]

---

204 See "The Sciences of Learning and the Practice of Teaching," *Guy Claxton* (blog), published March 18, 2024.

205 A Skourdoumbis & E Rowe, "A critique of 'Strong Beginnings' initial teacher education reforms: mandating neuroscience as core curriculum within the 'what works' movement" *The Australian Education Researcher* Jul 9 (2024).

206 Youki Terada & Stephen Merrill, "10 Studies Every Teacher Should Know About," *Edutopia* Jul 19, 2024.

The highly experienced mathematics education researcher and teacher Dr Peter Liljedahl compiled a list of fourteen pedagogical strategies that underpin his *Building Thinking Classrooms* approach[207]. His emphasis is on prioritising student thinking but few of his ideas would see daylight in classrooms governed by the dominant learning science of today. For example, Liljedahl believes students think best when they are standing up in loose groups, when problems are written on a whiteboard and not a screen or textbook, and when students are not treated as if they will all understand the same content at the same time. And don't get him started on the inefficiencies of conventional homework. Pity there seems to be no room for any of this in the teaching orthodoxies that are prevalent today.

A learning science that recognises the complexity and major contextual dependency of effective school teaching approaches would also acknowledge that teachers are the critical agency of good practice. Not state curriculums or authorities, regulatory bodies such as the Victorian Institute of Teaching, particular school sectors, partisan pedagogical directives, national assessment programs, tertiary institutions, technology, union ambitions, money, politically sourced education policies, think-tank advice or any other influence – simply the teachers.

Like the great slogan suggests, 'If you can read this, thank a primary teacher', it is teachers who make or break learning. Teachers who can draw from a rich and comprehensive learning science and not be welded to a rigidly mandated set of classroom practices, are best placed to assess the learning needs of their own students, implement appropriate pedagogies and evaluate the quality and extent of learning that occurs. Whether they run with a lot of direct instruction or lean heavily on inquiry, teachers should

---

207 See Peter Liljedhal, *Building Thinking Classrooms in Mathematics* (Corwin Mathematics, 2020).

be entrusted with making the best decisions for the learning of their students.

The deficit model that prevails in Australia, which regards teachers as needing heavy levels of direction, guidance and prescription rather than recognising their professional status and vocational commitment, is a failed perspective. Lack of autonomy, or freedom from mindless levels of accountability and control that have little to do with quality education, arises repeatedly as the killer issue for those leaving or contemplating departure from the profession. How many thousands more do we have to lose before authorities get this?

Ironically Professor John Hattie, despite his work contributing to the fabric of a deeply flawed learning science, offers wisdom for how a useful accumulation of transparent and openly curated evidence-based understandings may serve teachers. 'The major message, however, is that rather than recommending a particular teaching method, teachers need to be evaluators of the effect of the methods that they choose'[208]. Teachers will be evaluators of their chosen methods when they are given the trust, respect and autonomy that will allow their professional knowledge and abilities to flourish.

---

208 J Hattie, *Visible Learning*

APPENDICES
LESSONS ENCOURAGING INTRINSIC MOTIVATION AND CREATIVITY

'What our kids want isn't all that difficult to understand. They want to connect to their peers, and engage in work that is personally meaningful to them.'

— *Barbara Smith*

A SELECTION OF LESSON SUGGESTIONS WHICH WILL PROMOTE INTRINSIC MOTIVATION AND CREATIVITY. Many of today's teachers were not teaching before the standards movement hit, and know no other way of operating. Indeed, they may genuinely believe that the current methodology is 'best practice'. As teachers in a non-government school in Australia, with students whose parents are supportive of the school environment and the methods currently employed, they may believe that this is as good as it gets.

What follows are lessons which give students choice, encourage them to look at multiple perspectives, and propose innovative solutions. Open-ended lessons encourage creativity, critical thinking, and problem solving, all of which foster autonomy and intrinsic motivation.

If you must use rubrics – and not everything has to be assessed; not assessing a piece of work tells students that it has merit in itself. Involve the students in the creation of these rubrics. Students are a lot more likely to achieve learning goals and targets if they have chosen them and had input into their creation.

If you have set content that you need to get through, place these on a choice board and where possible allow students to choose when they study each. Any choice is better than none!

We also recommend the *Lesson App*, produced by a Finnish university. It creates and provides access to a wealth (some of it free of charge) of excellent lessons and other materials for all year levels and subject areas, and it's easily found with a quick google search.

SUBJECT SELECTION LESSON

This is a lesson I (Michael) have been taking which has proved to be popular with students, with many coming back the next day and enthusiastically speaking about the conversations it led to with their parents. Finnish schools have careers counsellors who regularly meet with even the youngest students. Helping the students discover their passions and giving meaning to their learning are considered as important as grades.

Like myself, my own children have gone through their school years with little or no career guidance. When I was at school, a career counsellor was not part of the school staff; while my own children's school did have a counsellor on staff, there were some 1300 other students and the careers part of the Humanities curriculum was not considered necessary a few years back. Consequently, I could see that my own children were, at best, unsure of a career path and forced to make life-shaping subject selections based on minimal guidance.

This lesson is designed to get students between Years 5 and 8 thinking about the subject choices they will be making in the coming few years.

Firstly, senior primary students have little or no knowledge of the subjects they will have available to them when they get to secondary school. Ask the class if any of them have been asked by relatives or friends about the career they would like to pursue in the future. Draw a table on the whiteboard like the one below with the two headings in bold text.

Explain to students that in the first years of secondary school they will study up to fifteen subjects as the idea is to give them a varied experience.

Ask students what some of these compulsory subjects will be and add them to the table on the whiteboard, with the grade levels at which they would study these (stress that this is approximate as it can vary from school to school, with the exception of English).

Both the compulsory and elective subjects will vary from school to school depending on the size of the school and many other factors, however I like to put as many subjects as I can think of on the list as I can see the importance in a student being aware of what their school *isn't* offering. Many students are not aware that some of these subjects even exist.

As we add each subject to the list, I ask the students if they can tell us what that subject is about. I also explain how the Humanities heading includes subjects such as Legal Studies, Politics, Economics, Geography and History which all become standalone subjects in the later years of secondary school, and similarly Science branches out into many other subjects.

The list does not need to be exact; it is the thinking it generates which is most important.

While this is in some ways doing the careers counsellor's work, it is in no way prescribing a career, rather generating thought and discussion about the student's talents, likes and passions. I also take the time to explain that the selection of some subjects may cancel the possibility of studying some others, or of studying certain courses at university level.

When a list like the one shown below is completed, I inform the students that if they complete Year 12 they can expect to have studied approximately half the subjects in the right hand column. Their final task is to select those subjects which they imagine they might choose to study.

If time permits, ask students to read their selections aloud and ask the students if they have any ideas on possible careers suggested by their subject preferences.

It is not reasonable to expect any form of intrinsic motivation if students are not aware of where the future might take them.

Compulsory Subjects	Elective and VCE/HSC Options
English (7-12) Mathematics (7-10) Humanities (7-9) Woodwork (7/8) Metal(work) (7/8) Language (usually 2 from French/Italian/Indonesian/Chinese or other) Art (7-10) Cooking (7/8) Science (7-10) Physical Education/Sport (7/8) Religion (particularly in non-gov school 7-12) Computing (7/8) Drama (7/8) Music (7/8)	Mathematics (up to 6 different math subjects from 9-12) Legal Studies (11-12) History (Australian and 'Revolutions ' – which is Russian history) (11-12) Geography (11/12) Accounting (11-12) Foreign Languages (see left column) Graphic Design and or Visual Arts (9-12) Physics (11-12) Hospitality (9-12) Physical Ed. (9-12) Outdoor Ed. (11-12) Automotive (9-12) Building /Woodwork (9-12) English Literature (11-12) Chemistry (11-12) Biology (11-12) I.T. (11-12) Drama (9-12) Dance (9-12) Music (9-12) Economics (11-12) Money (9-10) Media and/or Photography (9-12)

MATHEMATICS

The Four Fours

Order of operations, or the sequencing of mathematical processes according to both logic and protocols, is an important aspect of numeracy. Students can be led to explore the concept through an abstract challenge. The Four Fours requires them to assemble four repetitions of the digit '4' with interspersing mathematical operations so that the resulting expression equals one. Students are then tasked with the same challenge to produce outcomes of two, three and so on, all of the way to twenty.

Some examples of successful responses include:

- 4 + 4 x 4 - 4 = 16
- 4/4 + 4/4 = 2
- (4+4)/4 + 4 = 6
- 4^(4/4) + 4 = 8
- 44/4 + 4 = 15

The task is open-ended, with many possible solutions for each required outcome. It is inherently differentiating, being accessible for foundation through to advanced level students. It can be set from Years 2 through to 12. There is great opportunity for creativity, collaboration and student agency. Discourse can also be built into the task by requiring students to explain their thinking. As importantly as all of that, it can also be intrinsically motivating, satisfying and enjoyable.

The task encompasses a wide range of academic content. It includes order of operations and a variety of mathematical functions including the basic operations, indices, logarithms and factorials. Students can use calculator technology to support their solutions. There exists a vast difference between doing mathematics in this manner compared to direct instructional processes. The task can be seen as an opportunity for conceptual development and such learning can be supported by more formal notes and explicit elaborations.

A big point of the exercise, apart from driving academic understanding, is that students experience empowerment and ownership. Beyond task setting, they don't need to be told and shown what to do. Students have an opportunity to drive their own learning, fostering independence, resourcefulness and initiative. The teacher can also define their own role. They can offer minimal guidance or scaffold individual students to an extent that maintains accessibility and interest for them. This challenge is as close to a 'fail-safe' task as any worthwhile classroom activity may be. It is rich in the prompts and natural demands that can stir valuable thinking processes in students.

Rectilinear Perimeter and Area

This problem-solving lesson idea was sourced from Pehkonen et al (2013). The primary years lesson can be conducted as a prelude activity to formally learning rectangular area formulae. The formulae themselves may arise organically through engagement with the lesson task. The activity invites students to develop a conceptual understanding of rectilinear perimeter and area.

Lesson: When the class is calculating the perimeter and area of a rectangle, the teacher can ask pupils to investigate whether the following statements are true or not (through experimenting, drawing, concluding logically, etc.):

- Two rectangles that have the same perimeter always have the same area.
- If the area of a rectangle is enlarged its perimeter will also always get longer.
- For each rectangle there is another rectangle that has the same area but a longer perimeter.

The teacher can lead with one question at a time or release the three prompts at once. They could organise individual problem-solving followed by collaborative approaches. Rounds of student presentations to the class would be valuable in fostering verbal communication and thinking out loud. The teacher can support struggling students with leading questions such as 'can you think of a way to systematically measure areas?' Perhaps they could even supply students with pre-cut paper squares if they believed it appropriate for their class.

HISTORY

In Year 8 Humanities, the Australian Curriculum tells us that we will study the Middle Ages. This approach could be applied to other topics such as geography, or other subjects such as English, as discussed in the last dot point. The Middle Ages is a very broad topic, and I have devised an example of how a Finnish approach can be used to create some intrinsic motivation.

- Firstly, all students watch a fifteen-to-twenty-minute 'overview' video on the Middle Ages, which touches on many of the major events of this time including the Black Death, the feudal system and so on. A number of these can be found on YouTube and most schools have videos of this type.
- Before the viewing I ask students to write three or four 'juicy' questions about things in the video they find interesting. A 'juicy' question is a complex question with a 'how' or 'why' element to it, requiring some detail to explain it fully.
- Following the video, I ask around the room for at least one 'juicy' question from each student – there is often a lot of overlap here – and I write them all on the board.
- Once I have ten or so of these questions, I ask for a show of hands from students who would like to work in groups to investigate a particular question and report back to the class on their findings.

Students immediately have some intrinsic motivation because they have selected the topics to be studied, and the topic they themselves are investigating is one they have an interest in. A Year 8 student with no interest in medieval farming methods may find the gruesomeness of the Black Death fascinating (or 'lit', to borrow a term students sometimes use that certainly wasn't used in that sense in the Middle Ages).

The presentations students give the class are of a noticeably higher standard than they would be if students had been randomly allocated topics as they have some enthusiasm for the topic they are presenting and, of course, the student audience are watching classmates speak on a topic they are enthusiastic about.

Presentations can be varied: I encourage students to include a minute or two of appropriate footage sourced from YouTube or a similar platform and they can include quiz questions, audience participation activities, graphs, timelines etc. Tim Walker also suggests a 'gallery'-style approach where the presenters treat the room (or it could be another space) like an art gallery and have diverse visual material on the different walls and walk the 'audience' through it much like a curator at an art gallery, explaining each 'exhibit' as they go. This has the added benefit of getting the audience out of their seats, a method shown to improve learning in itself. There is evidence to support this 'gallery'-style presentation, with studies showing that memory is strongly associated with special awareness and place, so a change from the usual routine of learning in the same room or seat can stimulate learning.

Dr Jared Cooney Horvath points out that the brain cannot process both the written and spoken word at the same time, so presentations are strengthened by using pictures (he suggests a maximum of seven words per slide) rather than text projected behind the speaker. Copies of important parts of the text can be distributed after the speaker has finished, providing a second source for the material while boosting memory and learning in much the same way as coming back to it after a break does in the Finnish classroom.

In a similar way, a set novel in an English class can be broken down into various characters, themes and ideas. This is easier to do if the novel has a variety of character types and themes, all of which you would expect to find in a quality novel selected for study in an English course.

ENGLISH

Spelling

An effective way to make spelling lessons not only interesting, but fun and the motivation intrinsic: I would have spelling every week or fortnight, with one class' activities being preparation for the test at the beginning of the next spelling class. The test would then be followed by the activities for the next week's test.

- A sheet of lined paper is passed around the class and students are asked to write their name and suggest a spelling word that they sometimes have to guess when they're writing. Let them know that it is okay to misspell the word on the list – that is why they included it! Some students use this as an opportunity to write one of the most difficult words they can think of, but this only adds to the fun element of the challenge. This list becomes a primary source for the test and may need to be updated every few weeks.
- Using the students' completed list, select a dozen words to be tested in one week's time. I sometimes add a few related to whatever else we might be studying (a set text or theme) or common errors I have observed in the classwork, but I always try to leave at least half for the student's words.
- Write the twelve words on the whiteboard along with some activities which could include (and I try to vary these activities

every week, or ask the students for suggestions; the number of activities will depend on the length of the lesson and the number of words in the test may vary for the same reason).

- Find the dictionary meaning,
- Write the word in a sentence (this can be extended to combining two, three or more words in the one sentence that makes sense and is not just a list itself.)
- Deconstruct the words by jumbling the letters (if I do this I do so before I write the list – do as you see fit for the class' ability), so the students have to work out the list words.
- Find smaller words within each word: breakdown – break, down, own, do (let the dictionary be the judge in any dispute about the legitimacy of a word). This is a great way to encourage students to view words as smaller components placed together.
- Students construct a crossword puzzle with clues for each word. This can be done by hand (with a ruler!), with photocopied grid paper, or with a crossword generating program or the teacher constructs a crossword using an online program (there's several free ones) for students to complete.
- Take one of the words and create a nine-letter word puzzle (as seen in many newspapers) by mixing the letters on a Noughts and Crosses type grid. Students find as many words as they can using these letters (in the newspaper version they must include the letter in the centre space, with younger students don't bother with this rule). I draw columns for three, four, five-letter words on the board to write the answers before the end of the lesson and demonstrate to the students a suggested layout. I might fill in a few myself just to suggest a few possibilities and get them started. There is of course the nine-letter word. This is another activity I do before I have revealed the entire list.

- Collect the spelling tests after asking students to swap them with someone for correction. I would record each student's mark, but there was no section on the report card for spelling and I only mentioned it if there was a positive comment to come from it. The goal is intrinsic motivation and emphasising grades would destroy this. There is the learning of spelling happening too, but hopefully this is almost an unconscious event.

I knew the activity was having an impact when students who were not strong in spelling actually asked to do the spelling related activities when there was no test coming up as it was the last week of term. Students were having fun with words and it was no longer 'work'. Spelling has moved from a completely teacher-centred activity to an activity with purpose and meaning for students, and the most difficult words are accepted as challenges from classmates – attempts to trip each other up and part of a fun contest. Students now have some control over the words – the 'why do I have to learn these words?' is removed.

SCIENCE

The Distance to the Stars

Middle school or lower high school astronomy is an excellent topic to exploit children's natural curiosity and sense of wonder about the universe. Parallax is an astronomical range measuring technique that can be simply demonstrated and modelled on a school oval or broad outdoor space. As with most worthwhile lesson activities, careful planning and preparation is needed.

A rectangular grid must be measured out, about thirty metres by sixty metres. Two viewing positions are marked at one end and a background scale made of poles placed across the other end. A marker pole is placed somewhere in between, representing the 'star'. The pole is viewed against the background, and its position noted, from each of the two viewing positions. Using a scaled diagram (see additional book materials), the information can be used to find a parallax angle and pinpoint the location of the 'star' through basic trigonometry. The process is a neat, accurate and accessible reduction of authentic work in astronomy.

This lesson taps into the sense of awe and curiosity that all students possess. Standing on an expanse of grass and suggesting that every blade represents a galaxy, not just a star, that has been seen in our observable patch of the universe can be a wondrous experience for them. Pointing to a single blade and stating that our own solar system is just one microscopic cell within it gives students a humbling perspective of who and what we humans are.

Performing their own observations and generating useful scientific outcomes themselves are empowering experiences. The activity requires minimal amounts of prodding or pushing for students to be involved, it is intrinsically motivating. They usually want to see what it is all about. The practical exercise, based on standard curriculum content, carries meaningfulness and contextual appeal. It gives students a reason for believing that science, and maybe even school, can be relevant to them.

AN EXAMPLE OF STUDENT VOICE

Guest Author: Nethra Dave, Toronto, Canada (from Barbara Smith's book: *Urgent Care For Schools*)

Urgent Care For Schools is brimming with wonderful stories of student voice in all areas from the classroom to the school board to the United Nations. The goal must always be to design a purposeful and meaningful learning experience. To add to the need for learning in a social environment and in close proximity to interact and appropriate the understandings and behaviours of experts, the notion of 'situated responsibility' addresses the need for purpose as a motivating and engaging force for deepened and sustained learning. In other words, it matters what and how students learn.

'I recall watching one student leader stimulate discussion during a somewhat quiet session by grabbing a marker, flipping over a blank page on chart paper, and asking students to share any ideas they had around supporting recent refugees from Ukraine. Suddenly the room filled with noise...'

What was once a didactic conversation led by the teacher is now a pluralistic conversation facilitated by students. The classroom instantaneously springs to life.

As one student says in *Urgent Care*:

> ***'I'm starting to learn that global crises don't exist because they can't be solved, but because some people in power, with our trust, might not want to solve them. If we ask them why, if we hold them, and ourselves, accountable, if we treat our trust like it's as valuable as it is, I'm starting to think the whole world will change.'***

Student Health and Wellness Leader

Given the recent concerns during the COVID Pandemic about student, teacher and administrator wellbeing, it made sense to examine ways students could be health promotion leaders. At one school, Nethra – a Grade 5 student – had the autonomy to design her leadership role, as it was the first time the school encouraged students to apply for very specific job-embedded leadership positions.

Initially, Nethra planned to make bulletin boards to share tips about healthy living with her school community. The theme of her posters quickly turned to hand washing and physical distancing, when news of COVID became widespread. Her mother was a paediatrician, so she could rely on expert information. Nethra expanded her role as health promoter by initiating a podcast series that required using social media as the context for writing and presenting creative and informative messages about the need for sleep and flu shots.

The following transcript is from Nethra's podcast on the importance of getting a good night's sleep:

Hi, Welcome to the Why Podcast. This is your host Nethra Dave.

This Why Podcast is where we turn the 'Oh Why' to the 'Oh MY'.

Today's why topic is 'Why do children need a good night's sleep?'

At bedtime I liked reading a book, watching a movie or playing a board game, but my mother was always telling me to go to bed, saying that children my age need at least 10–11 hours of sleep each night.

So, I asked my mother 'why?' Also, my mother is a kid's doctor, a.k.a. paediatrician.

Sleep is very important for your physical and mental health. It helps your body and mind to rest and recover.

The circadian clock is a more complicated term for your body clock. I prefer to call it body clock.

> *It's like a regular clock which tells your body when to sleep.*
>
> *Did you know that children who get a good night's sleep are more creative, can concentrate better, and have more energy?*
>
> *Also, your brain needs sleep to get back everything it has used up in the day. Also, some of the areas of your brain are more active when your body is asleep. Surprising right? Now that I know all this, I crawl into bed and close my eyes and get a good night's sleep. Thank you for listening to this podcast. For more information about good night's sleep, visit About Kids Health.ca, trusted answers from the Hospital for Sick Children. Join me again for another episode of Why, where I turn the Oh Why is "Oh My". Bye-bye.*

Apart from her health promotion leadership role, Nethra also took on the task of co-writing the school's first student handbook. She met online via Zoom throughout the summer with another student to share their work and compile with the help of the school principal a guide to school using student voices. The questions and her responses about being a student leader complete this first chapter.

Question 1. When you were the Student Health leader, what were you most proud about doing?

As student health leader, I think my greatest achievement or what I was most proud of, was educating my fellow students on health facts and why certain things are important to keep you healthy.

Question 2. Where did you get your ideas for making healthy bulletin boards?

After my chain of podcasts, I pondered on what my next informative project would be. I needed something more organised that would catch the students' attention. Bulletin boards seemed like the perfect project. I got to work researching for more information that I could use. My two main sources were WHO (The World Health Organization) and my mother, a paediatrician. Using these two sources, I created my healthy bulletin boards, also adding lots of fun drawings and designs to make it more eye-catching.

Question 3. Why did you choose to make a podcast series?

As an avid listener of podcasts, I think they are a fun and interesting way to state beneficial and interesting facts, while also captivating the listeners' attention. My podcasts were health based, giving information on why certain things such as healthy sleep habits and influenza shots are important, whilst also adding funny jokes and stories, therefore giving the listener a little bit of both.

Question 4. How did you find your material for your podcast series?

I found my material for the podcast series through a singular website, the World Health Organization. In fact, if you are looking for any information on health, the WHO is an excellent source for the same.

Question 5. How did you feel about being a student leader?

In the beginning, my choice of becoming a student health leader was solely based on the fact that my mother was a paediatrician. Therefore, I assumed I would have a colossal amount of health-based information to pass on. After the first day I realised that this was the perfect position for me, not only did I have an actively involved principal who cheered me on, I also realised I loved medicine. In fact, I had a lot to learn! I was always interested in learning medical facts, and had an urge to learn more. This position helped me delve deeper into the vast amount of medical knowledge out there.

Question 6. Did you like the opportunity to be creative in your student health leader role?

Creativity is key for me in practically everything that I do, the fact that I got to be a student leader, that I was free and able to do what I wanted was perfect. I could use innovative ways to educate others, in methods they find interesting!

Question 7. Did you enjoy being a student leader? if so, why?

I truly enjoyed being a student health leader, it was an opportunity I had never had before and I loved the different things I could do within the role. It allowed me to expand my knowledge on medicine and find creative ways to help others do the same.

Question 8. Do you think these leadership experiences will help you in the future?

Yes, I think these experiences will help me in the future, it's always confusing to know how to be a good leader, as there are no specific rules. I think we learn through a variety of experiences. This was one of them for me.

FREQUENTLY ASKED QUESTIONS

The answers to many of these do appear in the main text of this book, but for those looking for a quick answer ...

In a nutshell, what is your message and why should educators listen to it?

Australian education can reinvent itself if it is prepared to let go of the practices used just because they have always been done that way. Dumbing down teaching to a scripted lesson format with less than university qualified teachers is an insult to current and future generations of children and teachers.

If we can make teaching a profession our brightest young people want to enter by giving the respect and professional autonomy they can get in other professions, then we can solve the 'teacher shortage' in a way that actually improves education for everyone, with hardly any increase in spending. Countries such as Finland and Estonia have shown that this can be done while creating a school environment where students actually enjoy school – teaching in these countries is one of the most popular career choices.

But we have to be prepared to cede control – control of teachers and the desire to micromanage them and all they do. We must also let go of the desire to control all aspects of students' lives.

Essentially, our message is that we need to make teaching an intellectual profession (as it once was) so that it attracts our best and brightest young people, and to make school a positive place, in such a way that young people want to be there and want to be involved in the learning that comes with it.

When the powers that be decided to mandate certain practices, we don't believe that they intended to 'dumb down' the teaching profession. Their goal was probably one of consistency: but a consistency that limits the individual expertise that teachers bring to their profession is not worth having.

You are both now at the end of your careers, why do you care what happens in the future in education?

We have seen hundreds of students whose lives have been altered – potentially ruined – because they were led to believe that education and learning at school was not for them. Across the country there are thousands of students who see our current system as a data collection factory that cares nothing for them as individuals, and they want to get out of it as soon as they can. In the last few years, we have seen thousands of teachers also decide that our education system has no place for them. They entered the field wanting to have a positive influence on the aforementioned children, and instead they found themselves as cogs in a data factory.

Education is the last expense a country should be willing to compromise.

At their best, schools can be exhilarating, inspiring, fascinating, lively, enriching and fun places to be. All schools have this potential because all students have the energy, verve, inquisitiveness, enthusiasm and dare that are gifts of their youth and essential elements of a positive and vibrant environment. Why would anyone not want to get involved? And why would anyone not want to address the issues that suppress the joys and benefits of education? These thoughts provide all the motivation we need to care deeply about the direction of future schooling.

What is the one big difference between schools in countries like Finland or Estonia and Australian schools?

This is probably the most common question we are asked. The answer is that in Australia we are still obsessed with how to best deliver the curriculum, how much can be remembered, the grades on standardised tests and the like. In Finland and Estonia, they have moved on from the curriculum obsession to looking at how we can make students more able to learn, able to own their learning and able to see learning as more than a way to achieve grades. Essentially, they have moved on from the idea of trying to pour as much content into an empty vessel to the idea of treating the 'empty vessel' as a thinking, feeling person who can learn a lot more efficiently if their interests, needs and attitudes are recognised and catered for.

How the students feel about their learning is never considered in Australian education. It is a big part of the thinking in Estonia and Finland.

Finland has reaped the benefits of having the country's brightest as teachers, and giving them autonomy to use best practice as they see fit for their students – with little or no political interference. The brightest don't require micromanaging or control, but we can't regulate our way to this. We have to make the profession an attractive space to the highest scoring secondary school graduates. We cannot say we will wait until the best are there. Firstly, the best of our current teachers are walking away from the profession in record numbers, and secondly, our top secondary school graduates are choosing professions which offer genuine professional autonomy, flexible working conditions (I (Michael) have a colleague who works in HR and points out the absurdity of sending well-paid professionals to mind students in the playground!), respect, innovative culture and a career pathway.

Doing this will not cost a lot of money, but we will have to redistribute education spending away from those who are among our society's most well-off to those who are least able to afford excellent educational opportunities.

How did countries like Finland get to where they are, or were they always like this?

Finland used to be a farming country and logging was the main export. Realising that this was not sustainable, it was decided (this was in the 1970s) that a focus on education was required to cultivate their greatest resource – their children. When the global recession in the early 1990s hit Western countries like Finland very hard, cuts to the education budget saw the decision to remove curriculum inspections of any type and give this responsibility to the teachers. This again increased the autonomy of teachers and the professional respect given to them. Decades of the country's best going into teaching, with the autonomy (and encouragement) to innovate, along with the professional body/union (they are one and the same) having control over the education system with very little government interference, has ensured a world-leading system which continues to evolve. Having the country's smartest people in the classroom has an enormous impact on how children see learning and education. The importance of role modelling cannot be overemphasised.

Simply judging the Finnish education system on test results would be a grave error. Once you witness students taking responsibility and ownership of their learning, displaying independence such as riding public transport at seven years of age or working diligently in the classroom while the teacher shows visitors around the school, you become aware that something beyond tests results is taking place. When COVID hit, Finnish teachers told me that their students were doing all they could to not let remote learning impact their studies. The Australian students I (Michael) was teaching deliberately used it as an excuse to avoid their studies.

Why have Finland's PISA scores levelled off from where they were before?

Several reasons. The challenges of successfully implementing inclusion policies have been a growing problem there. With a high priority on equity in school (and society), classrooms now include students with disabilities who were previously not part of the mainstream school system.

With suspension from school almost unheard of, Finnish teachers now believe that too much change occurred too quickly in this area, and you can be sure there will be action taken in the near future.

Two other issues were identified as significant in Finland's recently declining PISA performances. Population diversity has greatly increased over the last decade. We visited a Helsinki school where over forty native languages were now spoken, compared to a handful a few years prior. The sudden presence of so many different student cultural backgrounds has been a major challenge for Finnish education. The altering demographic has required Finnish teachers to adapt their pedagogical approaches, a work currently in progress.

Device distraction is the third damaging influence. Like other countries throughout the world, the now ubiquitous presence of mobile phones and computers has impacted the quality of educational outcomes in Finland. The potential educational benefits of such technology are recognised but this comes with a cost. Finnish students, particularly boys, often do not have the necessary self-discipline to partition mobile device educational applications from recreational activity in their use of phones. This has led to negative consequences for classroom attentiveness and focus. Encouragingly, Finnish educational leaders, as much as the Finnish public, are determined to restore their former quality.

Am I allowed to make changes to an Australian school? Who do I need to ask to do this?

Pasi Sahlberg (who is on the federal education minister's advisory panel) explained to us that he is often asked by Australian school leaders, 'Who do I ask about making changes at my school?' His response: 'You are the principal. If what you are doing is the right thing to do, then you are professionally entitled and likely *obligated* to do it.'

Indeed, in any other profession, failing to respond to relevant research and best practice would be a death knell, but somehow we have created an environment which, in many cases, seems to take great pride in maintaining outdated practices. Too often, we do not critically examine what we are told by our administrators, blindly accepting third party research and 'best practice' advocacy, even when we see evidence of it failing to assist those who need it most.

We need more leaders in Australian education to look at the bigger picture rather than follow the limited vision of politicians whose terms of office are too short for them to care beyond the next election cycle.

Unfortunately, many Australian educators have only witnessed a time when they forfeited all education policy decisions to those further up the chain. Many are leaving the profession, but change must start at the school level, and growing numbers of amazing school leaders are creating schools where students and teachers want to be.

What will happen if we continue to do what we have done before?

We fear for the future of education in this country. If we do not change, we could see the introduction of video-based teaching programs (postscript – this has already started!) produced by government departments of education (non-government schools will be the last to be impacted by the teacher shortage). There are already schools in the USA where mathematics is taught via an online program and the class only needs to be 'supervised', meaning the requirement of a qualified mathematics teacher is removed.

With estimates suggesting a shortfall of some 23,000 teachers by 2033, the future looks grim for those who cannot afford a place in an elite, 'teacher-staffed' school. Our two-tiered system will have an ever-increasing gap between the tiers. It appears that some states are pushing towards scripted lessons, which can allow teachers with less than university standard qualifications to work as 'teachers' as lesson preparation and actual teaching are reduced to the reading of a script. This would be disastrous for our children.

Aren't countries like Finland and Estonia very different societies than here? Surely this would mean their practices simply don't work here.

We have spent a lot of time in Finland, and this question about whether what we saw could be applied in Australia was at the forefront in our minds. Perhaps the easiest way to answer this is to look at the many schools in Australia where 'alternative' programs are running with great success. Big Picture Education schools such as the Croydon Community School, a government school where most of the students are from disadvantaged backgrounds, is one we've seen where some of the most 'difficult' students have thrived. In 2022 they were the second greatest improver in the state for NAPLAN results, and standardised test grades is not a metric they have concentrated on. If this can be done with our most challenging students, imagine the possibilities for the rest.

It is truly amazing to see children take control of their learning. Unfortunately, most Australian educators have little experience with this and believe that the factory model is the only way. We know: we were in the same place ourselves!

The basic needs and psychology of teenagers around the world are remarkably similar. A better question might be, 'Do we really want equity in education or are we happy to give the best educational opportunities to the most well-off financially in our society, and the worst educational opportunity to those born into economic disadvantage?'

What is wrong with standardised curriculum? Isn't it only fair and equitable that all students do the same things?

A standardised curriculum (and testing) is convenient for some educators, but not for the students. Indeed, both ignore the individual talents and characteristics of the students and place them in a big mass-production factory that makes data for the purposes of ranking and comparing students, schools and teachers. If we want to have schools where students want to be, it is important that they feel that the system is about them as individuals, not them as data points. If we want schools where teachers want to be, it is important that those teachers feel that they are trusted, respected and valued. Standardised tests give the message that the grades and assessments of teachers are not sufficient, and standardised curriculum tells teachers that they are not trusted to prepare appropriate curriculum materials (one of the main things they studied at university!). Another issue of course, addressed elsewhere in this book, is how fair a standardised curriculum can possibly be when there is zero priority given to standardised school resourcing?

We are very much of the opinion that making a big noise about academic outcomes is ignoring the elephant in the classroom in

Australian education. This blind chase for academic grades has been the very thing that created the teacher shortage. The danger is that the students most likely to suffer in a system lacking sufficient teaching numbers are those same students who have the least access to quality education materials outside of school; students who are already in under-resourced schools. We will be creating an underclass of under-educated who never had access to real quality teachers.

If all these ideas work so well, why haven't they already been done here?

An excellent question, and one we have been asking quite frequently. There are a number of factors at play in the answer to this:

- Many Australian school leaders do not recognise that their role is to be innovative. Innovation has not factored in their careers thus far and they do not see it as part of their future role. They may not even be aware that they are 'allowed' to be innovative. As a result, most of the practices – most of everything that happens – in Australian schools occurs because that's the way it's always been done.
- Some Australian schools (to be fair, mostly non-government schools) are doing quite well with the current system: they're making money and increasing enrolments. Whilst they may have many other issues, these can seem minor in comparison to those of the many schools not making money or maintaining enrolments (or teachers!).
- Very few Australian educators are aware of the innovation that is possible. Enquiries to me (Michael) regarding visits to Finland are usually from overseas educators, despite the fact that I have aimed promotional material at Australian audiences. Teachers in countries such as Singapore and most of Europe often have experience working in other countries, but it is rare in Australia, where anything other the mandated 'best practice' tends to be pushed aside.

- Some Australian schools believe that the practices they have used for over a century are what 'the market' wants from them.
- The top-down nature of Australian education does not encourage any innovation. While the main motivating method continues to be comparing and shaming schools, this requires that they all be doing something very similar in order to give some legitimacy to these rankings.

Australian schools' reluctance to change is akin to the United States' obsession with guns. Despite all the research and evidence pointing to a huge problem, both just continue as though change is impossible, regardless of the number of lives destroyed.

Nearly a century ago, a French sociologist wrote that every institution's unstated first goal is to survive and grow, not to undertake the mission it has nominally staked out for itself. Thus, the first goal of a government postal service is not to deliver mail: it is to provide protection for its employees. The first goal of a permanent military organisation is not to defend national security but to secure, in perpetuity, a fraction of the national wealth to distribute to its personnel.

This same principle applies to the existence of those organisations behind our national testing programs. Their first loyalty is to themselves surviving as institutions, not to schools, teachers, or students.

Schools need clear student rules and compliance, tight control over pedagogies and curriculum, and strongly enforced sanction regimes. Won't any alternative lead to chaos?

A common vision of good Australian education is fairly military in nature. It consists of strongly administered student behavioural protocols, micromanaged pedagogies, compliance with a given curriculum, and teachers drilled in the doctrine of conformity and uniformity. Such stringent management generally averts chaos, but at an enormous cost to educational quality, independence, resourcefulness, resilience and creativity for many students. Students should not be mainly viewed as objects to be tightly managed, but as fellow humans seeking to be richly educated. In blunt terms, if the main administrative and teacher focus is on maintaining control, then it is not on providing quality education.

Quality education will address many if not most of the issues that can arise with students. If students feel respected and cared for and levels of academic engagement, student and teacher happiness are high, then a good school will emerge. These schools do exist in Australia, just not enough of them. Student respect, allegiance and investment of effort are commodities that must be earned by schools, not ordered.

If we didn't have NAPLAN, how would we be able to monitor what our schools are doing and how they're going?

NAPLAN testing has been conducted in all Australian schools at Years 3, 5, 7 and 9 since 2008. The scheme is meant to provide an annual 'snapshot' of academic development. This is not a correct analogy. NAPLAN is anything but a camera click of where students are in their learning. It is more like a full-dress rehearsal followed by an opening night performance of a song and dance show. Schools typically devote at least a week or more, perhaps 5% of the total available teaching time for the year, to undertaking NAPLAN. The outcomes do not justify this level of disruption.

Many concerns exist. The 2021 Australian Education Union (AEU) State of Our Schools survey found 59% of principals think NAPLAN makes no difference to student outcomes, and 62% of teachers think the tests are an ineffective diagnostic tool for teachers. The Queensland Teachers Union has encouraged parents to boycott the exams in a bid to avoid 'high levels of stress and anxiety' in what it calls a 'high stakes, but low-value testing model'. Researchers recently found NAPLAN had 'strayed from its original purpose' of identifying struggling students by 'insidiously infiltrating everyday teaching and learning practices', which ultimately undermined student learning.[209]

A recent UNSW Business School study[210] found a disconcerting level of NAPLAN system 'strategic manipulation' within some Australian private schools. The researchers stated that in these schools, there was a far higher likelihood of academically struggling students to be absent during NAPLAN testing. The public image benefits to a school of ability-streaming their students who take NAPLAN are self-evident and have nothing to do with educational evaluation. But everything to do with junking NAPLAN.

So, if we reject NAPLAN but still want national level monitoring, what can we do? The most promising answer has been with us for decades. Several international assessment programs including the Progress in International Reading Literacy Skills (PIRLS), the Programme for International Student Assessment (PISA) and the Trends in International Mathematics and Science Study (TIMMS) are routinely implemented in Australian schools. Their outcomes are considered to be serious, accurate indications of academic achievement. These tests are conducted through sampling a low percentage of all students, just enough to be statistically significant.

An unobtrusive national test, done by a small proportion of students selected through random sampling, would seem a more benign alternative to the burdensome and damaging white elephant called NAPLAN. Finland and other countries with highly respected education systems have for many years successfully employed sampling methods to monitor academic achievement

---

209 See "A Naplan of Attack," *The Squiz*, 13 March 2024.

210 See "Private schools 'gaming' NAPLAN" *The Weekend Australian*, August 18, 2024.

trends. At the same time, we could also dispense with the odious practice of pitting schools against schools through the My School[211] comparison tables.

Why are we critical of a large amount of educational research conducted in Australia?

We are apprehensive about the 'ground-breaking' labels often attached to new educational research. These claims are rarely accompanied by elaborations about how and where the research was conducted, let alone details related to exactly what was measured. To simply state that 'this pedagogy will improve learning in any context' is not enough.

Australian educator Michaela Epstein cites the 'McNamara Fallacy' in describing the central issue plaguing many studies in Australian education[212]. She posted a LinkedIn observation summarising how seemingly relevant research can be meaningless in many contexts. Throughout this book we have touched upon how research findings can hold a much lower degree of universal application than is often claimed. Michaela writes in relation to the commonly misleading nature of educational research:

The McNamara Fallacy

1. *Measure whatever can be easily measured*
2. *Disregard what can't be measured easily*
3. *Presume that what can't be measured easily is not important*
4. *Presume that what can't be measured easily does not exist*

With the McNamara Fallacy, there is an over-reliance on measurable data. And this is to the exclusion of all other factors. Like curiosity. The underlying message becomes: those other factors no longer matter. So, what to do?

---

211 Visit myschool.com.au for more information.

212 See Michaela Epstein, "Curiosity Doesn't Exist," LinkedIn, posted 17 August 2024.

In the messiness of the classroom, data doesn't show a 'truth'. It hints at what's going on. Any piece of data is the starting point. The starting point for asking more questions and considering more factors.

Why is there a public and private school divide in Australia?

OECD data shows that about a third of Australian students attend private schools and the rest are in public schools. These proportions are about in the mid-range, with some countries having almost all students in public education and others having over half in private schooling. Private education in Australia generally pre-dates the provisioning of public schooling. It has been a foundational component of the Australian educational landscape, often in the form of Catholic and other Christian denominational schooling.

Traditionally, private education has included both a well-resourced sector and a sector that has long been financially challenged. The most advantaged private schools are significantly wealthier than almost all public schools, leading to tensions between supporters of each system. The contention mainly centres on the fair distribution of state funding and arguments exist for both positions, complicated by the high tiering of advantage within the private system. There is no easy resolution.

In most OECD countries, if private schools receive government funds they are not allowed to charge any tuition fees.

Award-winning writer and social commentator Jane Caro: '... almost no one outside the public education community appears to notice or care. Australians are blind to the damage our publicly funded but increasingly segregated education system is doing to our children and their future. I would argue that we are as blind about the long-term ramifications of our inequitable school system as Americans are about their lack of gun control. And our blindness is for the same reasons. It suits powerful vested interests that we do not see, or that at least enough of us don't see, so that it becomes political suicide to suggest change.'[213]

School choice is often touted as a key feature of our education system, but the ability to vote with your feet will always be directly related to your wealth. One of the strongest arguments for equity is that when the children of the country's wealthiest and most influential attend public schools, they ensure that these schools are of an excellent standard. Unfortunately (and we are both mainly from non-government school backgrounds) the cost of raising the standard of our government schools, combined with the cost of continuing the very generous funding we give the private schools, is something we cannot afford – we cannot have both.

We would suggest that there are also other important issues arising from divided educational institutions. A perspective of Australian education gained solely from highly advantaged schools would show that we have one of the best systems in the world. Viewed from struggling schools, we are third world in character. This immense degree of polarisation is associated with highly damaging cultural and socioeconomic consequences.

> ***'Education is used by the rest of the world to at least try to break down the class system. Almost alone in the developed world, Australia is using it to build one.'***
>
> *— Jane Caro*

Australian pedagogical research that is set within privileged schools, many of which charge high fees and practise selective entry for academically oriented students, can generate outcomes that are unhelpful to a majority of schools. It seems questionable

---

213 Jane Caro, "Class Warfare," *The Monthly*, July 2024.

to extrapolate findings that are based on a narrow student demographic to wider student populations. The differences are too great. We suspect that this issue diminishes the reliability of current Australian learning science, including the boundless promotion of direct instruction.

My own (Fabio) PhD study was based on a school cohort with histories of modest mathematics assessment results. This limits the extent of possible generalisation. In support of my conclusions, I argue that a sample of students who are not highly proficient in mathematics is more representative of average Australian mathematics students than a sample set of higher achievers. However, the contextual limitations remain and whatever I advocate based on my research, I need to always make this clear.

A high degree of demographic polarisation within a national education system can contribute to many unhealthy outcomes. In America we have seen book banning and attempts to control the narrative around history and religion. The need for this in Australia is minimised if most of our 'academically minded' students are in generously funded private schools where the chances of 'controversial' ideas being taught are unlikely. Independent schools founded on a religious ethos sometimes promote staffing and student practices that can appear inconsistent with established Australian values. Interestingly, a 2018 analysis of the period found that the 'type of school attended was not associated with academic achievement' and even years after leaving school 'there was no statistically significant association between type of school attended and employment status, occupation or earnings.' [214]

'If you've got students who have low literacy, low numeracy, low digital awareness – that's very expensive to provide the interventions required. Public schools usually don't have enough people in classrooms supporting those students with disadvantage.'[215]

---

214 J Robinson, "Schooled: A History of failure in education funding," *The Monthly*, August 2024.

215 J Robinson, "A Class Above, A Class Below," *The Monthly*, July 2024

But while an increasing number of parents are choosing to send their kids to schools with religious affiliations, there is a corresponding decrease in the number of Australians who identify as being religious themselves.

At almost every step over two centuries, we have put in place the building blocks of division. We have built one of the world's most socioeconomically segregated school systems because at every moment along this path we decided to do so. While once that was more about identity, the choices we are making now – both personal and political – are becoming less and less about reinforcing cultural values and more about entrenching privilege.[216]

What are some things an Australian school can take from your work and change immediately?

The fifteen-minute break every hour is supported by basic neuroscience and Finnish educators are shocked that we do not follow this. We implemented this in a number of primary schools in Orange, NSW with wonderful results.

The other thing we would suggest is to work towards creating a love of learning and school. Impressive grades are almost a complete waste if in achieving them we have killed the enjoyment of school, learning and the subject studied. Love of learning cannot be explicitly taught or measured by grades. It can be modelled or fostered by teachers who foster attributes in students including:

- Experiencing positive feelings about learning new things
- The ability to self-regulate efforts to persevere, despite challenge and frustration
- Autonomous behaviour
- Feeling challenged
- Having a sense of possibility

216 Robinson, "Schooled".

- Being resourceful
- Feeling supported by others in their efforts to learn[217]

This list of outcomes associated with 'love of learning' adds to our concerns in relation to the promotion of direct instruction as the main or only pedagogy that works. It cannot deliver many of the classroom opportunities that may lead to love of learning. We owe all students a lot more than direct instruction alone can ever give them. Such a message would well serve the teaching staff of any school.

What is best practice education?

John Dewey, a true American educational visionary of the late nineteenth and early twentieth centuries, lived in the era of Industrial Age, or 'factory model' schooling. Factory model education is designed 'to create docile subjects and factory workers'.[218] We fear current Australian educational trends are pushing us back in this direction. Dewey was a prominent advocate of a more humane and equitable approach towards the upbringing of children. His vision is as badly needed today as it was 100 years ago. The Finnish system, probably decades ahead of many current Australian approaches in terms of efficiency and outcomes, embraced Dewey's thinking a long time ago.

Dewey's beliefs are commonly described as 'progressive', and he is also often labelled as the 'father of progressivism'.[219] We consider his work more a matter of best practice. His philosophy centres on the direct interests of students, not the interests of curriculum content providers, educational administrators, perceived economic

---

217 List sourced from Ben Dead Ph.D, "Authentic Happiness," University of Pennsylvania, updated 2004.

218 See David Brooks, "The Relationship School," *The New York Times*, March 22, 2012.

219 See Dr Della Perez, "Chapter 6: Progressivism" in *Social Foundations of K-12 Education* (online: Centre for the Advancement of Digital Scholarship, 2022).

needs or political actors. Williams (2017)[220] describes aspects of the Dewey philosophy:

> *'In contrast to traditional classrooms, Dewey thought that schools and classrooms should be representative of real life situations, allowing children to participate in learning activities interchangeably and flexibly in a variety of social settings (Dewey, 1938; Gutek, 2014). He was of the idea that abruptly introducing too much academic content, out of context with children's social lives, bordered on unethical teaching behavior (Flinders & Thornton, 2013). This notion would be a point of conflict in education today, as it is vastly different from what is happening in classrooms with the strong emphasis on implementing the Common Core standards [a standardised curriculum and assessment program].'*
>
> — *Theobald, 2009*

Williams also identifies key features of Dewey's teaching advocacy, outlining a broader, holistic agenda compared to traditional teaching:

> *'When teachers plan for instruction, student interests will be taken into consideration and curricular subjects will be integrated with an emphasis on project learning. The educational experience encompasses the intellectual, social, emotional, physical, and spiritual growth of the whole child, not just academic growth.'*
>
> — *Schiro, 2013*

220 Morgan K. Williams, "John Dewey in the 21st Century," *Journal of Inquiry and Action in Education* vol. 9, no. 1, 2017.

Although a century old, Dewey's approach has weathered well. A large body of subsequent research on learning, some of it raised in this book, supports many of his ideas on schooling and educational outcomes, despite their summary dismissal by today's direct instruction enthusiasts. After all, Dewey was reacting to the same widespread pedagogy that had already reached its effective limits way back then.

THANKS AND ACKNOWLEDGEMENTS:

For some time I (Michael) didn't feel ready to write a follow up book to *Testing 3,2,1...* It was very difficult to write in 2018 and 2019 about the problems in our education system and get a completely indifferent response from most education leaders, despite the fact that the book received unanimously excellent reviews. In fact, one of the most common reactions was, 'What education crisis?'

When I first saw the amazing things happening effortlessly in Finnish schools, and I researched their appropriateness for Australian schools, I was excited at the possibilities. How to decide which schools can access this first was one issue I wrestled with. Here were cures for nearly every ill facing our schools – each with a wealth of research and neuroscience to support it – and with teachers and students losing interest in ever increasing numbers, how could we get this happening before too many more leave?

I had imagined that any follow-up book would be an analysis of the steps we took to improve the system, making it teacher and student friendly.

Reuniting with former teaching colleague Fab D'Agostin and finding that his Ph.D topic, 'Emotions In Education' aligned almost exactly with what I had found through my research into Finland's system was a wonderful synchronicity of the kind that always seems to precede a new book project. Fab joined me on a visit to Finland, and this book is really the result of countless hours of conversation there and here in Australia, often over a drink at the end of a week in schools. We were often joined by other teachers, and former teachers whose suggestions and encouragement informed us moving forward.

Thanks to all those teachers, and particularly Fab, whose enthusiasm often gave me the necessary jolt when I started to feel it was just too difficult a task. Make no mistake about that. I have had countless educators explain exactly how they have had zero improvement from the methods they have been using, many then dismissing the ideas of proven systems like Estonia and Finland despite the fact that they have never visited these or have any understanding of how they work. These are 'leaders' who are really just doing what they are told and expecting those in their schools to do the same. In the current environment where it seems nearly every teacher is leaving or considering leaving the profession, and student disengagement and mental health issues are at record highs, maintaining the status quo is simply not an option and cannot be justified. If you are not prepared to make a stand for students, teachers and the profession, then why are you working in education?

The entire #MeToo movement came from different women sharing their personal stories, as difficult as that was at the time for them. Why can we not do the same and share our difficult experiences in teaching to raise awareness and drive much-needed change?

A third visit to Finland cemented my view that Australian students and teachers can do everything Finnish students and teachers do.

The wonderful educators I have encountered in Finland: Mikko Turunen, Pia Friman, Juha Lehtinen, Pasi Sahlberg, Elina Syri, Saara Tahtela, Virpi Heinonen, Sharon Lierse and so many others who welcomed us into their schools and classrooms, and offered their time and expertise.

Thanks you also to David and Georgia at Melbourne Books, Melissa Georgiou (from *Finnish Education Perspectives* and Aalto University), Chris Gold, Pasi Sahlberg, Vaughan Cleary, Barbara J. Smith (Canada), Michael O'Keeffe, Graeme (Grim) Stewart, Aron Tremul, Robbie Moloney, Kimmo Hirvonen, Virpi Heinonen, Dr Sarah Aiono (in New Zealand), Ligia Learmonth, Michael O'Keeffe, Deborah Guissard, Bruce Connor, Brendan Nichols, Tristan

Phieler, Wade Zaglas, Robert Cameron, Amelia Clifford, Erin Morley, Nicole Brunker (Sydney University), and Robert Hattam (University of South Australia).

ABOUT THE AUHTORS

Michael Lawrence and Dr Fabio D'Agostin are experienced teachers who, after decades teaching in primarily non-government schools, through their experiences in Finnish education and research came to see that the education system they were a part of was not working for anyone other than a privileged few. They were particularly concerned at the obvious attempts to shut down innovative thinking in the system, and the dumbing down of the teaching profession. They are committed to making teaching a highly respected, desirable profession, and schools a place where students enjoy learning. They firmly believe that every child can be a successful student, this success may not be apparent on a standardised test; and that the future demands creative, independent thinkers rather than standard factory model students.

Michael's previous education title looked at the Finnish system and Fab's Ph.D research looked into the connections between student's emotions and effective learning.

Scan here for more information about Michael Lawrence and Dr Fabio D'Agostin.

BIBLIOGRPAHY

"A Naplan of Attack." *The Squiz,* 13 March 2024.

"Alarming reasons why more kids are skipping school." *The Herald Sun* 6 April 2024.

"Australian Student Wellbeing Framework." Student Wellbeing Hub.

"Critical and Creative Thinking (Version 8.4)." Australian Curriculum, Assessment and Reporting Authority. Accessed August 12, 2024.

"Final Report." Royal Commissions. published September 29, 2023.

"High Impact Teaching Strategies (HITS)." Victoria State Government Department of Education. Updated April 2023.

"Impact of Technology on Kids Today and Tomorrow." Western Governors University, published October 3, 2019.

"Information for Schools." Schools Victoria, September 9, 2024.

"Key Lessons: What Research Says About the Value of Homework." Reading Pockets.

"Legal Fight Over Help for Teacher." *The Age,* July 6, 2024.

"Pathways, Engagement and Transitions: Experience of Early School Leaver.," The Smith Family, published March 26, 2024.

"Private schools 'gaming' NAPLAN." *The Weekend Australian,* August 18, 2024.

"Some parents think their kids don't really need school anymore." *Manchester Evening News,* 17 March 2024.

"Teacher Wellbeing Index." *Education Support (UK).* Accessed August 2024.

"The Importance of Supporting Students with an Abundance of Care." Catapult Learning, February 8, 2021.

"The Most Important Qualities That Make a Good Teacher." Teachers of Tomorrow, 30 July, 2023

"The Sciences of Learning and the Practice of Teaching." Guy Claxton (blog), published March 18, 2024.

"Tips from Dr. Marzano." Marzano Resources. Updated 2024.

"Welcome to AERO." Australian Education Research Organisation.

"What Makes a Good Teacher?" Open Universities Australia, 3 June, 2022.

"When it Comes to Teachers, Respect Takes Many Forms – And All Matter." Monash University, 16 December, 2022.

A Keddie. "Disrupting the pathways of disadvantage: The problematic promise of John Hattie's Visible Learning." In T. Barkatsas & N. Binns (Eds.) *Teacher preparation and professional learning in Australia.* Singapore: Springer, 2016.

Aiono, Sarah (Dr). "Being Sold a Story: Teachers as Curriculum Designers – Teachers Are More Than Just Curriculum Deliverers." *Curiosity Creator* (Substack). June 27, 2024.

Aksela, Maija; Lundell, Jan & Ikävalko, Topias (eds). *LUMA Finland – Together We Are More.* Online book. LUMA Finland, December 2020.

Alton-Lee, Adrienne. "Meta-analysis in education: How has it been used?" *The Australian Educational Researcher,* 2003.

Amin, Mridula & Ettinger-Epstein, Sascha. "The Kids Who Fear School." *ABC News,* 29 April, 2024.

Ashenden, Dean. *Unbleaching the Whale: Can Australia's Schooling be Reformed?* Centre for Strategic Education, 2024.

Ashman, Greg. "Primary vs Secondary." Filling the Pail, August 16, 2015.

Australian Catholic University. "The Australian Principal Occupational Health, Safety and Wellbeing Survey 2023." Melbourne: Australian Catholic University, March 2024.

Australian Coalition for Inclusive Education. *Driving change: A roadmap for achieving inclusive education in Australia.* Australia: CYDA, 2020.

Bhandari, Pritha. "Control Variables: What are they and why do they matter?" Scribbr, published 1 March 2021.

Biesta, G. "Why "what works" won't work: Evidence-based practice and the democratic deficit in educational research." *Educational Theory* 57, no.1 (2007).

Bledsoe, T.S & Baskin, J.J. "Recognizing student fear: The elephant in the classroom." *College Teaching* vol. 62, no.1 (2014).

Blunden, Andy. "Vygotsky on the Development of Concepts." In *Concepts: A Critical Approach.* Leiden: Brill, 2012

Boaler, Jo. *Experiencing school mathematics: Traditional and reform approaches to teaching and their impact on student learning.* London: Routledge, 2002.

Bouriga, S & Olive, T. "Is typewriting more resources-demanding than handwriting in undergraduate students?" *Read Writ* 34, 2227–2255 (2021).

Bowers, Jeffrey. "The limits of meta-analysis in educational research." *Educational Researcher,* 2021.

Bracey, Gerald. "The Condition of Public Education." *Phi Delta Kappan,* October 2006.

Bradbury, Neil. "Attention Span During Lectures: 8 seconds, 10 minutes, or more?" *Advances in Psychology Education* vol. 40, no 4 (2016).

Brandenburg, R; Larsen, E & Simpson A. et al. "'I left the teaching profession ... and this is what I am doing now': a national study of teacher

attrition." *Australian Education Resource* (2024).
Britannia Online Dictionary. "means-end analysis." Accessed August 30, 2024.
Brooks, David. "The Relationship School." *The New York Times*, March 22, 2012.
Brown, M; Brown, P & Bibby, T. "'I would rather die': reasons given by 16-year-olds for not continuing their study of mathematics." *Research in Mathematics Education*, vol.10, no.1, (2008).
Brunker, Nicole. "Escape Oppression Now: Disrupt the Dominance of Evidence-Based Practice." *EduResearch Matters*, June 13, 2024.
Caro, Jane. "Class Warfare." *The Monthly*, July 2024.
Chee Soon, Tan. "Test Anxiety." Nanyang Technological University, published September 16, 2024.
Conway & Andrew, et.al. (eds). *Variation in Working Memory*. New York, 2008.
Cooney Horvath, Jared. "Aside from nobody knowing what a 'memory' is, this definition counts forgetting (which is a change in memory) as learning. I don't think Alzheimer's should be lumped with learning." LinkedIn, July 2024.
Cooney Horvath, Jared. "The Limits of GenAI Educations." *The Harvard Business Review* July 16, 2024.
Cooney Horvath, Jared. "Why You're Probably Wrong About the Science of Learning." *Tes Magazine*, 1 May, 2024.
Cooney Horvath, Jared. *Stop Talking, Start Influencing – 12 Insights from brain science to make your message stick*. Dunedin: Exisle Publishing, 2019.
Costello, Ellie and Morgan, Fran. *Square Pegs: Inclusivity, Compassion and Fitting In – A Guide for Schools*. Independent Thinking Press, 2023.
Creswell, John. "Challenges of meta-analysis in educational research." *Review of Educational Research*, 2017.
D'Agostin, Fabio. Task-Related Emotions in Mathematics Education. Deakin University. 2020. Thesis.
Daliri-Ngametua, Rafaan (Dr)."NAPLAN's covert influence on teaching and learning." *Australian Catholic University*, November 2023.
Darling-Hammond, Linda. *The Flat World and Education*. New York: Teachers College Press, 2010.
Deci, Edward; Koestner, R & Ryan, Richard. "A meta-analytic review of experiments examining the effects of extrinsic rewards on intrinsic motivation." *Psychological Bulletin* vol. 125, no. 6 (1999).
Dewey, J. *Experience and education*. New York: Macmillan, 1938.
Dietrichson, Jens et. al. "Targeted school based interventions for improving reading and mathematics for students with, or at risk of, academic difficulties in Grades 7–12: A systematic review." *Campbell Systematic Reviews* vol. 16, no. 2 (2020).
Epstein, Michaela. "Curiosity Doesn't Exist." LinkedIn, posted 17 August 2024.
Ewing, B. 'Open Your Textbooks to Page blah, blah, blah':'So I Just Blocked Off.' In *Proceedings of the 27th Annual Conference of the Mathematics Education Research Group of Australasia Inc (MERGA). Mathematics Education for the Third Millennium, Towards 2010*. Mathematics Education Research Group of Australasia, 2004.
Ferlazzo, Larry. "Resources for Starting a New School Year Strong." Larry Ferlazzo's Websites of the Day, posted July 31, 2016.
Ferlazzo, Larry. *The Student Motivation Handbook: 50 Ways to Boost an Intrinsic Desire to Learn*. Routledge, 2023.
Fleming, William J.."Employee well-being outcomes from individual-level mental health interventions: Cross-sectional evidence from the United Kingdom." *Industrial Relations Journal* 55, no. 2 (2024).
Flinders, D., & Thornton, S. *The curriculum studies reader. (4th Ed.)*. New York: Routledge 2013.
Fromm, Erich. *Escape From Freedom*. Discus Books, 1965.
Gatto, J. T. *Dumbing Us Down, The Hidden Curriculum of Compulsory Schooling*. Canada: New Society Publisher, 1992.
Giroux, Henry. "Global Education Magazine: Non-Violence and Peace (January 30th 2013)." Global Education Magazine.
Gray, Peter (PhD); Lancy, David (PhD) & Bjorklund, David (PhD). "Decline in Independent Activity as a Cause of Decline in Children's Mental Well-being." *Journal of Paediatrics* vol 260, February 23, 2023.
Gray, Peter. "Letter #41. How the Leash Chokes the Spirit." Substack, 22 May, 2024.
Gredler, M.E. "Understanding Vygotsky for the classroom: Is it too late?" *Educational Psychology Review vol.* 24, no.1, (2012).
Green, Peter. "ICYMI: Memorial Day Washout Edition (5/26)." *Curmudgucation (blog)*, May 26, 2024.
Greeno, J. G. "Situations, mental models, and generative knowledge." In Klahr, D. and Kotovsky, K. (eds) *Complex information processing: The impact of Herbert A. Simon*. Lawrence Erlbaum Associates, 1989.
Greer L. et.al. "Publication bias in education research: A meta-analysis of meta-analyses." *Educational Research Review*, 2020.
Gutek, G. *Philosophical, ideological, and theoretical perspectives on education. (2nd Ed.)*. New York: Pearson, 2014.
Hagemeister, Volker. "A critical analysis of the section on class size in Hattie's Visible Learning." *Open Journals*, 2020.

Hannu L. et al.. "Three Orientations for Understanding Educational Autonomy: School Principals' Voices from Australia, Finland, and Jamacia." *Journal of Educational Administration and History*, vol. 53, 2021.

Harari, Y. N. *21 Lessons for the 21st Century*. London: Vintage, 2019.

Hattam, Robert. LinkedIn. July 22, 2024.

Hattenstone, Alix. "Move to home schooling biggest since pandemic." *BBC UK* 3 June 2024.

Hattie, John. "*Hattie Ranking: 252 Influences and Effect Sizes Related to Student Achievement*," 2017.

Hattie, John. *Visible learning for teachers: Maximizing impact on learning*. London: Routledge/Taylor & Francis Group, 2012.

Hattie, John. *Visible learning: A synthesis of 800 meta-analyses on achievement*. London: Routledge, 2009.

Heikkinen, Hannu; Wilkinson, Jane & Bristol, Laurette. "Three orientations for understanding educational autonomy: school principals' voices from Australia and Finland." *Journal of Education Administration and History vol.* 53, no. 4 (2021).

Heller, Blimie. 'The less autonomy a child is given, the more they will try to assert control over every tiny little thing, in an attempt to get it back. And the reverse is also true. The more autonomy a child is granted, the less they feel the need to assert control over every detail.' Facebook, November 2021.

Henebery, Brett. "Global study highlights critical importance of teacher wellbeing." *The Educator Australia*, April 11, 2024.

Hennessey, Beth & Amabile, Teresa. *Creativity and Learning: What Research Says to the Teacher*. Washington DC: National Education Association of the United States, 1987.

Hennessey, Beth. "Rewards and Creativity." In *Intrinsic and Extrinsic Motivation*. Academic Press, 2000.

Hermant, Norman and Yussuf, Ahmed. "Andrew Tate's Ideology Driving Sexual Harassment, Sexism and Misogyny in Australian Classrooms." *ABC News*, published April 2, 2024.

Hernik. J and Jaworska, E. "The effect of enjoyment on learning." In *INTED2018 Proceedings* 2018. IATED. 2018.

Hidi, S & Renninger, K.A. "The four-phase model of interest development." *Educational Psychologist* vol. 41, no.2 (2006).

Hinton, C; Miyamoto, K & Della-Chiesa, B. "Brain research, learning and emotions: Implications for education research, policy and practice. *European Journal of Education vol.*43, no.1, (2008).

Hmelo-Silver, C. E.; Duncan, R.G & Chinn, C. A.. "Scaffolding and Achievement in Problem-Based and Inquiry Learning: A Response to Kirschner, Sweller, and Clark (2006)." *Educational Psychologist* vol. 4, no.2 (2007).

Howard, Joshua et. al. "Student motivation and associated outcomes: a meta-analysis from self-determination theory." *Perspect Psychological Science* vol. 16, no. 6 (2021).

Hunter, Jane & Carter, Don. "Disquiet in the playground: Explicit teaching and other buzzwords." *The Education Review*, July 16, 2024.

Hunter, Jane Louise. "Is There a 'Right Way' to Teach? Recent Debates Suggests Yes, but Students and Schools are Much More Complex." *The Conversation*, published July 25, 2024.

Ideagen. "Education Crossroads: Navigating Teacher Shortages, Safety Concerns and School Refusal Trends." Australia: School Governance, 2024.

Information Management and Management Science. 2nd International Conference on Information Management and Management Science 2019. New York: Association for Computing Machinery, 2019.

Karnovsky S and Gobby, B. "How teacher wellbeing can be cruel: refusing discourses of wellbeing in an online Reddit forum." *British Journal of Sociology of Education*, 2024.

Kaukko, A. "*Finland relies on teachers' pedagogical solutions – in Australia, class teacher Arto Kaukko had to print lesson plans on the classroom wall.*" *Opettaja Magazine*, 2021.

Kauppila, R. *The way people learn: socio-constructivist learning*. Jyväskylä: PS-Kustannus, 2007.

Kemmis, S; Wilkinson, J; Edwards-Groves, C; Hardy, I; Grootenboer, P & Bristol, L (eds). *Changing Practices, Changing Education*. Singapore: Springer, 2014.

Killian, Shaun Patrick. "What Everyone Needs to Know About High-Performance, Teacher Student Relationships." *Evidence-Based Teaching*, accessed July 23, 2024.

Kohn, Alfie. "Teaching Strategies That Work! (Just Don't Ask 'Work to Do What?')" Alfie John, published August 10, 2011.

Kohn, Alfie. "The Siren Song of 'Evidence-Based' Instruction." published May 23, 2024.

Kohn, Alfie. *Feel-Bad Education*. Beacon Press, 2018.

Kuestenmacher, Simon. "A growing problem looms for Australian schools as teachers flee." *InDaily News*, April 15, 2024.

Kuhn, D. "Is direct instruction an answer to the right question?" *Educational psychologist*, vol. 42 no.2, (2007).

Langenbern, Adam. "University of Tasmania vice-chancellor Rufus Black sounds alarm over state's public education system." *ABC News* Thu 6 Jun 2024 at 7:10pm.

Liljedhal, Peter. *Building Thinking Classrooms in Mathematics*. Corwin Mathematics, 2020.

Lingard, B. "Policy borrowing, policy learning: Testing times in Australian schooling." *Critical Studies in Education* vol. 51, no.2 (2010).

Lonka, K. "*Education lifted Finland out of poverty, but we need to keep developing to remain at the cutting edge.*" *University of Helsinki*, December 2019.
Lovitt, Charles & Lowe, Ian. *RIME*.
Lowe, Ian. "Mathematics at work: Modelling your world." *Australian Academy of Science* vol.1, no. 2, (1988).
Maroun, Jamil and Tienken, Christopher. "Research Shows What Standardized Tests Actually Measure." Quoted in *Forbes Magazine*, Feb 10, 2024.
Martin, E. P. et al.. "Positive Education: Positive Psychology and Classroom Interventions." *Oxford Review of Education* vol. 35, no. 3 (2009).
Mason, Shuman & Cook. "Comparing the effectiveness of an inverted classroom to a traditional classroom in an upper-division engineering course." *IEEE Transactions on education*, vol. 55 (2013).
Mavros, Larissa. "Tonight: leaders to explain the Gonski 2.0 education revolution." *UNSW Sydney Newsroom*, 24 May 2018.
McDonough, Sharon; Brandenburg, Robyn & Moran, Wendy. "A Study of Teacher Educator's Work: Complexity and Confrontation." *Educational Forum vol.* 87, no. 4 (2023).
McLeod, Saul. "Constructivism Learning Theory & Philosophy of Education." *Simply Psychology* February 1, 2024.
Meier, Deborah et al.. *Many Children Left Behind*. Beacon Press, 2004.
Mockler, Nicole; Stacey, Meghan; Colledge, Claire & Watt, Helen. "Professional Development: The Minister Claims She Trusts Teachers. But Does She Really?" *EduResearch Matters*, 23 August, 2024.
N, Alexis. "South Korea and Finland – role models for the ideal education system?" *The International School of the Sacred Hearts Student Publication*, January 11 2023.
Nordengren, C. "New educators want opportunities for teacher-leadership, too." Online: ASCD, 2016.
OECD. "PISA 2022 Results (Volume I and II) – Country Notes: Australia." Australia, 2022.
OECD. Students Well-Being: What it is and How it can be Measured. PISA 2015 Results Volume III (2017).
Owen, R. "Can we make real transformative change in education?" *Greater Good Magazine*, Berkeley University of California, April 21, 2022.
Pandya, Sachin. "My Students Can't Meet Academic Standards Because the School Model No Longer Fits Them." *EdSurge*, Jan 24, 2024.
Pehkonen, Erkki; Näveri, Liisa & Laine, Anu. "On teaching problem solving in school mathematics." *CEPS Journal* 3 (2013).
Pekrun, R. "Academic emotions." In T. Urdan (Ed.) *APA Educational Psychology Handbook, Vol.* 2. Washington, DC: American Psychological Association, 2010.
Pekrun, R. *Emotions and learning*. Educational Practises Series. Geneva, Switzerland: International Academy of Education (IAE), 2014.
Pekrun, R. *Emotions and Learning*. Geneva, Switzerland: International Academy of Education (IAE), 2014).
Perez, Della (Dr). "Chapter 6: Progressivism." In *Social Foundations of K-12 Education*. Online: Centre for the Advancement of Digital Scholarship, 2022.
Piaget and Vygotsky. "Powerful Inspirators for Today's Students in Early Education and Developmental Psychology." In N Veraksa, & I Pramling Samuelsson (eds) *Piaget and Vygotsky in XXI Century*. Germany: Springer Cham, 2022.
Polesel, John and Teese, Richard. *Undemocratic Schooling*. Melbourne: Melbourne University Press, 1999.
Pondiscio, Robert. "*A new lost generation: Disengaged, aimless, and adrift,*" from the Thomas B. Fordham Institute.
Richman, Talia. "Computers to Score Written Answers to Texas' STAAR Test." *The Dallas Morning News*, February 14 2024.
Riordan, Sally. "Improving Teaching Quality to Compensate For Socio-Economic Disadvantages: A Study of Research Dissemination Across Secondary Schools in England." *Review of Education* 10, no. 2 (August 2022).
Riordan, Sally. "Schools are Using Research to Try to Improve Children's Learning – But It's Not Working." *The Conversation*, published April 3, 2024.
Ripley, A. *The Smartest Kids in the World*. New York: Simon & Schuster, 2013.
Ripley, Amanda. *The Smartest Kids in the World*. Simon & Schuster, 2014.
Ritchhart, Ron. *Creating Cultures of Thinking: The 8 Forces We Must Master to Truly Transform Our Schools*. Jossey-Bass, 2015.
Robinson, J. "A Class Above, A Class Below." *The Monthly*, July 2024.
Robinson, J. "It's Pay School: The Price parents pay for their children's education has become the key measure of a school's quality, and this approach is costing us all." *The Monthly*, September 2024.
Robinson, J. "Schooled: A History of failure in education funding." *The Monthly*, August 2024.
Roffey, Sue. *ASPIRE to Wellbeing and Learning for All in Early Years and Primary: The Principles Underpinning Positive Education*. Melbourne: Routledge, 2024.
Rosenshine, B. "Principles of instruction: Research-based strategies that all teachers should know." *American Educator* vol. 36, no.1 (2012).
Ryan, Richard & Deci, Edward. "Self-

Determination Theory and the Facilitation of Intrinsic Motivation, Social Development and Well-Being." *American Psychologist* vol. 55, no. 1 (2000).
Sahlberg, Pasi. "Sata 24". Presentation, Croatia 2024.
Sahlberg, Pasi. "The good news is bad news when it comes to Australian pupils' Pisa scores. But there's no need to panic." *The Guardian*, Dec 6 2023.
Sahlberg, Pasi. *Finnish Lessons* 2.0. New York: Teacher's College Press, 2015.
Sarkar, Jayanta and Sarkar, Dipanwita. "What Happens When You Pay Year 7 Students to do Better on NAPLAN? We Found Out." *The Conversation* July 19, 2024.
Sawyer, W. "Critiquing the evidence-based education movement: The dangers of "what works" approaches." Presented at the American Educational Research Association Annual Meeting, Washington DC, 2016.
Schiro, M. S. *Curriculum theory: Conflicting visions and enduring concerns.* (2nd Ed.). Los Angeles: Sage Publications, 2012.
Schoenfeld, A.H. "When good teaching leads to bad results: The disasters of 'well-taught' mathematics courses." *Educational Psychologist* vol. 23, no.2 (1988).
Schwartz, Daniel et al. "Constructivism in an Age of Non-Constructivist Assessments." in Sigmund Tobias & Thomas Duffy (eds) *Constructivist Instruction.* London: Routledge, 2009.
Senek, Simon. "How great teachers inspire action." TED Talks, September 2009. Video, 17:47.
Sheninger, Eric. *Disruptive Thinking in Our Classrooms.* Chicago: ConnectEDD Publishing LLC, 2021.
Shochet, Ian; Dadds, Mark; Ham, David & Montague, Roslyn. "School connectedness is an underemphasized parameter in adolescent mental health: results of a community prediction study." *Journal of Clinical Child and Adolescent Psychology* vol. 35, no. 2 (2006).
Skourdoumbis, A & Rowe, E. "A critique of 'Strong Beginnings' initial teacher education reforms: mandating neuroscience as core curriculum within the 'what works' movement." *Australian Education Research* (2024).
Sloan, Karen. "7 Strategies to Teach Conceptual Understanding in Math." Carnegie Learning (blog), April 17, 2023.
Smith B. J. *The Gatekeepers: Why School Systems Should Rethink Resisting Change.* Maryland: Rowman & Littlefield, 2023.
Smith, B.J. *Teacher Shortages and the Challenge of Retention.* Maryland: Rowman & Littlefield, 2023.
Spacey, John. "94 Examples of School Traditions." *Simplicable,* April 14, 2024.
Spicer, Andre. "Work 'wellness' programmes don't make employees happier – but I know what does." *The Guardian*, January 18, 2024.
Spiro, R. J. & Jehng, J. C "Cognitive flexibility and hypertext: Theory and technology for the nonlinear and multidimensional traversal of complex subject matter." In D. Nix & R. J. Spiro (Eds.) *Cognition, education, and multimedia: Exploring ideas in high technology.* Lawrence Erlbaum Associates, Inc, 1990.
Stagg Peterson, Shelley. "Letting Teachers Choose What They Want to Learn Supports Teacher Morale – And Yields Better Teaching." *The Conversation*, 23 August, 2024.
Stevens, Robert & Ructtinger, Liliana. *Cultivating Critical and Creative Thinking.* NSW: NSW Department of Education, 2018.
Swain, Nathaniel et al.. "What We Want to Say Right Now to Sahlberg and Goldfeld." *EduResearch Matters*, May 29, 2023.
Sweller, John. "Why Inquiry Based Approaches Harm Students' Learning." *The Centre for Independent Studies*, August 11, 2021.
Tall, David and Thomas, Michael (eds.) *Intelligence, Learning and Understanding in Mathematics: A Tribute to Richard Skemp.* Post Press, 2002.
Tancredi, Haley; Killingly, Callula & Graham, Linda J.. "'My Brain Leaves the Room': What Happens When Teachers Talk Too Much?" *The Conversation*, 17 July, 2024.
Teacher Tom. "Why Schools are so Threatened by Children at Play." *Teacher Tom* (blog). August 16, 2024.
Terada. Youki & Merrill, Stephen. "10 Studies Every Teacher Should Know About." *Edutopia* Jul 19, 2024.
The Australian Education Union. "Summer 2023." *The Australian Educator Magazine* Issue 120, 2023.
The Australian Government. *The Productivity Commission, 2024.* Canberra: The Australian Government, 2024.
The Australian Youth Barometer. Developed by the Monash Centre for Youth Policy and Education Practice (CYPEP) in the Faculty of Education at Monash University, Aug 2024.
Theobald, P. *Education Now: How Re-thinking America's Past Can Change Its Future.* Colorado: Paradigm, 2009.
Toivola, M; Peura, P & Humaloja, M. *Flipped Learning in Finland.* Helsinki: Edita Publishing, 2020.
UNESCO. Recommendations and summary of deliberations of the United Nations Secretary-General's High-Level Panel on the Teaching Profession. Geneva: International Labour office, 2024.
United Nations Office of the Human Rights Commissioner. Finland: UN expert says education system must address new challenges

to continue to deliver on its promises. 29 November 2023.
University of Waterloo. "Teaching Problem-Solving Skills." Centre for Teaching Excellence. Accessed 2 September 2024.
Valentine, Stephen and Cooper, Patricia. "The Dangers of Meta-Analysis in Educational Research: A Critique." *Educational Research Quarterly*, 2016.
van Merrienboer, Jeroen & Krischner, Paul. *Ten Steps to Complex Learning*. New York: Routledge, 2017.
Waghid, Zayd. "Teachers Change Lives – But What Makes a Great Teacher?" *The Conversation*, 7 March, 2023.
Walker, T. D. *Teach Like Finland*. London: W.W.Norton & Company, 2017.
Walker, T.D. *Teach Like Finland*. New York & London: W.W.Norton & Company, 2017.
Walker, Tim. "The Simple Strength of Finnish Education." This is Finland, 2016.
Webb, N. "Peer interaction and learning in cooperative small groups." *Journal of Education Psychology* vol. 74, no. 5 (1982).
Webb, N. "The teacher's role in promoting collaborative dialogue in the classroom." *British Journal of Educational Psychology*, vol. 79 (2009).
Wehe, Hillary; Rhodes, Matthew & Seger, Carol. "Evidence for the negative impact of reward on self-regulated learning." *Quarterly Journal of Experimental Psychology* vol. 68, no. 11 (2015).
Weiss, B. "STUDENT VOICE: Teachers assign us work that relies on rote memorization, then tell us not to use artificial intelligence." In *The Hechinger Report*, Feb 2024.
What is the Science of Learning?, Analysis Paper 63, February 2024.
Williams, Morgan K. "John Dewey in the 21st Century." *Journal of Inquiry and Action in Education* vol. 9, no. 1 (2017).
Willingham, Daniel. "On the dangers of meta-analyses in education." *Education Next*, 2015.
Wrigley, Terry. "Learning in a Time of Cholera: Imagining a Future for Public Education." *European Education Research Journal vol.* 21, no. 1 (Dec 2020).
Yassine, J. et al.. "Building Student-Teacher Relationships and Improving Behaviour-Management for Classroom Teachers." *Support for Learning*, vol. 35, no. 3 (2020).
Zhao, Yong. *What Works May Hurt: Side Effects in Education*. Teachers College Press, 2018.
Zheng, Zoey. "Pasi Sahlberg: Teachers need a sense of mission, empathy and leadership." LinkedIn, February 3, 2018.

www.ingramcontent.com/pod-product-compliance
Lightning Source LLC
LaVergne TN
LVHW050952080826
845145LV00005B/1477

* 9 7 8 1 9 2 2 7 7 9 3 6 6 *